United Nations Development Aid

DIGAMBAR BHOURASKAR has worked in the United Nations in New York for thirty two years (1957-1989). He held several senior positions including Director of the Development Administration Programme in the Department of Technical Cooperation. He was closely associated with several aspects of UN development aid and was responsible for managing a sizable programme of aid.

He served as Financial Adviser to the Government of Jamaica (1989-1990). He was a Fellow at the Center for Management of Baruch College, CUNY, in New York (1991-1993) and was Adjunct Professor of Economics at Baruch College (1993-1998). He also served as consultant to UN and UNDP.

The author holds a Ph.D. in Economics from the University of Bombay. He was also a Post-Doctoral Research Fellow at Princeton University, NJ, USA.

United Nations Development Aid

A Study in History and Politics

Digambar Bhouraskar

ACADEMIC FOUNDATION
NEW DELHI

First published in 2007
by :

ACADEMIC FOUNDATION
4772-73 / 23 Bharat Ram Road, (23 Ansari Road),
Darya Ganj, New Delhi - 110 002 (India).
Phones : 23245001 / 02 / 03 / 04.
Fax : +91-11-23245005.
E-mail : academic@vsnl.com
www : academicfoundation.com

Cataloging in Publication Data--DK
Courtesy: D.K. Agencies (P) Ltd. <docinfo@dkagencies.com>

Bhouraskar, Digambar.
United Nations development aid : a study in history and politics / Digambar Bhouraskar.
p. cm.
Includes index.
ISBN 8171885330

1. United Nations--Technical assistance.
2. United Nations--Economic assistance. 3. United Nations Development Programme.
4. Technical assistance--Developing countries.
5. Economic assistance--Developing countries.
I. Title.

DDC 338.910 917 24 22

Typeset by Italics India, New Delhi.
Printed and bound in India.

10 9 8 7 6 5 4 3 2 1

To

Ishan and Gulab

Contents

List of Tables and Annexures

TABLES

ANNEXURES

Note on Document Symbols

A/--	Documents relating to the General Assembly
A/PV/--	Proceedings of the General Assembly
A/C.2/--	Documents of the Second Committee of the General Assembly
A/C.2/SR.--	Summary Records of the Second Committee
E/--	Documents of the Economic and Social Council
E/SR--	Summary Records of the ECOSOC
E/AC.6/--	Documents of the Economic Committee of the ECOSOC
E/AC.6/SR.--	Summary Records of the Economic Committee
E/TAC/--	Documents of the Technical Assistance Committee
E/TAC/L.--	Limited or Draft Documents of TAC
E/TAC/SR.--	Summary Records of the TAC

Acronyms

ACABQ	Advisory Committee on Administrative and Budgetary Questions
ACC	Administrative Committee on Coordination
CCAQ	Consultative Committee on Administrative Questions
DESA	Department of Economic and Social Affairs
ECAFE	Economic Commission for Asia and the Far East
ECLA	Economic Commission of Latin America
ECOSOC	Economic and Social Council
EPTA	Expanded Programme of Technical Assistance
EDF	Economic Development Fund
FAO	Food and Agricultural Organization
GA	General Assembly
GC	The Governing Council of the Special Fund and later of the UNDP
IAEA	International Atomic Energy Agency
IBRD	International Bank for Reconstruction and Development
ICAO	International Civil Aviation Organization
ILO	International Labour Organization
IMCO	Intergovernmental Maritime Consultative Organization
IMF	International Monetary Fund
IMO	International Maritime Organization
ITO	International Trade Organization

ITU	International Telecommunications Union
OAS	Organization of American States
OPEX	Operational and Executive Personnel
SUNFED	Special United Nations Fund for Economic Development
TAB	Technical Assistance Board
TAC	Technical Assistance Committee
TACOC	Technical Assistance Committee of the Council
TAPC	Technical Assistance Policy Committee
UAR	United Arab Republic
UN	United Nations
UNCTAD	United Nations Conference on Trade and Development
UNDP	United Nations Development Programme
UNESCO	United Nations Educational, Scientific and Cultural Organization
UNRRA	United Nations Relief and Rehabilitation Administration
UNTA	United Nations Technical and Assistance
UNTAA	United Nations Technical Assistance Administration
UNTAAD	United Nations Technical Assistance and Administrative Department
UPU	Universal Postal Union
WHO	World Health Organization
WMO	World Meterological Organization

Acknowledgements

I want to express my high appreciation and gratitude to my friend Prof. Muchkund Dubey, President, Council for Social Development, New Delhi, India, for organising excellent logistic support during the preparation of this manuscript and for giving valuable and insightful comments on the manuscript. I wish to thank Mr. Harpal Singh for typing the entire manuscript with high level of accuracy and speed. I am also grateful to Ms. Medha Dubey for initial editing of the manuscript.

At the United Nations library in New York, where all the work was done, Mr. Alan Aalto, Mrs. Rosalba Butler, Mr. Peter Leonard and Ms. Elisa Gagliano were unfailingly helpful, over the years, in providing me with all the relevant documents. They showed not only considerable patience but also extended warm friendship to me. I owe them deep gratitude.

Preface

Contrary to popular perceptions, the United Nations undertakes a wide variety of actions than one can imagine. It is not surprising since the UN is the single most universal organisation and engages itself with a wide range of continuing and current issues of international and national concern. The UN works basically in three areas: political, economic and social, and humanitarian. In each of these areas, it performs mainly two functions: policy and operational. The Member Governments work to evolve policy consensus on current and contemporary issues which are common to all or to large groups of countries. They don't always succeed but they keep trying and rarely give up. In most cases, the outcome is positive though not always optimal.

Operational activities are of two types. Some are responses to emergencies such as intra-country conflicts, civil wars, or inter-country conflicts, and natural disasters. Others are of a continuing nature based on certain policies adopted by the UN in the past. Examples of the first kind are peacekeeping operations and disaster relief operations. Among the continuing operational activities, the pre-eminent one is the provision of development aid in the form of technical assistance to developing countries to enable them to accelerate their pace of economic and social development. Other operational activities deal with prevention such as efforts in disaster reduction or with monitoring of policies or agreements reached in the past such as in the field of narcotics and drugs.

UN development aid started almost since the founding of the UN in 1945. The founders attached great importance to it and had high hopes about its contribution to economic development in developing countries. When the first International Conference on Technical Assistance was convened to establish the Expanded Programme of Technical Assistance (EPTA), the Secretary-General characterised the

Conference as "potentially one of the most significant ever called by the United Nations." He told the delegates that "You are participating in what should become one of the world's greatest achievements for lasting peace and for the social progress and better standards of life in greater freedom proclaimed in the Preamble to the Charter of the UN." Mr. Santa Cruz, President of the Conference, echoed a similar sentiment. "This task," he said, "in my opinion, together with the Universal Declaration of Human Rights, the most important task the UN has accomplished in the five years of its existence."

In spite of its size and scope, no serious attempt has been made either from inside or outside the UN to evaluate its impact and effectiveness since its inception, to learn from the past experience and to assess its relevance for the present and the future.

This book presents, for the first time a comprehensive survey and a critical analysis of the United Nations development aid from its founding in 1945 until 1966 when several parallel programmes of aid were merged into the present United Nations Development Programme. In order to provide a most authentic account, I have used exclusively only the primary sources which include records of discussions and decisions in the General Assembly and Economic and Social Council (ECOSOC); the two principal legislative bodies responsible for all aspects of policy and management of UN development aid. The sources also include records of the Technical Assistance Committee, a subsidiary body of the ECOSOC constituted to assist ECOSOC in the management of development aid; reports and studies prepared by the Technical Assistance Board, principal operations arm of the EPTA; and those prepared by the Secretary-General, *ad hoc* working groups and committees, and by functional commissions. The treatment is thematic with a blend of chronological account. I have focused on policies and political considerations underlying decisions. I have explained implementation at the macro level and discussed at length legislative concern over the impact of the programmes on economic and social development of developing countries.

The analysis in this book is based on my long association, 32 years, with the UN. I was directly involved with the substantive support and management of technical assistance in my areas of responsibility. This and the interaction with the legislative bodies enabled me greatly not only to understand the functioning of the UN from inside but also to gain insight into underlying political processes.

The demand for multilateral capital and technical assistance gained momentum immediately after the founding of the UN. Several developing countries had attained independence after the Second World War and needed assistance, free of political strings, from the UN to launch their national development plans. At the UN any operational activity requiring finance needs the support of a majority of developed countries, especially the US. However, initially developed countries, which were then preoccupied with the rehabilitation and reconstruction of European economies devastated by the war, resisted demands for development aid. However, persistent struggle by developing countries paid off and it was agreed to include a very modest sum in the UN budget in 1948 to provide technical assistance for advisory services and training to developing countries. This programme was known as the United Nations Regular Programme of Technical Assistance. However, it was hardly enough in the light of the volume of aid required. Developed countries were against providing capital assistance from the UN.

The subsequent growth in development aid was not without a considerable element of luck. In 1948, President Truman, in his inaugural address, recognised the economic interdependence between developed and underdeveloped countries and the impact of economic conditions in underdeveloped countries on international peace and stability. He expressed strong interest in providing substantial technical assistance to them for their development through multilateral channels. He appealed to other developed countries to join him in this international endeavour and promised to make a substantial contribution. Soon after the US Government brought the issue to the UN and asked Member States to establish an EPTA. This strong US initiative radically changed the attitude of other developed countries and they also joined in the US effort.

The ECOSOC requested the Secretary-General and the specialised agencies to prepare a detailed plan for assistance. However, this plan turned out to be rather vague, imprecise and not very innovative. It was essentially an enlargement of the work that was already being done under the UN Regular Programme of Technical Assistance. The ECOSOC reviewed and revised the Plan and worked out details of its institutional and operational arrangements. Subsequently, EPTA was established in 1950. Contributions were to be on a voluntary basis and in national currencies if so desired.

At the first International Conference on Technical Assistance, governments pledged $ 20 million for the first year of which the US contributed 60 per cent. The rest of the contributions were mostly in non-convertible currencies and posed problems in their utilisation. The real beginning of the UN development aid dates from the US initiative because EPTA represented a quantum jump from the modest start in 1948 when the UN budget provided for only $ 250,000. Subsequently, the UN did increase provision in its budget but it was still small. Later, it was almost accepted that all technical assistance should be financed from voluntary funds. As a result of this, support for provision in the UN budget diminished and it shrank considerably over time.

EPTA differed in some important respects from the UN Regular Programme. Whereas EPTA received substantial amount of resources in national non-convertible currencies, the UN Programme received funds from the UN budget which were fully convertible. The UN Programme did not have country targets like EPTA and that gave it considerable flexibility in determining priorities for assistance and also enabled it to respond to emergencies such as later in the 1960s in Africa. At the same time its major weakness was that it gave too much discretion to UN bureaucrats to design the programme without giving much say to the recipients countries.

In subsequent years, EPTA grew steadily in terms of its volume, number of countries assisted, and the range of its economic and social activities though it was never commensurate with growing demand for assistance. It provided assistance for formulation and implementation of integrated and coherent national development plans, policy and administrative reforms, for improving productivity of public sector personnel, for institutional building in training, for improving education and health standards, and for enhancing productivity in various sectors of economic activity—notably in agriculture.

However, EPTA's growth was not linear. It encountered problems arising from its original conceptualisation and practical difficulties in implementation. I have discussed in depth its early financial crisis owing to inexperience of its management, difficulties in management of non-convertible currencies, especially political storm over utilisation of Soviet currencies, initial political compromise over distribution of resources among recipient countries, the leverage exercised by specialised agencies, and EPTA's failure in developing an adequate methodology for evaluation of its activities.

The creation of the Special Fund to provide pre-investment assistance was not in the cards and its birth owed mainly to a renewed effort by developing countries to seek capital assistance through the UN. Developing countries suggested establishment of a Special United Nations Fund for Economic Development (SUNFED) in the UN. From the beginning developed countries were against provision of capital assistance observing that such assistance should be sought from international lending institutions, private capital markets and from private foreign investors. However, developing countries continued their struggle for a long time. I have explained in detail how developed countries advanced a variety of reasons to oppose it, how the US tried to link its support for such assistance to global verifiable disarmament, a condition developing countries could hardly satisfy. But as this issue lasted for almost for a decade, the US pulled out a magic card. The US volunteered to provide substantial amount of additional resources for pre-investment assistance and to set up a Special Fund for this purpose without any commitment to the establishment of a SUNFED. Other developed countries joined the US in supporting the creation of a Special Fund. The US offer split the unity of developing countries and many accepted the US offer. The Special Fund was established in 1960. Several developing countries continued to ask for a SUNFED and did succeed later in having a resolution adopted in the General Assembly for the establishment of a Capital Development Fund. But all developed countries had voted against it and so the Capital Development Fund was born with scant resources.

Unsurprisingly, there was considerable overlap between activities of the Special Fund and EPTA and agitation was growing for their merger. I have discussed the merger in detail and pointed out how incomplete it was at the time. Developing countries were keen to safeguard EPTA and so the two Programmes with their separate identities were simply put under one umbrella. It is perhaps of historical interest to ask the question whether the present UNDP would have been established if the Special Fund did not have to be created. But in reality nothing has been lost. There is full integration now and UNDP keeps growing in monetary terms though not much in real terms.

The UN observed its 60th anniversary in 2005. On any important anniversary, it is customary, in public as in private life, to reflect on achievements as well as failures in the past, to learn lessons for the future. I thought it might be useful to provide a comprehensive account of one of its most important activities on this occasion. Moreover, I hope that the book will make a contribution to the institutional memory in the UN which, as I said before, is sadly lacking, especially in the economic and social fields. Scholars might not be completely satisfied with my treatment of the subject but I shall be gratified if they recognise the merit of this activity and take more interest in it.

Digambar Bhouraskar

1

Establishment of the United Nations Regular Programme of Technical Assistance

The Second World War was finally over, leaving behind vast devastation and an unsettled world. Though the human and material toll was confined mainly to Europe and the Pacific, the war did have widespread and serious repercussions elsewhere. The colonies of Allied Powers suffered the deprivation arising from the mobilisation of their resources for the war which depressed their chronic slow rate of growth. With the world greatly chastened by the war, the mood was sombre when United Nations General Assembly opened its first session in London on 10 January 1946. There was, inevitably, lot of soul searching and deep probing into the tragic consequences and experiences of the war to distill lessons for the future. What emerged, unsurprisingly, was a strong desire for a peaceful, prosperous, just and a secure world and all Member States, while extolling the UN Charter, pledged themselves to strive ceaselessly to attain these goals.

In his welcoming address,[1] Prime Minister C. R. Attlee of the United Kingdom advised that "The United Nations must become the overriding factor in foreign policy" and stressed the importance of the 'Rule of Law' in world affairs. Forcefully invoking the UN Charter, he declared that "social justice and the best possible standards of life for all are essential factors in promoting and maintaining the peace of the world", and underlined the importance of making "Èconomic and Social Council an effective international instrument." Though Mr. Attlee's aspirations were widely shared, the main preoccupation of the developed countries at the time was with rehabilitation and reconstruction of countries, mostly European, ravaged by the war and not with social and economic development of underdeveloped countries. Taking up Mr. Attlee's theme, Mr. Lleras Restrepo of

1. Official records of the First Part of the first session of the General Assembly, 10 January-14 February 1946, London, pp. 39-43.

Colombia pointed to the glaring diversity in economic development among members and stressed the need "to correct inequalities and provide justice".[2] He dwelt at length on linkages between economic interdependence, global growth with equity and international peace and stability. These linkages were now to constitute the anchor of future discussions on multilateral aid and economic development of underdeveloped countries.

The first step for technical assistance for economic development was taken during the second Part of the First session of the General Assembly held from 23 October-16 December 1946 at Lake Success, New York. During this session, Mr. Charles Malik of Lebanon placed on the agenda of the General Assembly the item relating to the creation by the United Nations of Advisory Boards to provide expert advice and guidance to underdeveloped countries in the various fields of economic and social development.[3] The General Assembly referred the subject for detailed examination to its Joint Second and Third Committee.

In the Joint Committee, Mr. Malik introduced a draft resolution[4] on the creation by the United Nations of Advisory Boards to provide expert assistance. In constructing the analytical framework of his case,[5] Mr. Malik referred to the Preamble of the Charter of the United Nations wherein "it had been agreed to employ international machinery for the promotion of the economic and social advancement of all peoples". He then cited Articles 60 and 66 which underlined the unique role of the United Nations in promoting economic and social development and the responsibility of the General Assembly in approving and meeting requests for assistance from member nations. He drew attention to gross inequality in development of Member Nations and classified countries into four groups: developed, non-self governing, trusteeship territories, and sovereign but underdeveloped countries. The developed countries obviously needed no assistance

---

2. *ibid.*, p.146.
3. Official records of the Second Part of the first session of the General Assembly, 23 October-16 December 1946, Lake Success, New York.
4. Document A/C.2 & 3/32.
5. For Mr. Malik's statement and discussion on the Lebanon's draft resolution, see summary records of the 10th meeting of the Joint Committee of the Second and Third Committees on 6 December 1946. Document A/C.2 & 3/38.

and, moreover, they had the responsibility to promote development in the non-self governing countries and trusteeship territories under their care. It was only the last group—independent but less developed—which lacked financial and technical resources for accelerated development and needed outside assistance. Bilateral assistance agreements, in spite of their usefulness, he argued, "created a real danger for the economic independence of the assisted countries which were not in a position to resist too exclusive an influence such as might be exerted by the protecting countries". United Nations was in a unique position to provide effective and disinterested assistance. His formal proposal, in the first place, would have the General Assembly refer the matter to the ECOSOC for study and recommendation to the next session of the General Assembly a plan to render effective advisory assistance in various fields of economic and social development for countries desiring such assistance. Secondly, his proposal included some general guidelines to serve as a framework for discussions in the ECOSOC. The guidelines would have the ECOSOC take into account, in studying this question, the unique role of the UN in providing such assistance, the need for the highest quality of advice and assistance and coordination of such activities with those of the UN specialised agencies. In the discussion that ensued reactions from others ranged from subtle but firm opposition to guarded support, to enthusiastic endorsement.

Representatives from Australia, Canada, Chile, Norway and USSR opposed the Lebanese proposal on the ground that the ECOSOC would be overburdened especially in its early stages when it had already a number of high priority items to deal with. Around this time ECOSOC had also decided to set up sub-commissions of the Economic and Employment Commission established at its first session. One of the sub-commissions was to be on Economic Development which, this group suggested, could also deal with expert assistance. Australia and others also tried to deflect attention by pointing to the assistance provided by the specialised agencies. These countries would agree to refer the matter to the ECOSOC provided there was no time limit set on action by the ECOSOC. Venezuela, India, Syria, and France were in full agreement with the Lebanese proposal, whereas others while agreeing in principle submitted some amendments. USA wanted a recognition of the "responsibility of the specialised agencies in their respective fields." Stressing the importance of bilateral aid, USA also suggested that ECOSOC develop the proposal in cooperation with the specialised agencies and Member Governments. France believed that the reference to Member Governments was contrary to the spirit of the Lebanese proposal which had pointed out certain dangers of bilateral assistance. Despite attempts at clarification by the US representative on the importance of bilateral aid the US suggestion to include cooperation with Member Governments in the development of a plan did not receive much support and hence was rejected. There seems to have been some confusion regarding the premises upon which this particular discussion was based. The supporters of the Lebanese draft resolution interpreted the reference to the pitfalls of bilateral aid as Lebanese rejection of bilateral aid and its substitution by aid from the UN. This certainly could not have been the intention of Lebanon but Lebanon failed to clarify and let the misunderstanding stand. Indeed, while presenting the joint Committee's report to the General Assembly, the Rapporteur of the Joint Committee explained that the US suggestion was not adopted as "the aim of the draft resolution, as presented by the delegation of Lebanon, was to substitute the expert advice of international organisations, such as the United Nations and the specialised agencies, for the bilateral arrangements which often resulted in the undue technical dependency of one nation upon another." The Chinese delegate suggested a separate memorandum on guidelines to the ECOSOC instead of including them in the operative part of Lebanese draft resolution. The Lebanese delegate accepted this suggestion and on his own dropped the idea of setting a time limit for action by ECOSOC as well as his specific institutional reference to creation of central advisory boards. He was content with a general study of advisory assistance and was willing to leave the question of ways and means to the ECOSOC. Following the acceptance of the US proposal to include a reference to cooperation with the specialised agencies and of the Chinese suggestion to delete reference to guidelines in the resolution, added to Lebanon's readiness to compromise, especially on the time limit, some of the countries which had originally opposed the Lebanese proposal were now willing to vote for it. The Lebanese proposal, with the Chinese and US amendments, was thus adopted by overwhelming majority in the

Committee. However, Byelorussian Soviet Socialist Republic, Peru, Ukranian Soviet Socialist Republic and the USSR registered their silent disagreement by abstaining from voting. In the General Assembly, there was hardly any discussion on the draft resolution recommended by the Joint Committee. The General Assembly adopted it unanimously at its 65th plenary meeting held on 14 December 1946.[6] The final decision represented a compromise and differed in three important respects from the original Lebanese proposal. It did not prescribe any time limit for the ECOSOC to study the matter. Second, it did not specify any particular institutional arrangement, methods or mechanism to render assistance. Finally, it provided no policy guidelines for directing the discussions in the ECOSOC. Thus stripped of some of its essential elements the original Lebanese proposal ended up as a general request to ECOSOC giving the latter complete flexibility and freedom in how to deal with the matter. Nonetheless, this constituted a first step in the right direction.

Before this matter came up for discussion at the ECOSOC, the Council had already agreed to set up Economic and Employment Commission and two sub-commissions on: (a) Employment and Economic Stability, and (b) on Economic Development.[7] The Commission was to advise the Council, *inter alia,* on general economic conditions, world economic situation, economic reconstruction of war devastated countries, promotion of full employment, and problems of economic development particularly relating to underdeveloped areas. The sub-commission on Economic Development was expected to deal with (i) principles and problems of long-term economic development, (ii) full and effective use of all resources, (iii) raising levels of consumption, and (iv) effects of industrialisation and technological changes on world economic situation.

With the institutional framework under way, the Council took up the question of expert advisory services at its fourth session. Before the debate on this subject commenced during the Council's fourth session, the discussion on the First Report[8] of the Economic and Employment Commission had already provided some indication of the

6. GA Resolution 52(I).

7. ECOSOC Resolution 6(I).

8. Document E/255.

general feelings prevailing with regard to the issue of aid to the underdeveloped countries. The developed countries and the Commission continued to emphasise full employment and economic stability, especially in their countries, and economic reconstruction of countries seriously affected by war. The underdeveloped countries underlined not only interdependence between these goals and economic development of their countries but also warned about threats to international peace and security posed by their abysmally low levels of living. They regretted the delay in setting up the Sub-Commission on Economic Development and Lebanon even went further by charging that "there seems to be a conspiracy of silence on problems of development".[9] The Economic and Employment Commission did refer to technical assistance for economic development but stated that it should be provided "within available resources". It referred the issue for further study to the Sub-Commission on Economic Development.

The attitude of the developed countries remained rather lukewarm. The representative of Norway said that despite some speeches neither The General Assembly nor ECOSOC was in a position to finance development projects. The US representative appeared to inject a positive note into the discussions by stating that problems relating to development should receive greater emphasis in international discussions and UN should play a preponderant role in this field. However, the major elements of UN policy which he outlined did not seem to accord with his intentions. These elements[10] were: (i) right of underdeveloped countries to initiate separate action on their own, (ii) use of technical advice and assistance from specialised agencies, (iii) role of ECOSOC in ensuring coordination and integration of work to avoid overlap and duplication, and (iv) direct arrangements between countries and by private arrangements for the supply of technical and capital assistance. Thus, the responsibility and initiative for development were placed squarely on underdeveloped countries. The latter were to seek financial and technical assistance from sources outside the UN which would play only a passive role of coordination—hardly a promising prospect.

---

9. ECOSOC, fourth session, summary records, Document E/SR.56.

10. *ibid.*, E/SR.58.

During the fourth session of the ECOSOC, Venezuela together with Chile, Cuba, India, Lebanon and Peru submitted a draft resolution[11] on expert assistance to Member Governments following the lead given by the General Assembly in its Res.52(I). Perhaps sensing the general mood, the sponsors of the draft resolution submitted a very modest proposal. It simply asked the Secretary-General of the UN to (a) act as a catalyst or intermediary by collecting and providing relevant information on availability of experts to Member Governments, (b) arrange assignments of teams of experts to requesting countries for study and solution of their specific problems, and (c) bring experts' recommendations to the attention of other interested Member Governments which may want to help in the execution of programmes. The Secretary-General's initial response to this was somewhat neutral. In his note[12] to the Council, he referred to the technical assistance provided by the League of Nations, ILO and other specialised agencies and to the observations on expert assistance made by various Commissions of the Council such as Population, Social and Economic, and Employment Commissions. He pointed out that services of experts on UN staff were used periodically by governmental representatives on an informal basis. However, he asked for "guidance of the Council concerning the general principles which should govern his actions" when formal requests received involved "extended services and substantial expenditures on the basis of mutually agreed financial arrangements with the governments concerned". He suggested that the Council should ask the Coordination Committee of the Administrative Committee on Coordination (ACC) to submit a report on this entire question during the Council's next session and the Council give careful consideration to this matter on the basis of that report.

Initiating the discussion[13] in the Council, the representative from Venezuela stressed the fact that all the UN Commissions were unanimous on providing technical assistance to the underdeveloped countries. He reminded the Council of the enormous needs of underdeveloped countries and pointed to the modesty of the proposal

11. Document E/324.

12. Document E/328.

13. For discussion on the six power draft resolution submitted by Venezuela (E/324), see ECOSOC, fourth session, summary records, E/SR.56-58 and E/SR.77-82.

as it would entail very little cost to the Secretariat. "The initial advisory operations," he said "would be on a modest scale and would expand to the extent that their success proved their value to Member Governments." The Indian delegate, being a cosponsor, strongly supported the draft resolution. He, too, emphasised its modest character and even offered to delete a provision in the draft resolution whereby recommendations of experts would be brought to the attention of other Member Governments interested in rendering special aid for implementation. The Peruvian representative found the proposal too modest and felt it was, in fact, "a rather weak attempt to change the economic trends in underdeveloped countries". The US delegate supported the resolution but reserved the right to make comments on the organisation of assistance, role of specialised agencies and the terms of assistance. The other developed countries were in general agreement with the draft resolution. Thus, in principle, there seemed to be at least general agreement on the ideas contained in the draft resolution.

The Secretary-General estimated the cost of carrying out the activities during 1947, until the Council considered the whole question at the fifth session next year, at $ 14,800. The draft resolution was redrafted in the light of the comments in the Council and the observations made by the Secretary-General. Specifically it omitted the reference to consideration of experts' recommendations by other governments. The Council's decision was contained in its resolution 51(IV) of 28 March 1947. In a separate resolution, acting on the recommendations of the Economic and Employment Commission, the Council expressed the view that "technical assistance should not be used for the purpose of exploitation or of obtaining political and other advantages exclusively for countries rendering such assistance".[14]

During the fifth session of the ECOSOC, the Fiscal Commission, which was established in October 1946, submitted its first report in which it asked the Secretary-General to provide, *inter alia* technical advice, information and assistance on fiscal matters to especially less developed countries. The mounting chorus on technical assistance emanating from various Commissions such as Social Commission, Population Commission, the Economic and Employment Commission and now the Fiscal Commission alarmed developed countries which

14. ECOSOC Resolution 27(IV).

expressed concern about additional expenditures involved and suggested establishing priorities. At the same session, the Economic and Employment Commission came out with its second report[15] in which it continued to harp on reconstruction and stability, paying lip service to economic development. It argued that loans and credit should be given exclusively for reconstruction and stability. The commission also introduced a new concept of economic self-sufficiency and argued that industrialisation in underdeveloped countries should be self-reliant. Some of the developed countries strongly criticised the neglect of economic development and preferential treatment envisaged for loans and credits for economic stability and reconstruction. The majority of developed countries also disagreed with the Commission's proposal that underdeveloped countries should be encouraged to industrialise themselves in order to attain an increasing degree of self-sufficiency. They argued that development should be economically efficient and self-sufficiency should not be a goal. These countries also felt that loans and credits should not be given exclusively for economic stability and reconstruction, to the exclusion of resettlement and development.

Also during this session the Secretary-General submitted an 'Interim Note'[16] on expert assistance to Member Governments. The Note, essentially a response to the ECOSOC Res. 51(IV) of 28 March 1947, explained the arrangements made by the UN Secretariat and specialised agencies for implementing the resolution. It also reported on the progress, or rather lack of it, made by the Coordinating Committee in preparing the report requested by the Council in its resolution 51(IV) and included the Secretary-General's observations on general procedures and terms, including financial arrangements, followed in rendering technical assistance.

The UN Secretariat and the specialised agencies had not set up any specific machinery for dealing with the requests for expert assistance. These were handled by staff on an *ad hoc* basis. The Secretary-General outlined some factors determining the extent to which the UN and the specialised agencies could provide expert assistance. These included constitutional provisions of UN organisations, budgetary allocations, availability of experts, and financial arrangements between

15. Document E/445 and Add.1.

16. Document E/471 and Adds.1&2.

organisations and Member Governments requesting assistance. An Addendum (E/471/Add.2) to his Note listed number of fields in which the United Nations and specialised agencies could provide expert assistance. The Coordination Committee's report was still not ready and would come before the Council only at its sixth session. On the question of procedures and terms of assistance, as requested in the Council's resolution, the Secretary-General had initially said that he would report after the meeting of the Coordinating Committee to be held towards the end of September or October 1947 but he did make a statement on 29 July 1947. According to him the total cost of expert assistance, from both within and outside the UN, were to be borne by the requesting Member Governments only with two exceptions. The UN will pay the salaries of staff deployed on missions provided no temporary replacement was needed and would not charge for assistance provided through correspondence. While the Secretary-General's statement seemed to reflect financial constraints, oddly enough, the UN budgetary provision allowed for technical assistance to all Member Governments in the field of social welfare, according to General Assembly resolution 58 (I). Such aid was given even to developed countries such as Austria, Finland and Italy. In fact, all the resolutions adopted on technical assistance till then, both by the General Assembly and ECOSOC, referred to Member Governments and not specifically to the underdeveloped countries.

The Secretary-General's note proved to be quite a disappointment for representatives from developing countries.[17] Venezuela remarked that it "Departed in substance from the intention of the Council's resolution." Other representatives were unhappy with the fact that no machinery had been set up to provide expert assistance. The President of the Council ascribed this to budgetary difficulties. USSR was in favour of making ad hoc arrangements in individual cases rather than adopting a general policy on the issue as a whole. However, as the Secretary-General's note did not really encourage further action, the Council simply took note of his Interim Report in its decision 96 (V) of 12 August 1947 on expert assistance. The Council reported its discussion on expert assistance to the second session of the General Assembly but did not ask for any action by the General Assembly.

17. For comments on the SG's Note, see E/SR.113.

Finally, during the sixth session of the Council, the Coordinating Committee submitted its first report.[18] It pointed out that conditions of assistance and its nature varied greatly from case to case, and the experience of different countries could not be generalised. According to the report each request had to be handled as a special case. The Committee, therefore, concluded that "the opportunities for cooperation between Secretariats as described in the Secretary-General's Interim report were satisfactory". Thus, even though the Committee had been given a substantial amount of time to make a detailed study of the issue of assistance, it failed to come up with any new ideas on the arrangements to be made in this respect; it preferred to confine its role to studying future experiences in the field. This was rather a strange position especially in view of the fact that the Secretary-General had already outlined basic elements of financing technical assistance. As the Secretary-General had not considered any structural or institutional factors, the lessons of the future experiences would be severely limited, simply mirroring the past. Perhaps the only likely development would be an increase in the volume of assistance sought.

The Coordinating Committee's report did not provide a basis for a decision by the Council and hence the question was postponed to the next session. During its seventh session, the Council made some observations on expert assistance within the framework of its discussion on the Report of the third session of the Economic and Employment Commission. In its resolution 139 (VII) of 26 August 1948, the Council, merely decided to give wider circulation to information on the availability of expert assistance and the terms on which it would be rendered. The UN Secretariat's lack of sensitivity and its failure to recognise the urgency of the problem thus significantly retarded any further progress in this area.

Meanwhile, during its second session in June 1948, the Sub-Commission on Economic Development discussed extensively the question of technical assistance for economic development. The Secretary-General had submitted a paper surveying technical assistance activities of the Secretariat and the specialised agencies. He described activities other than provision of funds and relief supplies.

---

18. Document E/614.

This was expected because the UN did not provide funds anyway. In its report,[19] the Sub-Commission observed that it, "Does not believe that the role of an international agency should merely be a passive one." The Sub-Commission put forward the following basic principles for the provision of technical assistance:

(a) All technical assistance should be provided only at the request of the country concerned.

(b) Any technical assistance provided should meet the needs of the country concerned and in a form desired by the country.

(c) Technical assistance should not be used for economic or political interference and should not be accompanied by any considerations of political nature.

(d) Technical assistance should be given only to or through governments.

(e) Countries requesting technical assistance should, as far as possible, define in advance the nature and the scope of the problem involved.

(f) Technical assistance should be rendered in such a manner as to utilise and instruct local personnel to the maximum extent practicable.

(g) Technical assistance should be of high quality and competence.

These principles were to govern future policies and operations relating to technical assistance.

The Sub-Commission also outlined several forms of technical assistance for promoting economic development. These included teams of experts, fellowships, training of local technicians, international conferences of experts, and other forms of exchange and dissemination of knowledge and information.

While examining the variety of arrangements that could be made for defraying the cost of providing technical assistance, the Sub-Commission realised that it was not practicable for the UN or the specialised agencies to have on their staff the whole range of experts that may be required. It noted that the specialised agencies did bear varying portions of the cost. The UN, which did not do so, could only

19. Document E/CN.1/Sub.3/22.

detail a few staff members periodically for short duration, provided no replacements were needed. A majority of the members of the Sub-Commission observed that the UN rule "Might act as a deterrent to requests for technical assistance because it implies that the rule will be followed rigidly and that, in every case, practically all the cost would fall on the requesting government irrespective of its ability, at the moment, to meet all the cost involved." The Sub-Commission, therefore, suggested that, "The UN should, under approved and agreed conditions, be prepared to share some of the costs of TA." It also urged Member Governments, which were in a position to render technical assistance, to increase their assistance through appropriate UN organs and agencies.

The Sub-Commission's detailed examination of this issue provided the underdeveloped countries with the needed ammunition to intensify their campaign for technical assistance at the General Assembly's third session.

Citing the UN budgetary provision for social advisory services, the delegates of these countries now pitched for technical assistance for economic development by the UN. Burma, Chile, Egypt, and Peru submitted a draft resolution[20] in the Second Committee of the General Assembly, dealing with economic questions, seeking assistance up to $ 500,000 in 1949, to provide for teams of experts, organisation of local training facilities, organisation of international conferences, organisation of exhibits, compilation of bibliographies and exchange of information on technical publications. The text of this draft resolution was based largely on the advice of the Sub-Commission on Economic Development which, at its session in June 1948, had discussed in depth the question of technical assistance and submitted its recommendations to the Economic and Employment Commission.

Introducing the draft resolution, the delegate from Venezuela referred to all the previous resolutions adopted by the General Assembly and the ECOSOC on this subject, and pointed out that they were of no practical value in the absence of financial provision. Despite the technical assistance provided by the specialised agencies in their respective fields there was still a broad area of development in which technical assistance was needed and could be provided only

20. A/C.2/129.

by the UN. Commenting on the draft resolution, the UN Secretariat explained[21] that it had neither administrative nor financial resources to carry out the functions described in the draft resolution. It could at best organise one team of experts every two years. It would need substantial financial resources to undertake the functions. In this context, the Secretariat referred to the substantial funds expended on fellowships under social advisory services and by WHO and UNRRA.

Most of the developed countries cautioned the Second Committee about the pace of expenditures. They wanted the fifth committee to decide on the financial provision. However, the Second Committee appointed a sub-committee to prepare a final text of the draft resolution. After considering various amendments suggested to the draft resolution, the Sub-Committee finally agreed to submit two separate draft resolutions to the General Assembly: Draft Resolution 'A' on technical assistance and 'B' on training of apprentices and technical workers.

The draft resolution 'A' was finally adopted by the sub-committee. It deferred from the draft resolution of the original sponsors in one important respect. The sub-committee deleted reference to the specific amount of $ 500,000 during the first year of operation and instead decided to 'appropriate the funds necessary to perform the functions'. Thus, though the ceiling appeared to have been lifted, yet in practice the question was left open, without seeming to negate the intention of the sponsors. The other changes made in the draft resolution were more editorial in nature. The policy framework contained in the original was kept intact. In addition to resolution 'A', the sub-committee also agreed on a statement and requested the Rapporteur of the Second Committee to include it in his report to the General Assembly. This statement dealt primarily with two issues: financial provision in 1949 and pace of the programme in the first year. On the financial question, the Second Committee would express its desire to the General Assembly "that enough funds should be included in 1949 budget of the UN to permit the SG to initiate the functions and services set forth in the resolution." With regard to the pace of the programme, the basic thrust of the various observations on its individual elements was on what was practicable. However, on

21. A/C.2/138.

comprehensive economic missions, such as the one sent to Haiti earlier, the statement included a strong qualification. It prescribed that such missions be undertaken "Subject to the principle that the full operation of the programme should not be attempted in the first year." This was probably in deference to the Secretariat which had explained earlier the complex and time consuming process of organising such missions. It was also part of the attempts of the developed countries to restrain the level and pace of expenditures on technical assistance. But this limitation on capacity proved to be controversial and this part of the statement barely made the sub-committee. It was adopted by a vote of four in favour, three against, one abstention, and two absent. This margin of success was too thin to survive.

When the report of the sub-committee came before the Second Committee, the latter also had financial estimates of the programme prepared by the Secretary-General. In preparing these estimates the Secretariat also adhered to the 'principle' on the operation of the programme during the first year. The Secretariat stated that it could not undertake more than three comprehensive missions in the first year and anticipating under performance asked for $ 70,000 for missions though the total cost of three missions was estimated at $ 100,000. The total budgetary provision required for all elements of the programme was estimated from $ 324,000 to $ 384,000 depending on the amount to be spent on fellowships. The discussion in the Second Committee centred mainly on the pace of the programme in the first year and on the total financial provision to be made for the programme. The developing countries reopened the discussion on the first issue and refused to accept the 'principle' enunciated by the sub-committee. While they agreed on doing what was practicable, they did not want deliberate under utilisation of the potential capacity. Chile moved a formal amendment for its deletion from the report of the Second Committee to the General Assembly. Despite some protests by Australia and USA, the Chilean amendment was adopted. As for the financial question, though the Secretary-General had submitted estimates, the developed countries did not want to commit themselves to any particular figure. Instead, they wanted the question to be referred to the Fifth Committee. Some of them, especially Netherlands and USA, found Secretary-General's estimates of fellowships rather too high. Netherlands commented that UN should not expand fellowship programme unduly "thus becoming a vast Rockefeller Foundation." Among the developing countries, surprisingly India took a contrary position on the financial question.[22] Saying that no clear principle was laid down by any organ of the UN on financing technical assistance, India believed that the UN and specialised agencies should bear only administrative costs and not be responsible for carrying out of technical assistance programmes. India was of the opinion that developing countries could afford to pay. This approach, India argued, would enable the Secretariat to accomplish larger share of work and avoid recriminations from countries. India suggested that the entire question be sent back to the ECOSOC for further study without General Assembly taking any action at that stage. Evidently, developing countries did not share India's views on this subject. At the end, the Second Committee adopted resolution 'A'[23] while referring the financial question to the Fifth Committee.

When the General Assembly considered the report of the Second Committee, it had three financial estimates for the year 1949 on technical assistance. The Secretary-General had submitted an estimate of $ 348,000; The Advisory Committee on Administrative and Budgetary Questions (ACABQ) scaled it down to $ 85,000 and the Fifth Committee agreed on a budgetary provision of $ 288,000. Belgium supported the ACABQ recommendation and argued that the Fifth Committee provision was voted by 26 Members who contributed only 10.23 per cent of the total budget while others contributed 90 per cent and bore the actual burden. The Belgium delegate even suggested tying voting to the size of contributions. This was perhaps a lone and harsh note of dissent at that time but the argument was to become a rallying point for developed countries in the 1980s. However, the General Assembly, in its Resolution 200(III) of 4 December 1948, did approve resolution 'A' on technical assistance submitted by the Second Committee and accepted Fifth Committee's recommendation for budgetary provision of $ 288,000 for the year 1949. This resolution by the General Assembly marked the first, modest but historic, step in providing multilateral aid by the UN to developing countries. The General Assembly also requested the

22. A/C.2/SR.80.

23. A/C.2/157.

Secretary-General to report to each session of the ECOSOC on the progress made in the implementation of this resolution and further requested ECOSOC to review such reports by the Secretary-General and "when necessary, formulate recommendations concerning policy and budgetary action required by the General Assembly to carry on the functions instituted by the present resolution."

Thus, in one form or another, the question of providing technical assistance through the UN and specialised agencies had been before the UN legislative bodies, General Assembly and ECOSOC, since 1946. In 1946 Lebanon had set the ball rolling by asking for the creation by the UN of Advisory Boards to provide expert advice and guidance in various fields of economic and social development to underdeveloped countries. Later a milder version of this did survive. Several Commissions of the UN had recommended provision of technical assistance in their respective fields. The programme, however, grew only incrementally but without any budgetary appropriation in the UN for provision of technical assistance. The UN basically played a passive role providing information on experts and on their availability. The developed countries, using various arguments, blocked appropriation of budgetary funds for technical assistance in the ECOSOC. Both the ECOSOC and the UN Secretariat had failed to provide dynamic leadership. The representatives of underdeveloped countries continued to voice their frustration regarding the ECOSOC's indifference and its poor performance in the General Assembly's discussions. The Socialist countries were also least enthusiastic. Instead of discussing the merits of the case, they persistently indulged in Cold War rhetoric, focusing more on criticism of the Marshall Plan and neglect of eastern European countries. They placed all the blame for the state of world affairs on western developed countries. The continuing efforts by underdeveloped countries finally got a big push after the Sub-Commission on Economic Development studied the subject of technical assistance at great length during its second session in June 1948 and made strong recommendations for its provision in different forms. The Governments of Burma, Chile, Egypt, and Peru immediately picked up these recommendations and packaged them in a draft resolution which they introduced during the third session of the General Assembly, leading to the adoption of the GA resolution 200(III). It was an irony that the ECOSOC and the Economic and Employment Commission had not even discussed the report of the Sub-Commission on Economic Development on its second session which was devoted almost entirely to the discussion of technical assistance. The underdeveloped countries managed to pre-empt the ECOSOC and succeeded in persuading the General Assembly to approve financial provision for technical assistance in UN Regular Budget for 1949. This was the real beginning of what was to be called in later years as the United Nations Regular Programme of Technical Assistance.

2

Establishment of the Expanded Programme of Technical Assistance (EPTA)

In his inaugural address on January 20, 1949, President Truman spoke at length on the problems of economic development in the underdeveloped countries. He outlined a programme to provide substantial and broad-based assistance to them to facilitate the task of rapid economic development. In 'Point Four' of his programme, he laid special emphasis on the importance of technical assistance for economic development and pledged to launch an ambitious programme for its provision, both separately and jointly through international cooperation. He said, "We invite other countries to pool their technological resources in this undertaking. Their contributions will be warmly welcomed. This should be a cooperative enterprise in which all nations work together through the United Nations and its specialised agencies whenever practicable."[1]

Later, on 24 June 1949, President Truman sent a strong message to the Congress on technical assistance for the underdeveloped areas of the world. In it, he described the dismal economic conditions in these countries, the rising aspirations of their populations, the economic interdependence of the underdeveloped and developed countries, and the beneficial effects which rapid development in such countries would have on the future growth prospects of the developed countries, as well as on international peace and security. He asked the Congress to enact legislation "to authorise an expanded programme of technical assistance for such areas, and an experimental programme for encouraging the outflow of private investment beneficial to their economic development."[2] For the first year of the programme, he

1. Development of Technical Assistance Programs, US Senate Committee on Foreign Relations, November 22, 1954, p.54.

2. *ibid.*

recommended an appropriation of $ 45 million. This would include both the US contribution to the programmes of international agencies, as well as the assistance to be provided directly by the US.

During the eighth session of the ECOSOC (February 1949), the US delegation placed President Truman's ideas at the centre stage of the deliberations. Referring to the broad concept of economic development embodied in 'Point Four' of President Truman's address, Mr. Thorp, the US delegate, said, "The immediate task, however, was not the contemplation of goals but the more prosaic discussion of means."[3] While discussing various aspects of economic development, he stressed "two international factors in economic development: the international flow of capital and the international flow of technology".

With regard to technical assistance, his second point, Mr. Thorp emphasised the importance of better use of resources in the development process and of the knowledge needed to develop those resources. "The clear conclusion," he said, "was that technical cooperation was a basic type of outside assistance whereby the underdeveloped countries could be helped in their progress towards a better economic life. To meet that objective, the concept of technical cooperation had to be broad in substance and in method, and had to embrace many and varied activities." He believed that genuine international cooperation in the field of technical assistance could result in the mobilisation of greater resources. Therefore, he urged the Council "to plan such expanded programmes and perhaps to revise operating and administrative procedures."

The US submitted a draft resolution[4] incorporating three proposals:

(i) The Secretary-General, in cooperation with the ACC, should prepare "a concrete programme for enlarging the activities of the United Nations and specialised agencies in the field of technical assistance for economic development".

(ii) Examination of ways and means of financing an expanded programme, including consideration of special project budgets.

---

3. For Mr. Thorp's complete statement, see document E/SR.251 of 25 February 1949.
4. Document E/1191.

(iii) Recommendations for the coordination of planning, execution and control in the field.

The US delegation suggested that at its ninth session, the Council should review the comprehensive report to be prepared by the Secretary-General on the three proposals, and also, formulate recommendations for decisive action by the General Assembly and specialised agencies. It urged the Member States to be patient while assessing the impact of an expanded programme on economic development. "The timetable for the attainment of the objectives of economic development should be measured not in years but in decades," Mr. Thorp said.

Mr. Thorp's speech was received warmly by the other delegates. The speech, coming as it did from the US, seemed to impart a sense of certainty to the issue of technical assistance. In the ensuing discussion, several comments were made on various aspects of the US proposal. These essentially consisted of suggestions regarding the in-depth study to be prepared by the Secretary-General. France came up with an important addition to the US proposal, i.e., that the study should take cognizance of social factors which directly condition economic development. The French proposal was accepted and the US draft was adopted by an overwhelming majority in the ECOSOC.[5] Only the socialist countries opposed it as they thought that the ideas contained in it were too vague and non-operational.

After consultations with the UN agencies, the ACC appointed the Working Party of Experts to prepare a draft of the report. The Working Party received suggestions from the Member Governments and also consulted the Organization of American States (OAS). The final report[6] consisted of two parts. Part I set out the objectives and nature of the programme, fields of work covered, and organisational and financial arrangements. There was complete agreement on the text in Part I among all participating agencies. Part II contained detailed proposals by the UN and the specialised agencies in their respective functional areas. Each agency took responsibility only for its own proposals. In his Preface to the report, the Secretary-General

5. ECOSOC Resolution 180 (VIII) of March 1949.

6. Report by the Secretary-General on a Comprehensive Plan for an Expanded Programme of Technical Assistance for Economic Development, Document E/1327/Add.1, 27 May 1949.

cautioned that "problems of economic development do not fall neatly into classes which correspond to the respective functions of individual organisations" and, therefore, some development problems may have ramifications that concern a number of them. In other words, some overlap and duplication was perceived as natural and unavoidable.

The following pages summarise the various aspects of the report.

PART I OF THE REPORT

Objectives of the Programme

Pointing to the rapid technological evolution in the developed countries and its beneficial impact on productivity and standards of living, the report took note of the increasing economic inequality between the developed and developing countries. It said the process of development in the latter was a complex one and required a broad-based approach. The report emphasised the importance of enhancing productivity in all fields through the application of capital and the technical knowledge and experience available, so as to facilitate rapid economic development. Stating that technical knowledge could be shared through technical assistance, it went on to say, "The problem immediately at hand is to organise it [technical assistance] and direct it into the channels where it can produce the speediest and most constructive results."

The principal responsibility for development would rest with the recipient developing countries. Their attempts would be bolstered by sustained efforts by the developed countries and by the UN and its specialised agencies. The report laid particular emphasis on the role of the underdeveloped countries' governments in the development process. They would plan, promote, direct and assist the process. The report said, "The accumulation of capital and organisation of technical skills on the scale necessary for effective economic development is often possible, especially in underdeveloped countries, only through governmental action."[7] It elaborated that the governments concerned would have to manage stress, promote balanced development, ensure optimum growth and secure widespread distribution of benefits. The

7. *ibid*, p.7.

report's emphasis on the role of the state in economic development was a reflection of the times. This was a period when development economists and policy makers, both in the developed and underdeveloped countries, as well as multilateral and bilateral programmes highlighted the role of the state. They expected the underdeveloped countries to formulate their development plans, and spell out their priorities and needs for assistance. The report drew attention to various channels of providing technical assistance. It made particular mention of the role of direct private foreign investment, universities, foundations, research institutions, bilateral assistance and multilateral assistance provided by the UN and specialised agencies. Coordinated action on the part of these agents, would significantly enhance the volume and effectiveness of technical assistance to the underdeveloped countries.

Nature of the Programme

The report recognised the importance of bilateral assistance. It was felt that in the light of the needs of the underdeveloped countries and the volume of assistance needed, there was room for both bilateral and multilateral assistance, which could grow simultaneously. The report specified, "there should, however, be a progressive increase in the relative importance of international action in the amount of technical assistance provided,"[8] since in the UN charter and the constitutions of the specialised agencies, the Member Governments have pledged themselves to promote "higher standards of living, full employment and conditions of economic and social progress and development" in all countries. "A worldwide programme of technical assistance for economic development cannot succeed without effective international cooperation,"[9] it said.

Stressing the importance of the exchange of knowledge and experience among all countries, the report cited examples of fields in which international and regional action was indispensable.

The following five conditions were mentioned for ensuring "the effectiveness of the proposed technical assistance programme in stimulating and accelerating sound economic development."

---

8. *ibid*, p.11.

9. *ibid*, p.12.

(i) A Practical Approach

This required each country to tailor its design of development to its particular needs, desires and potentialities, and to refrain from borrowing a development pattern, however successful, from another country. A technical assistance programme had to be so designed as to respond effectively to a country's specific goals, objectives and pattern of development. The report added that in some cases, it might not be practical to support a comprehensive programme of technical assistance and it might be necessary to proceed on a piecemeal basis in selected fields. Another element of this practical approach was the need for balanced development. This caution was probably influenced by the prevailing theories of economic development. In the 1950s, there was considerable discussion in the academic circles on balanced development in underdeveloped countries.[10]

(ii) A Favourable Environment

This called for modernisation of social and economic institutions, changes in social and economic attitudes and habits, and observance of sound macroeconomic policies.

(iii) Personnel

The report emphasised the importance of having an adequate number of qualified experts, supplemented by trained and experienced local staff. The experts would include public officials in advanced countries, and personnel drawn from research institutions, foundations and other entities in the private sector. Ensuring an adequate supply of experts required the full cooperation of governments, especially those of the advanced countries.

(iv) Supplies and Equipment

Apart from capital investment, equipment and supplies were required for technical assistance projects, such as training and research institutions and demonstration projects in agriculture. Such supplies were essential for the successful implementation of programmes and projects.

---

10. Prof. Ragner Nurske of Columbia University was the principal exponent of the theory of balanced development.

(v) Continuity

Economic development was viewed as a long-term process, requiring a progressively growing volume of technical assistance. Therefore, the report said, governments should also consider expanded programme as part of a long-term commitment to development. Though it did not anticipate long-term budgetary provisions by advanced countries, it suggested such commitment, at least in principle. The governments of the underdeveloped countries were expected to sustain their commitment to development, adopt the recommendations of the experts to the maximum extent feasible, make efficient use of resources, and ensure proper maintenance of the institutions and facilities created under technical assistance programmes.

In the light of different types of technical assistance and the various agencies and organisations participating in it, the report did not find it "feasible to suggest any uniform terms on which international technical assistance should be furnished". The underdeveloped countries were expected to make some contribution, at least in local currency, to the technical assistance programmes. Other arrangements would have to be made on an *ad hoc* basis, depending on the circumstances in each country. The administrative, political and economic arrangements made were expected to be consistent with the resolutions passed by the General Assembly and ECOSOC in earlier years, especially GA resolution 200 (III).

Fields of Work

While Part II set out detailed programmes of technical assistance proposed by the UN and specialised agencies, chapter 3 of Part I contained a brief description of these fields, providing the rationale for assistance and highlighting its major objectives and the scope for it in each field. The formulation of the broad objectives of technical assistance was rooted essentially in a recommendation for balanced development. The major objectives in various fields were as follows:

- Estimation of needs and formulation of programmes of development taking into account external factors.
- Improvements in agriculture to increase domestic supplies of food, raw materials and exports.

- Expansion and diversification of non-agricultural industries.
- Expansion of power, transport and communications.
- Large and growing investment in health for eradication of diseases and provision of effective health services.
- Provision of technical education and promotion of scientific research.
- Building basic social services to deal with needed adaptation to new ideas, techniques and methods of work.
- Improvements in the life and labour of working men and women.
- Establishment of sound monetary system, and credit machinery, and promotion of sound macroeconomic policies.
- Strengthening national administrative services.

Forms of Technical Assistance

The report identified five forms of technical assistance: advisory services, training, demonstration projects, pilot plants and dissemination of technical assistance.

The advisory services would be both of a short-term and long-term nature. They would comprise individual experts, as well as teams of experts. They would also undertake, if requested, general assessment of human and material resources for development. The training was to include training of nationals at home and abroad, besides the establishment of training institutions. Demonstration projects were considered another useful means of imparting training. According to the report, "These may take many forms, ranging from demonstrations executed by single persons to highly complicated projects involving the development of a sizeable productive undertaking." Pilot plants would be undertaken to initiate research and processes for the adaptation of technology used in the advanced countries to the specific developmental needs of the underdeveloped countries. The report recommended the dissemination of the latest technical and scientific information to the industrial and agricultural organisations, in addition to research and teaching institutions, in the recipient countries.

Organisation and Finance

The report called for a cooperative effort, but emphasised the need to avoid overlap and duplication among executive agencies. It highlighted four areas in which action was required to ensure effective coordination in the execution of the Expanded Programme of Technical Assistance (EPTA).

(i) Relationship between Recipient Governments and International Organisations

The report did not provide any concrete guidance in this area. Stating that the type, extent and timing of technical assistance may vary from country to country, it did not consider feasible to formulate specific guidelines for action. It suggested that in some cases a general agreement would suffice, while in others, a formal agreement covering various aspects might be required. It did suggest that there was a need to create a national coordinating mechanism—a concept which has endured over time.

(ii) Relationship between International Organisations

For facilitating coordination, review and evaluation activities under the expanded programme, as well as for the submission of periodic reports to the ECOSOC, the report suggested the establishment of a Technical Assistance Committee (TAC) under the ACC. The Committee would be aided by a small full-time and qualified staff. The staff would collect and analyse all the relevant information on the programme, act as a clearing house for information and service the TAC. The latter was conceived essentially as a consultative body, rather than an operational arm of the ACC. The technical assistance projects and requests falling within the competence of individual specialised agencies was entirely left to them for execution.

(iii) Relationship with Programmes of Bilateral Assistance

While stressing the need to strengthen this relationship, the report did not suggest any mechanism for doing so. It merely requested aid-giving countries and recipient countries to keep international organisations informed of their bilateral activities.

(iv) Finance

The recommendations on finance represented the lowest common denominator of the preferences expressed by the UN and the specialised agencies. This so-called consensus led to the formulation of a decentralised method of financing the expanded programme. Each agency could have, if necessary, its own special budget for technical assistance. It could expect the recipient countries to make some contribution, at least to meet the local expenditures.

The special technical assistance budget of the UN could be in two parts, covering: (i) a programme of technical assistance to be carried out by the UN itself; and (ii) a supplementary fund to be used by the Secretary-General, in consultation with the ACC, to finance technical assistance projects to be carried out jointly by the participating organisations, and to supplement the technical assistance budgets of these organisations when additional funds were required for facilitating the execution of essential projects. The fund was not to be used to finance the regular technical assistance activities of the specialised agencies, which would finance such activities from their own budgets. However, the report left some scope for this in case the executive heads of the agencies made such a request. The report did not elaborate on the type and extent of joint projects, or on the nature of the essential projects for which supplementary funds were to be provided.The executive heads of the agencies would use the TAC to consult each other on their proposed programmes and budgets before finalising them. While making its reviews, the TAC would focus on coordination and would attempt to ensure that the agencies' various activities harmonised with the system's overall programme. The ACC would then issue and submit a report on the programmes and budgets to the ECOSOC, General Assembly and the governing bodies of the specialised agencies.

PART II OF THE REPORT

Part II described the kinds of technical assistance activities to be undertaken. The presentation was in the nature of 'projects', but gave no indication of their character, size, location and costs. All the details of the so-called projects were to be determined later, in consultation with individual governments desiring assistance. The report stated that these projects were essentially extensions of the technical assistance activities then being carried out under the GA resolution 2000 (III), and also included accumulated requests which had not been met. The description of the projects was based mainly on illustrations of what could be done in various areas with the help of the accumulated experience and expertise of the organisations. There was no mention of any survey of needs or extensive consultations with the recipient governments. The projects as described were mere extrapolations of the limited range of activities then being carried out by the organisations, and did not reflect the entire spectrum of needs.

The total cost of the programme, to be implemented by the UN and five specialised agencies,[11] was estimated at $ 35.9 million for the first year and $ 50.1 million for the second. The UN share was $ 5.9 and $ 9.2 million for the first and second year, respectively. Just as the concept and formulation of the projects were very weak, so were the estimates of the costs. The project inputs included experts, consultants, equipment and supplies. The estimates for manpower were based on the prevailing UN salary scales. The anticipated costs of equipment and supplies were a matter of guesswork. The estimates were very rough and were meant to indicate only the approximate order of magnitude. They were not intended to serve as a basis for the preparation of formal budgets. Though it was argued that the Secretary-General's request for greater flexibility was based on the complexity of the development process, it can be perceived to have sprung more from the imprecision and vagueness in the formulation and costing of projects.

The UN Programme of Technical Assistance was "proposed as an expansion of the programme undertaken in accordance with the resolution 200 (III) of the General Assembly" and included the same services as authorised in that resolution. Since similar services were to be rendered both in the technical assistance programme of the regular budget and in the EPTA, the total estimated cost for the latter was to be reduced by the amount provided for technical assistance in the former. This budgetary approach, which failed to differentiate between technical assistance in the regular budget and the EPTA, opened a political window which probably encouraged the donor countries in later years to attempt to eliminate provision in the regular budget for project related technical assistance.

The major types of services included in the EPTA were comprehensive exploratory surveys; technical advisory services;

11. WHO, UNESCO, FAO, ILO, and ICAO.

scientific and industrial research; training; pilot and demonstration projects; and dissemination of technical information. Since the specialised agencies also provided these services in their fields of competence, the UN would render assistance mainly in 'unassigned' areas. Such fields were considered to include manufacturing, power, transport and communications, preparation of development plans, public finance, statistics, government administrative reforms, macroeconomic policies, social welfare services, population and housing. Where necessary, projects in some of these fields would be carried out in cooperation with the specialised agencies. For each major type of service, the Secretary-General's programme presented estimates of output in the first and second years. The total outlay on economic development was estimated at $ 15.12 million. The UN share, $ 12.5 million, formed 82 per cent of the total. The balance of the expenditure was to be incurred by the specialised agencies on economic development.

The programme proposed by the Secretary-General as well as those of the specialised agencies, neither dealt with specific sectors, nor did it indicate any order of priorities. It did not differentiate between various levels of development, and failed to indicate how much a country could expect to receive and in what fields. The programme's proposals discussed only inputs—experts, fellowships and equipment—which were common to all projects and sectors. The operational aspects of programming had no relevance to the objectives discussed earlier, such as the integration of technical assistance with economic development, balanced development, and so on. Later, this would pose difficulties in the evaluation of the programme. It is a pity that the Secretariat did not seize the initiative and put in extra efforts to project a clear vision for the future of technical assistance. Essentially, it proposed to provide the same inputs that had been provided in the UN Regular Programme, with the difference that it covered more fields for assistance.

During the ninth session of the ECOSOC, the delegate from the US opened the discussion on the EPTA. In a comprehensive and far-ranging statement,[12] he commented on all the major aspects of the programme that were contained in the Secretary-General's report. His

12. For comments by the US on the SG's report, see E/SR.303.

comments, he said, were based on an in-depth review by over 500 US government officials of their understanding and past experience in this sphere, as well as their perception of the future possibilities. This exercise had clearly pointed especially to "the impossibility of formulating exact and complete programmes far in advance." On 24 June 1949, President Truman had submitted legislation to the Congress: the first part dealt with technical assistance and the second with private investment. The US favoured technical assistance through the UN and in cooperation with other governments, and underlined the importance of rapid action by the Council. Praising the Secretary-General's efforts, he noted that the ACC had not found it possible to comment on the proposals, or their practicality, bearing on economic development, or suggested any omissions. While calling it an unfinished programme, the US delegate softened the remark by saying, "in fairness, it should be added that no guidance had been given to its authors as to the limits within which they should work."

The US delegate believed that a programme of $ 36 million, as proposed in the Secretary-General's report, could not be carried out efficiently in the first year as there would be several limitations and delays in the recruitment of expert personnel. He proposed a range of $ 15 million or $ 25 million for the first year. He suggested that within this range, the Economic Committee of the ECOSOC should develop sectoral priorities and distribution of resources. Alternative balanced programmes could be formulated at budgetary levels of $ 15 million, $ 20 million and $ 25 million, in consultation with the UN and specialised agencies. He further suggested that the Economic Committee should consider proposals from agencies which could make an effective contribution to economic development. However, this criterion was not fully explained, nor was any guidance given on how to measure or assess 'effective' contribution.

The US was unwilling to discuss the question of financing, i.e., whether there should be a central special budget or separate budgets for each agency, until the General Assembly decided on the scope of the programme. It suggested that after the Assembly had taken a decision, the UN should convene a technical assistance conference to decide upon (i) the total contribution, (ii) contributions to each agency, (iii) the amount each government would contribute, and (iv) an understanding by each government that it would pay its contribution to the agency to which it was pledged. At the conference, allocations should be made in terms of agencies, keeping in mind the relationship between the UN and the agencies. On the subject of coordination, the US agreed to the formation of a Technical Assistance Committee (TAC) of the ACC, but wanted the ECOSOC to play a role as well. Finally, the US emphasised coordination with non-governmental organisations, especially the OAS.

In the discussion that followed, practically every country, except the Socialist countries, welcomed the strong support voiced by the US for expanded multilateral technical assistance. Some of them made a few observations of their own. Australia would contribute only in kind for payment in Australian currency or sterling. It believed that the specialised agencies were not really concerned with economic development and worried about how they would coordinate with each other. Australia was of the view that initially, the UN would have to play a greater role in the sphere of undertaking surveys and formulating programmes, and later, the balance might shift in favour of the agencies. This clearly showed a lack of true understanding of the developmental process and of the importance of contributions from different sectors, such as agriculture, health and education. Also, Australia was not in favour of forming the TAC. Instead, it advocated a central fund and the establishment of a governmental committee to formulate broad policies and principles, as well as to allocate funds for projects.

Lebanon believed that technical assistance could not produce effective results in the absence of capital investment. Investment finance was more important. It disapproved of the US suggestion to scale down the programme from $ 36 million to $ 15-25 million for the first year, arguing that delays in the recruitment of personnel could not pose such a serious problem. Lebanon attached importance to assistance in project execution.

The USSR and other Socialist countries saw the Secretary-General's report as a mere collection of projects. They were against an international conference and a central fund. They believed that the EPTA needed further serious study and that the Secretary-General's proposals lacked the finality to be implemented.

Accepting the US proposal, the ECOSOC referred the matter to the Economic Committee for detailed review. When the Committee commenced its discussions,[13] the US identified three major problems: (i) the type of activities to be included in the programme and the priorities in the initial stages; (ii) the formulation of a best possible programme in terms of the objectives and resources available; and (iii) administration, coordination and financing of the programme. As for financing, the US sought clarifications on the concept and working of a central fund, the management of local monies contributed by donors, and the methods of raising and disbursing resources. All these issues were discussed by the Economic Committee.

The Secretary-General's representative, Mr. David Owen, explained the proposals set out by the former in the seventh chapter of his report. He pointed out that the proposals for an EPTA were essentially formulated within the framework of the GA Resolution 200 (III). The difference was that they now made provision for supplies and equipment, which had not been envisaged in the earlier resolution. Moreover, the Secretary-General's proposals on EPTA also included activities to be carried out under the GA Resolution 200 (III)—Regular Programme of Technical Assistance—but the EPTA budget will be reduced by the amount separately authorised by General Assembly for technical assistance activities under Res. 200 (III). "The proposals," he said, "were a statement of facilities and opportunities which could be offered to underdeveloped countries, not a blueprint of technical assistance for any particular country." Programmes for individual countries would be prepared in close consultation with the governments concerned. Mr. Owen felt that while experts would come from countries at various levels of development, those coming from countries at an intermediate level might be of greater use, since their experiences would be closer to those of the developing countries. With these remarks, Mr. Owen had sown, perhaps inadvertently, the seed for a future programme for the exchange of technical assistance between the developing countries, an independent programme which was later established by the UNDP.

While explaining the various types of services to be provided, Mr. Owen pointed out that it was essential to first assess the needs of individual countries. Therefore, he emphasised the importance of

---

13. For discussion on SG's Report in the Economic Committee during the Ninth Session of ECOSOC, see E/AC.6/SR.55-59, 68-70, 72 and 75-80.

comprehensive exploratory surveys, which he hoped would identify needs that could be met within a short period. Referring to the fact that the Secretary-General had planned four missions for the first year and five for the second owing to difficulties which may crop up in administration and recruitment, he cautioned that "the proposals had been drawn up in a short time, and could be regarded only as tentative; indeed, the first two or three years of the programme should be regarded as experimental, for modifications would certainly be required".

Supplementing Mr. Owen's remarks, Mr. Laugier, another representative of the Secretary-General, remarked that the whole programme was tentative and drawn up without an exact idea of the time frame, the countries which were to benefit and the availability of funds. He proposed three procedural approaches: (i) one could wait till the governments expressed their needs; (ii) the Council could decide on the geographical coverage of the programmes; and (iii) intergovernmental bodies could decide on the substantive priorities.

The discussions that followed included some general comments on the size and nature of the programme, as well as on its individual elements. France and Belgium pointed out that the fact that the programme dealt only with forms of technical assistance, and not with fields of application, made it difficult to allocate resources and ensure a balance between supply and demand. They felt that the Council might have to establish priorities at some stage. India and Denmark found the programme modest and believed it deserved more resources. On the other hand, the US and Venezuela described the programme as unduly ambitious, especially as far as the first year was concerned. They argued that the Secretariat had no administrative experience in several fields of technical assistance and this would delay the execution of the programme. For this reason, they suggested that the provision for the first year be modified. The USSR wondered if the governments of the underdeveloped countries had been invited to participate in the preparation of the programme, and believed that it had been prepared from the top down. It also considered the programme vague and abstract, as well as inadequate in terms of the distribution of resources among countries. For these reasons, the USSR called for greater dialogue with the developing countries.

With regard to the individual elements of the programme, there was wide agreement on exploratory surveys, advisory services and training. However, there was a lot of scepticism regarding scientific and industrial research centres, pilot projects, and technical publications and the dissemination of such information. These reservations would imply that a large number of countries, especially the developed ones, were not yet ready to move beyond the core activities specified in the GA Resolution 200 (III).

In reply to these comments, Mr. Owen re-emphasised the tentative nature of the programme and the Secretariat's readiness to respond to the needs of the various governments. He said that the provision of information on sectoral distribution would entail the creation of appropriate administrative machinery, which would delay the pace of execution. He was confident that the need for experts would be met in the first year. He asked the Council to accept pilot and demonstration projects on an experimental basis, subject to review in due course.

In general, the main difference between the underdeveloped and developed countries was that whereas the former emphasised aid for industrialisation, preferably with finance, the latter wanted basically to expand the existing technical assistance activities included in the GA Resolution 200(III). The resistance of the developed countries to pilot projects, institution-building and dissemination of technical publications stemmed essentially from this.

Administration, Coordination and Finance

There was extended discussion on these three aspects of the EPTA. The focus was largely on coordination mechanisms, a central fund for the collection and disbursement of monies, the need, if any, for the distribution of resources among the UN and its agencies, and the question of holding an international pledging conference for technical assistance. The discussion on the main issues of coordination and finance centred around three proposals, presented by Australia, New Zealand and the US. Australia outlined a highly centralised approach, as opposed to the decentralised one suggested by the Secretary-General. The proposals put forward by New Zealand and the US stressed decentralisation in the implementation and administration of projects.

(a) Coordination

Australia suggested that the ECOSOC should be responsible for overall policy, under the supervision of the General Assembly. The Council should set up a commission to interpret and execute policy. This commission could be a body of the whole or limited to the principal donors and recipients. The Secretary-General and the specialised agencies would be responsible for day-to-day administration. Each agency should fund its own projects from its own budget. As for joint and large-scale projects, they should be reviewed by the commission.

New Zealand submitted that the agencies should formulate annual programmes, to be reviewed by the ACC or TAC of the ACC. The ACC or TAC should submit the programmes that have been agreed upon to a special committee of the Council, which should review them and make recommendations to the Council. The special committee should have limited membership. It should be responsible also for oversight and conflict resolution. The ECOSOC should focus especially on the size of the programmes submitted to it and the policies underlying them. The General Assembly should undertake an annual review.

The US proposal did not differ much from that of New Zealand. The US, too, suggested that the agencies and ACC, or TAC, should play a role in the formulation and collation of programmes. It opined that a special committee of the Council should review the programmes accordingly and make recommendations to the Council. In addition, the special committee should be in charge of evaluating past performance. The Council should examine the reports submitted to it and present its conclusions to the General Assembly. The US emphatically opposed centralised administration of the projects by the special committee or any central body, as proposed by Australia.

Several countries supported decentralisation as proposed by the US, but made a few suggestions on certain other aspects. The UK proposed that the ECOSOC could state a few general principles to guide the execution of the projects by the UN and its agencies. Later, the UK even submitted a draft of such guidelines. Lebanon did not like the concept of a special committee with limited membership, as it could be liable to take decisions on political grounds. Similarly, China preferred the TAC to a commission or special committee of the Council as the former would be non-political in nature. India and Chile were in favour of a special committee of the whole to one with limited membership. Only Belgium adopted a completely different stance. Doubting the effectiveness of multilateral technical assistance, it advocated only bilateral aid. It preferred an administrative set-up which would serve only as a liaison between the donors and recipients.

(b) Central Fund and Reserves

There was near unanimous agreement on having a common central fund financed by voluntary contributions. There was also general agreement that contributions should be accepted in national currencies. New Zealand and Denmark cautioned against any separate solicitation by the agencies. New Zealand felt that contributions should not be tied to any specific agency, country or project. France alone suggested special, separate budgets for each project, so that governments could participate in projects of their choice. This was obviously not accepted.

Although there was general agreement on the need to have reserves, the suggestions regarding their size varied. The suggestions ranged from 5 per cent (India) to 40 per cent (Brazil), while some countries (notably, the US) were in favour of having reserves in excess of a certain amount, without specifying the amount.

(c) International Technical Assistance Conference

Initially, the US suggestion to hold an international conference on technical assistance, specifically for the mobilisation of resources, received a rather lukewarm reception. Australia, India and New Zealand were not particularly enthusiastic. Australia felt that such a conference would create problems of coordination. It held that confusion would ensue if the conference were called upon to divide the contributions among the participating agencies. New Zealand considered a conference too cumbersome and India found it unnecessary.

(d) Percentage Distribution of Funds among UN and Agencies

Except for the UK which was not initially convinced, there was hardly any opposition to the idea of such distribution. New Zealand wanted the shares to be fixed for only the first six months, while China expressed the need for some flexibility in compliance. The Chairman decided to poll the views of all the members of the committee. He received 12 proposals and summarised the results as follows:

Table 2.1

Summary of Proposals

Percentages

	Country Proposals (a)	*Average*	*Mode*	*Chairman's Recommendations*
UN	16-30	23.2	25	23
ILO	4-18	10.6	10	11
FAO	23-35	27.7	25	27
UNESCO	10-25.5	16.5	20	17
WHO	14-30	20.8	20	21
ICAO	0-3	1.2	1	1

Note: (a) represents the range reflected in the proposals.

The proposals made by the delegates stemmed from their perceptions of the importance of work carried out by different agencies. The wide range in each case reflected glaring differences in perceptions, which, in any case, were probably based more on impressions than careful analysis. Only the FAO seemed to have scored high on everybody's watch. Once the ranges contained in the countries' proposals were known, the Chairman's task turned out to be purely mechanical. He suggested 'average' percentages for agreement. Statistically, modal figures would have been more relevant, given the pull of high numbers on 'averages'. However, the committee could not reach an agreement at that stage and the matter was postponed to a later date.

(e) UK Paper[14]

The UK paper, proposed as a draft report on the basis of the Secretary-General's report, aimed at laying down principles or

14. Document E/AC.6/42.

guidelines for the execution of programmes and projects by the UN and specialised agencies. It suggested principles for the standard of work, coordination of efforts, economy of effort and selection of projects. The paper proposed that whatever work was to be carried out should be of the highest possible quality. It called for coordination of efforts between the UN and its agencies, especially in respect of large-scale, joint and training projects. With regard to the selection of projects, the emphasis was on projects which would yield early returns in the sphere of economic development.

It was in the area of economy of effort that some of the UK suggestions proved to be contentious. The main premise was that the UN and its agencies "should not themselves engage upon any activities on their own account, if use can be made of the activities of governments or private undertakings". The paper, therefore, suggested that the UN and its agencies should not undertake demonstration projects, both in the non-profit making as well as profit-making fields. The UK was also against the establishment of international training institutions and would instead, have the national or sub-regional institutions strengthened. These suggestions failed to receive the support of all the members of the Committee.

After the general discussion on the Secretary-General's report, Australia, New Zealand and US-Chile introduced their respective draft resolutions. All three proposals were in favour of a unified central fund for technical assistance.

As expected, the Australian draft[15] advocated a high degree of centralisation. It vested in the ECOSOC the entire responsibility for the allocation and use of funds. A commission of the whole of ECOSOC would advise it (the Council) on the principles and procedures to be used with respect to funds, and the procedure for dealing with requests. It would also make recommendations to the Council. The proposed TAC (of the ACC) would assist the commission by providing it with the annual programmes of the participating agencies and by giving it relevant reports and data on the progress in the execution of projects. In 1950, the Council would allocate up to $ 5 million and the balance of the amount collected would be reserved for subsequent allocation, to be made on the basis

15. Document E/AC.6/41.

of experience. The Australians also saw a need for formal agreements with the specialised agencies to ensure compliance with the principles and procedures laid down by the ECOSOC for the expanded programme. Australia did not make any reference to an international conference on technical assistance.

New Zealand's proposal[16] was in the form of a long draft resolution for adoption by the General Assembly. It advocated a decentralised structure and laid down general policies for governing operations. The proposal included policies relating to the responsibilities of the agencies and recipient governments. It visualised the establishment of a Technical Assistance Board (TAB) as a coordinating mechanism of the ACC. The TAB would assist a Technical Assistance Committee of the Council (TACOC). The TACOC would consist of just nine members of the ECOSOC. It would supervise general policy, review programmes and the progress made in their execution, and make recommendations to the ECOSOC. It would also be in charge of conflict resolution. The initial allocation of funds made by the Council for 1950 would be up to smaller of the half of the funds received or $ 10 million. The balance would be carried over and allocated in subsequent years by the TAB, on the advice and with the consent of the TACOC. The proposal was in favour of an international conference on technical assistance. It authorised the Secretary-General to collect funds and administer them in coöperation with the TAB, subject to general policy supervision by the TACOC.

The US-Chile proposal[17] resembled that of New Zealand in many respects. It endorsed an international conference on technical assistance, suggested a coordinating mechanism, and advocated the establishment of a TAC of the ACC and a Technical Assistance Policy Committee (TAPC) of the ECOSOC. The difference was that the TAPC was conceived as a standing committee of the ECOSOC. Also, the TAPC would be a body of the whole, unlike New Zealand's TAPC, which was limited to nine members. The major differences between the US-Chile and New Zealand proposals pertained to financial arrangements for the disbursement of funds and the size of the

16. Document E/AC.6/47 and Rev.1.

17. Document E/AC.6/48.

reserves. The US wanted the first $ 10 million and 80 per cent of the next $ 10 million to be made available immediately, with the rest going into the reserves. It also envisaged somewhat greater decentralisation in the administration of the funds. For example, the ACC "shall be authorised to allocate monies in the reserve as it may decide and at such times as it may decide". Only disagreements within the ACC were to be resolved by the TAPC. A feature which distinguished the US-Chile proposal from the others was that it accorded the ECOSOC primacy in the overall management of the EPTA and did not want the programme to emanate from the General Assembly.

After some discussion, the Economic Committee formally decided to consider the US-Chile draft resolution as a working paper for discussion.

The US-Chile proposal, which invited the ACC to set up a TAC, provided that the TAC should work through the ACC, and the latter should submit programmes and financial reports to the ECOSOC. Several members were uncomfortable with this arrangement. They believed that the ACC was purely an advisory body and should not be assigned this function. They were in favour of establishing a body that would be independent of the ACC, but would obviously include representatives from each participating agency. New Zealand, however, still wanted the body to consist of only those agencies which would be participating in the EPTA.

As for the proposed TAPC, some members wanted clarifications on its composition, that is, whether it would be a committee of the whole or one of limited membership. Some countries also cautioned that the TAPC should not meet too frequently in a year.

The discussion on the international conference focused mainly on its terms of reference and its relationship to the General Assembly. The US suggestion to invite all members of the specialised agencies, including non-members of the UN, raised questions about the General Assembly's sovereignty *vis-à-vis* non-members of the UN. However, this doubt was quelled by Chile's observation that in such a conference, the members of the UN would nonetheless have a majority. With regard to the terms of reference, the general view was that the conference should deal mainly with the total contribution and contributions by individual countries. A drafting committee was set up to work out a compromise.

There were four issues to be dealt with in the area of financial management: the size of the programme in the first year; the size of the reserves; subsequent allocation of reserves; and the shares of the UN and specialised agencies. Unlike the US, some members were in favour of a smaller programme for the first year, so as to gain experience. As for the size of the reserves, it was agreed that 20 per cent of the funds should be put in reserve. Regarding the subsequent allocation of the funds in reserve, many members wanted the TAPC, and not the ACC, to make such allocations. However, the US argued convincingly that it did not want a political body (TAPC) to exercise control over subsequent allocations. It added that given the percentage shares of the agencies to be fixed, the ACC was better suited for the job as it could have the necessary data to plan ahead, instead of starting after receiving the funds. Finally, the committee agreed upon the financial arrangements proposed in the US-Chile draft.

The discussion on the question of fixing percentage shares of agencies in the provision of technical assistance was influenced by subjective perceptions of the Members of the Committee. At the outset, the Chairman restated his list of the 'averages' he had arrived at following the earlier poll among the members. However, several members felt that these 'averages' did not reflect consensus. This observation was based on the members' own preferences, as some would rather give more to certain agencies and less to others. Eight countries suggested different percentages especially for the ILO, WHO, FAO and UNESCO. Taking these suggestions into account, the Chairman submitted revised proposals which identified the 'range', 'averages', 'modal value' and 'median'. There was some discussion on the relevance of these concepts, but the members could not agree on a common scale. Finally, they left the decision to the Chairman, who gave the following figures:

UN	23 per cent
ILO	11 per cent
FAO	29 per cent
UNESCO	14 per cent
WHO	22 per cent

ICAO	1 per cent

These were essentially 'median' values, preferred by many, but as they amounted to only 98 per cent, the Chairman added the remaining 2 per cent extra to the share of the WHO. The committee adopted the scale by a vote of 12-0-6. The US, however, abstained as it wanted a much higher share for the WHO and less for UNESCO. The final scale thus represented a mechanical result and not the consensus. By drawing up percentage shares for the agencies, the Committee also ended up deciding the allocation of resources among different fields of activity, while leaving it to the agencies to work out the country shares and their composition.

Finally, the Committee took up the question of setting priorities for the selection of projects by the agencies. The majority of members was against setting priorities at that stage and wanted to wait till more experience was gained. The US and India, however, felt that priorities should be set, especially with regard to marginal projects. According to them, it would be useful to the agencies. In the absence of wide support, merely a paragraph on priorities was included in the draft resolution. It must be noted that the members really did not have any method or criteria for spelling out priorities and the issue was discussed in very general terms.

The discussion then moved on to a joint draft resolution,[18] prepared by the US, Chile and New Zealand. It incorporated the amendments submitted during the discussion of the US-Chile draft resolution. The US submitted an amendment to this resolution, suggesting principally that the General Assembly, rather than the ECOSOC, should authorise the Secretary-General to set up the TAC, and that the international conference should also approve the financial arrangements proposed by the Council. In addition, India and the US wanted the resolution to contain a reference to 'guidelines'.

The UK and Brazil felt strongly that the TAC should report to the ECOSOC through the ACC, and not directly. Further, they held that the Secretary-General should not appoint the executive secretary of the TAC without consulting the heads of the participating agencies. However, this was opposed by several other members, notably, New Zealand, India, Australia and Lebanon. These countries viewed the

18. Document E/AC.6/56/Rev.1.

ACC as merely an advisory and coordinating body, without any executive functions. They wanted the TAC to have a legal status, and to be independent, powerful and focused on economic development. The critics carried the day and the UK-Brazil amendment was not accepted.

Australia tried unsuccessfully to reduce the percentage of resources to be made readily available for disbursement. Similarly, New Zealand failed to persuade the members that the TAPC should exercise general policy supervision over the TAC's activities. The members felt that there was already enough provision for the TAPC to perform this function. The members also rejected a US amendment whereby the international conference would approve the financial arrangements. Asserting the primacy of the General Assembly, they said there was no need for the conference to approve recommendations which had already been adopted by the Assembly. The US had argued that governments at the conference might not contribute to a programme over which they had no control. The US, however, reserved its position on this issue. Finally, after going through the other sections without amendments, the Economic Committee adopted the entire US-Chile-New Zealand draft resolution (E/AC.6/56/Rev.1), with the understanding that several members might raise some issues in the plenary meetings of the ECOSOC.

In the meantime, a subcommittee of the Economic Committee had submitted a report,[19] setting out "principles to serve as guide to the United Nations and specialised agencies participating in the expanded programme of technical assistance...", in the formulation and execution of their programmes. The report, which drew largely on the paper presented earlier by the UK and on the Secretary-General's report (E/1327/Add.2), dealt with various operational questions. The economic committee adopted it after taking into account some minor suggestions made during the discussion. It was then incorporated as Annex A in the resolution adopted by the Committee.[20]

Throughout the discussion on the EPTA, Belgium was the only one to argue strongly in favour of bilateral aid. It tried to seek legitimacy

19. Document E/AC.6/54.

20. E/1526.

for bilateral aid by agreeing to channel it *via* the TAC, while observing the 'principles and guidelines' enunciated by the Economic Committee. Needless to say, the position taken by Belgium was not accepted.

The Economic Committee submitted its final report[21] to the ECOSOC which included the US-Chile-New Zealand draft resolution as amended and adopted by the Economic Committee. There was still considerable discussion on the report of the Economic Committee in the ECOSOC.[22] Lebanon reiterated its concern about the small size of the programme in its first year of EPTA. The USSR repeated its objections to almost everything and attributed the underdevelopment of the underdeveloped countries to the policies pursued by the colonial powers. New Zealand identified certain issues on which agreement had been reached by a narrow majority. Australia insisted on the desirability of a highly centralised framework for policy and administration, arguing that decentralisation would result in considerable waste of resources. France was still in favour of contributing to specific projects that would be of interest to the governments concerned, rather than to 'an anonymous fund'.

Several amendments were moved to the draft resolution. These related principally to renaming the TPAC and TAC; appointment of the Executive Secretary of the TAC; percentage allocation of resources among the participating agencies; and approval of financial arrangements. At the suggestion of France, the TPAC was renamed the Technical Assistance Committee of the Council and the TAC was renamed the Technical Assistance Board (TAB), comprising only the UN and the agencies participating in the EPTA. It was also agreed that the TAC of the Council should be set up after the international conference on technical assistance. The Executive Secretary of the TAB was to be appointed by the Secretary-General in consultation with the agencies.

With regard to percentage distribution of resources, the USSR and Poland totally opposed the idea. They believed that resources should be allocated only after assessing their availability. France, too, reiterated its strong reservations on the 'secret and piecemeal method used to arrive at percentages'. However, no amendment relating to

21. *ibid.*

22. E/SR.310, 340-343.

percentages was accepted. An amendment suggesting that the international conference should approve all financial arrangements was accepted.

The discussion on the 'guiding principles' resulted in a few procedural and editorial changes, in addition to some changes of emphasis. Other than that, the whole text was accepted. The ECOSOC thus adopted the entire draft resolution submitted by the Economic Committee.[23]

This resolution and the underlying plan for EPTA marked a quantum jump in the provision of development aid by the UN. This was a historic achievement, clearly due to President Truman's vision and the initiative taken by the US in the UN. The volume of UN development aid continued to grow in future years.

In general, the Council's resolution was received favourably by the Second Committee of the General Assembly.[24] However, amendments were submitted by Poland, Mexico and Australia and later, Lebanon. Poland wanted the committee to state explicitly that the TAC of the Council would have the power to review and make recommendations on any question before the TAB. However, some members believed that the Council's resolution had already recognised the TAC's primacy, while a majority argued that such an explicit statement might lead to excessive and unwarranted political interference in the administration of the programme. Poland withdrew its amendment in the absence of majority support. A Mexican amendment sought to give the Secretary-General some flexibility in convening the international conference. However, as pointed out by Lebanon, since the Secretary-General had already been given the discretion to do so in paragraphs 12 and 13 of the Council's resolution, it was agreed to make a reference to these paragraphs in the Second Committee's draft resolution. An Australian amendment wanted the committee's draft resolution to reiterate mandatory acceptance of the 'principles and guidelines' by the participating agencies. This was agreed upon unanimously.

Before the matter reached the plenary session of the General Assembly, the USSR had come around to support the EPTA, on the

23. ECOSOC Resolution 222.A.(IX) of 14 & 15 August 1949.

24. For discussion in the Second Committee, see A/C.2/SR.95-97.

condition that there would be no political interference and exploitation while giving aid. It also agreed to the proposed international conference. Now that there was agreement among all parties, the Second Committee's draft resolution on the EPTA, with its amendments, was adopted unanimously.[25]

The atmosphere in the General Assembly's plenary session was charged with considerable emotion and a feeling of triumph. Everybody was happy with the major breakthrough in the field of technical assistance and there was a feeling of gratitude to the US for its forceful initiative. The general mood was summed up in a comment by the President of the Assembly, who said, "The discussion on EPTA concerned one of the noblest efforts towards international economic cooperation ever made." The US, on its part, expressed its readiness to play a substantial role in the EPTA through the UN and its agencies. It hoped that all countries, including the developing countries, would participate and contribute to the common fund. Pointing out that the ECOSOC had not provided any criteria or guidelines to the agencies for determining their priorities, the US suggested that the agencies should prepare statements to that effect and indicate activities which could make the maximum contribution to economic development, at least in the short run. Having savoured the joy of triumph, the General Assembly unanimously adopted the Second Committee's draft resolution.[26]

International Technical Assistance Conference

The Technical Assistance Conference was held from 12 june to 14 June 1950 at Lake Success in New York. It was convened to pledge contributions to the Expanded Programme, and to approve the financial and allocation arrangements proposed by the ECOSOC in its Resolution 222(IX) and endorsed by the General Assembly at its fourth session. The conference was attended by 54 countries. Notably, all the Soviet Bloc countries were absent at the Conference.

At the conference, the developments and discussions leading up to the creation of the EPTA were briefly reviewed in papers[27] submitted

25. Report of the Second Committee, A/1064 of 7 November 1949.

26. GA Resolution 304(IV) of 16 November 1949.

27. E/CONF.10/2-4.

by the Secretary-General. The papers also mentioned the financial and allocation arrangements approved by the ECOSOC, and informed the conference that all the specialised agencies concerned had received authorisation from their respective governing bodies to participate in the programme. Further, the papers drew the participants' attention to the form and conditions under which contributions would be made to the special account of the EPTA. No contributions were to be made with limitations "as to use by a specific agency, or in a specific country or for a specific project." With regard to domestic currency credits, it was hoped that no restrictions would be imposed on the type or quantity of services and materials, as this would hinder the programme.

The conference opened on a high note of optimism. The Secretary-General characterised it as "potentially one of the most significant ever called by the United Nations."[28] The EPTA, he said, would help in arresting the widening gap between the developed and underdeveloped countries, besides enhancing global interdependence, world peace and stability. He was pleased that the Programme embodied universality of participation, contribution and benefits, and that it was designed to stay above politics. He told the delegates, "You are participating in what should become and can become one of the world's greatest achievements for lasting peace and for the social progress and better standards of life in greater freedom proclaimed in the Preamble to the Charter of the UN."[29]

Mr. Santa Cruz (Chile), President of the conference, echoed a similar sentiment. He said the EPTA "...in my opinion, together with the Universal Declaration of Human Rights, is the most important task the UN has accomplished in the five years of its existence." He also declared that the conference would "mark an epoch in the history of international collaboration and in the history of human progress."[30]

Several countries expressed their readiness to agree to a partial conversion of their domestic currency credits into other currencies, mostly non-dollar currencies. The US estimated that the requirements for the programme's first year would be $ 20 million and agreed to

---

28. E/CONF.10/PV.1.
29. *ibid.*
30. *ibid.*

contribute 60 per cent of the amount. The total contributions pledged at the conference amounted to the equivalent of approximately $ 20.01 million. Only six countries, including the US, pledged contributions in US dollars, amounting to US$ 12,040,500. Of this, the US share was $ 12,007,500. All other countries promised contributions in domestic currency credits. Managing such tied credits and matching them with the needs of the underdeveloped countries would, in later years, pose a challenge to the administration in terms of ensuring economy and effectiveness in the implementation of the programme. Cuba was the only country to draw attention to the restrictions that tied credits might place on their effective utilisation.

In its final act, the conference approved two resolutions: one on contributions, and the other on financial and allocation arrangements. These endorsed the recommendations made by the ECOSOC.

In his closing remarks,[31] the President emphasised change in international attitudes and responsibility, and spoke of the movement towards collective economic security. He said the EPTA would make an important contribution to the economic development of the underdeveloped countries and expressed his optimism about greater expansion of UN Technical Assistance in the future. He regretted the absence of the Soviet Bloc countries, ascribing it to political reasons. He hoped they would return to participate in the future.

Thus came to fruition the idea first proclaimed by President Truman and piloted energetically and successfully by the US delegation at the UN.

31. Document E/CONF.10/PV.5, p.10ff.

3

Country Programming and Coordination (EPTA)

The Technical Assistance Conference, as we have seen, approved the allocation of resources among the participating organisations according to the percentage shares recommended by the ECOSOC. Initially, in the ECOSOC, the member countries had expressed their own ideas on the matter. These were evidently based on their individual perceptions of the importance that the recipient countries might attach to assistance from different agencies. The developed countries' preferences were perhaps also based partly on their understanding of what contributes effectively to economic development and partly on their experience of bilateral assistance. At that stage, no serious effort had been made to consult the developing countries, even on a sample basis, on their needs and priorities. Of course, some developing countries were represented in the ECOSOC, but there is nothing to suggest that the delegates from such countries had articulated the needs of countries other than their own. Ultimately, in the absence of a consensus on a scale of distribution, the Chairman had worked out a compromise reflecting the maximum accommodation. There had also been some discussion on devising criteria for project priorities within different fields of activity, but the effort was abandoned since no consensus could be reached.

The participating agencies were now free to develop projects at a country level, within the limits of the quotas assigned to them. Thus, the developing countries were at the mercy of the participating agencies and could not be sure either of the total value of assistance they might receive, or its composition. The ECOSOC had given the agencies a general directive to ensure, as far as possible, a fair geographical distribution of the total assistance, but there were no benchmarks. The total expanded programme of technical assistance thus became a summation of individual programmes, prepared independently by the participating agencies in their respective fields of competence.

Initially, operative difficulties were encountered in the sphere of allocation since a substantial portion (40%) of the total contribution was in non-convertible national currencies. The problem was eased, to a large extent, by the fact that the US alone made 60 per cent of the total contribution. However, the non-convertible contributions were clearly in the nature of tied aid, though there were no restrictions on the use of such currencies for specific projects, or specific countries, or specific agencies. The EPTA's administration, which had no prior experience in the management and utilisation of non-convertible currencies for providing project inputs in different countries, had to struggle and juggle around for quite some time before it could ensure nearly full utilisation of the resources.

As implementation proceeded, there was growing concern among the legislative bodies[1] about ascertaining whether the programme was meeting the recipient countries' priority needs with respect to economic development. During the fourth session of the General Assembly, the Second Committee (in charge of economic and social questions) asked the recipient governments to clarify and prioritise their needs. Noting that the participating organisations had rather a free hand, the ECOSOC, during its 50th session, recognised the importance of full and continuous consultations between the recipient governments, representatives of the agencies, and resident representatives to facilitate the preparation of a programme for technical assistance at the national level. It also emphasised the need to assist the developing countries in preparing coordinated country programmes. As a result of an initiative taken by the USA, the TAC requested the Executive Chairman of the TAB to submit "(i) proposals for improving the procedures whereby coordinated country technical assistance programmes for approval by TAB may be developed at the country level, (ii) and a statement of responsibilities of the resident representatives and the corresponding responsibilities of the participating agencies."[2]

---

1. Document E/TAC/L.18 of 9 April 1952.
2. E/TAC/L.31.

The year 1953 marked the beginning of the planning of technical assistance at the country level. The TAB formulated some guidelines[3] for 1954, with a view to improving coordinated country programmes. The TAB would indicate a range of possible expenditure at the country level for all countries. Once the pledges for 1954 were known, the TAB would provide more definitive figures to the resident representatives, who would assist the respective governments in preparing coordinated programmes. Finally, the board would receive, review and approve the programmes. If the actual resources available for a country turned out to be less than the figure originally indicated by the TAB, the government concerned would be requested to delete projects which it accorded lower priority. The members of the TAC, however, were still not clear on the role to be played by the governments, resident representatives and representatives of the agencies in the preparation of coordinated programmes.

During the 16th session of the ECOSOC, Australia came up with a most telling criticism of the prevailing method of distributing resources among the UN agencies.[4] Australia held that the predetermined allocation of resources to the agencies on a percentage basis was flawed and felt this hindered a country's freedom to formulate its own priorities. The Australian delegation, therefore, suggested that the allocations be made after the preparation of integrated programmes. The Chairman of the TAB agreed that making percentage allocations seemed illogical in the case of country-level programming. He, too, suggested that the allocations to the agencies be made after the respective governments had prepared their programmes.

The portion of the total resources to be considered for automatic allocation to the agencies was discussed at some length. Initially, eight countries suggested in a joint draft resolution[5] that 80 per cent of the total funds available in 1954, 'after' allowing for an increase in the reserves and for the necessary minimum expenses of the TAB and field offices, should be made available to the agencies. However, a majority of the TAC's members argued that provision for the agencies

3. Document E/TAC/12.

4. E/TAC/SR.43.

5. E/TAC/SR.47 (annex).

should be made 'before' considering the reserves and expenses of the TAB and field offices. Finally, the TAC agreed[6] that 75 per cent of the total resources would be made available for the agencies 'before' allowing for all other expenses. This probably gave the agencies and country programmes a little more financial scope as it placed a ceiling of 25 per cent on the other expenses. Moreover, the TAC expected that some more of the money earmarked for resources and administrative expenses would be made available for further allocation to the programmes.

In view of the growing concern[7] over the automatic procedure for allocating funds to the agencies, the US suggested that such allocation be made according to a permanent formula, which would require only periodic review by the TAC rather than annual adjustments every year. It mooted the appointment of a Working Party to study the matter in detail. The US believed that the present percentages for the agencies were not optimal but along with the UK argued that there was no conflict between percentage allocation to the agencies and the concept of country programming. On the other hand, Belgium held that percentage allocation to the agencies would nullify the preparation of country programmes, endanger coordination, discourage initiatives by the recipient countries and ultimately, result in programming by the agencies. The countries would thus be more or less presented with a *fait accompli*. However, Belgium was prepared to compromise if the percentages for 1954 could be reduced. France, too, emphasised the importance of country programming and coordination at the country level, and wanted the agency percentages to be reduced to 60 per cent so as to permit greater flexibility. Since no specific agreement could be reached on this question, the ECOSOC agreed with the TAC recommendation, based on the suggestion made by the US, to appoint a Working Party "to consider in due course the system of allocation of funds to be applied as from 1955, taking into account ...the development of technical assistance programmes at the country level."[8]

The following year, France submitted a detailed proposal[9] to the TAC and the Working Party on the allocation of resources. It

6. E/TAC/SR.50, Annex II, B and ECOSOC Resolution 492(XVI).

7. E/TAC/SR.46,48 and 50.

8. E/TAC/SR.50, Annex II, C and ECOSOC Resolution 492(XVI).

9. Memorandum by France on allocation of EPTA Funds, E/TAC/ 32 of 11 January 1954.

suggested mainly two measures: (i) the elimination of automatic allocation of funds to the participating agencies, and (ii) setting up of an intergovernmental body to approve the programmes before they were put into effect.

The French delegation argued that the difficulties being faced now were rooted in the institutional arrangements made in the ECOSOC Resolution 222(IX), under which the EPTA had been established. It asserted that automatic allocation of substantial resources to the agencies would deter a country from formulating programmes consistent with its developmental plans. Predetermined allocations to agencies limited the options of the recipient governments and were unlikely to encourage programmes which the countries might have proposed in the absence of such limitations. Moreover, the governments would feel compelled to accept or promote such allocations lest they did not get what they truly needed. The French proposal pointed out, and rightly so, that the current system was adopted when the Council had no knowledge of the recipient countries' needs, the availability of experts or the feasibility of implementing the programmes. No crisis had arisen so far because in the early years, implementation had lagged behind available resources. Now, however, the resources made available could not match the requests, and automatic allocation did not provide an effective criterion for project selection. The system was arbitrary and there was a need to find a rational manner of allocating funds.

With respect to the setting up of an inter-governmental body to approve programmes, the French proposal defined the nature of the body and also, the procedure for approving programmes. The inter-governmental body was intended to replace the TAC in order to avoid overlapping, and was to be considered an administrative council, rather than a committee, of the ECOSOC. It would include some of the contributing countries that were not members of the UN so as to reflect their interests. As for the programming procedures, the French proposed that the recipient governments draw up their lists of requests on the basis of their needs, regardless of any balance established in advance by an outside agency, in different fields of activity. Country programmes would be sent directly to the TAB, which would have the main responsibility of reviewing them and preparing an annual programme. The proposed administrative council would review the annual programme and, in approving it, only give directives to TAB and not indulge in second guessing. It would also "settle the problems arising from divergences of opinion which may occur in the TAB between the various Participating Organisations during the discussion of the annual programme"[10]. The French proposal provided for flexibility by allowing for substitutions of projects during the year. It also allowed for the resubmission of a project during the following year if it was approved but not implemented during the year in question. In addition, France wanted to curb interference in the work of the agencies during the phase of implementation, and also aimed at avoiding 'too violent fluctuations' in the shares of the agencies in the total programme.

In the course of the discussions of the French proposal, the Working Party,[11] appointed by the TAC, recognised that "there appeared to be a lack of consistency between the establishment of comprehensive country plans of technical assistance best suited to advance the development of the countries concerned and the present system of automatic allocation."[12] It added, "The total annual programme of technical assistance as finally approved should reflect, to the maximum extent compatible with the need for some long-term planning by the participating organisations, the technical assistance programme that each government wishes to see carried out in its country."[13]

The Working Party deferred its decision on the French proposal on the ground that since the latter had never been applied, it was difficult to assess the divergence that would arise between the system of automatic allocation and the formulation of programmes according to the proposal. This was rather a flimsy excuse, especially in view of the fact that the Working Party had already recognised the inconsistency between country programming and automatic allocation. Furthermore, it had agreed that the recipient countries had the right to formulate their own priorities for assistance, and that such an arrangement was desirable.

10. *ibid.*, p.6.

11. E/TAC/37—Report of the Working Party.

12. *ibid.*, p.7.

13. *ibid.*

The Working Party went on to invite comments from the recipient countries. It asked the TAB, too, for its comments and requested it to provide information on (i) the difficulties that the adoption of the French proposal might create in coordination between the Regular Programmes and the agencies' activities under the Expanded Programme, and (ii) the state of the coordination machinery within the recipient countries.

Though the Working Party could not reach any definite conclusions, it did, however, put forward some alternative suggestions. These included the outright elimination of automatic allocations; giving 25 per cent of the available funds to the TAB for discretionary allocation; annual and continuing review and adjustment of agency percentages; and a phased elimination of the system of automatic allocation.

Regardless of whether an alternative would be adopted, the Working Party did recognise the need for a "competent inter-governmental body to be associated more closely than in the past with the drawing up and review of the comprehensive annual programmes." It also felt that the programmes should "be drawn up sufficiently far in advance to allow the participating organisations sufficient time to finalise their annual programmes of operation". As for the French suggestion that the TAC be replaced by another inter-governmental body for supervision of the EPTA, the Working Party took no action as it doubted whether it had the "competence to deal with such a proposal." Finally, it requested the TAC to defer its final recommendations on the French proposal to its next session in order to give the Secretary-General and ACC more time to consider it.

In June 1954, as requested by the Working Party, the TAB provided information[14] to the TAC on the agencies' reactions to the French proposal. Most of the agencies said they would have no difficulty coordinating the activities under the Regular Programme and those under the EPTA. The ILO and FAO said that as they had a large staff working on the latter, any significant fluctuations in its resources would create difficulties. The WHO's position on the issue was very vague. With regard to the coordination machinery in the recipient countries, the TAB pointed out that its efficacy varied from country to

14. E/TAC/31.

country, but there was consensus on discussing the technical aspects of the projects with the agencies concerned.

The French proposal provoked considerable discussion[15] and encountered divergent views. Most of the underdeveloped countries supported the elimination of automatic allocation, whether outright or in a phased, flexible manner. They believed that the present system did not guarantee a fair geographical distribution as the agencies had the money and did their own 'country programming.' The UK found the French proposal logically sound, but felt that more experience was needed before its application could be considered. The present system, the UK believed, prevented interagency competition and provided some measure of assurance to the agencies. Surprisingly, it was Australia which had serious reservations. It argued that there was no need for change since the legislative bodies had not expressed any dissatisfaction with the present system. The ECOSOC Resolution 222 (IX), Australia pointed out, did not mandate any fixed percentage of contributions for automatic allocations. The retained money was distributed according to agency percentages as no other method was available. The proposed French system of allocation would result in only marginal improvements, while entailing a considerable cost in terms of administrative complications, an increase in administrative costs, uncertainty regarding the agencies' respective shares in the programme, and fluctuations in the size of the agencies' programmes. The Australian government deemed it fit to wait until the resident representatives and agency representatives gained sufficient experience to be able to handle any changes. In countering the criticism, France reiterated its arguments in defence of the proposal. Further, it remarked that the money retained in the special account was always distributed again later according to the percentage shares of the agencies, as the same agencies sat in the TAB and would not have agreed on anything else. The French argued that the present system left the governments with no initiative. The governments could make requests only if the agencies had the money and the agencies insisted on their fixed shares; thus, the system perpetuated itself. France wondered, "Why the logic of its proposal should be considered its fault when in the opinion of some delegates the main and the only advantage of the present system was the mere fact of its existence."[16]

15. On the decision of the French proposal in TAC, see E/TAC/SR. 60, 61 and 65.

16. E/TAC/61.

Finally, in its report[17] to the ECOSOC, the TAC did reflect the general recognition of the inconsistency between automatic allocation and country programming, as well as the need to develop programmes on the basis of the recipient countries' needs and wishes for technical assistance. It asked the TAB and agencies for the same information which had been sought previously by the Working Party. It also endorsed the Working Party's suggestions for considering various alternatives. The TAC agreed that whichever alternative was finally adopted, it was desirable and necessary for the TAC and the TAB's and agencies' representatives in the field to be associated more closely with the preparation of the annual programme. A number of governments, members of the TAC, agreed with the French suggestion that some members of the participating agencies which were non-members of the UN should be associated with the EPTA activities, but many had doubts about setting up a new intergovernmental body. They proposed that the membership of the TAC be enlarged.

The Committee felt the question of the allocation of funds was intimately connected with that of setting up an intergovernmental body. It decided to defer a final decision on these issues until the 18th session of the ECOSOC. It, however, urged the ECOSOC to consider associating some members of the participating organisations that were not members of the UN with the work of the TAC, possibly by including them in the membership of an enlarged TAC.

In the plenary, some governments expressed their preference for the alternatives suggested by the TAC for the allocation of funds, while some cautioned against trying an untested system. While the majority agreed on associating non-members of the UN with annual programming, almost everyone preferred to enlarge the TAC rather than create a new intergovernmental body, as proposed by France. The Council adopted recommendations of the TAC on these questions.[18]

During the 18th session of the ECOSOC, the TAC again considered the question of the allocation of funds, and that of associating some members of the agencies which were non-members of the UN, as well as Member States which were not members of the ECOSOC, with the administration of the EPTA.

---

17. E/2558 of 25 March 1954.

18. ECOSOC Resolution 521B. (XVI) of 5 July 1954.

France and five others countries, including the US, introduced a joint draft resolution[19] which outlined certain procedures and principles to govern the allocation of funds from 1 January 1955 for the 1956 programme and in subsequent years. The joint draft resolution, on the one hand, aimed at abolishing predetermined shares for the agencies and gave the recipient governments full freedom to express their needs and priorities during the formulation of their programmes. Yet, on the other hand, it maintained that the agencies should have the principal role in programme implementation, and accepted the need to avoid sudden and sharp variations in their shares. The draft resolution envisaged a process with sequential steps, culminating in the approval of an annual programme by the TAC. To begin with, the TAB would provide guidance on the availability of resources. Programmes would be prepared at the country level, with the recipient governments being given full freedom to express their needs and priorities. The formulation of these programmes would not be bound by the notion of predetermined shares. The TAB would receive and review the programmes, then draw up the overall programme for the following year. While doing so, it would ensure that the agencies were not assigned less than a certain percentage (later agreed at 85 per cent by the TAC) of their share for the current year. The TAC would then review and approve the programme submitted by the TAB. Five per cent of the estimated resources were to be allocated to the Executive Chairman to "meet any urgent needs which may arise during implementation of the annual programme." Finally, the TAC would allocate resources to the programmes, and the General Assembly could confirm the allocations later.

The first draft of the resolution came in for considerable criticism.[20] The most important objection related to the apparent abolition of the agencies' percentage shares and the restriction of variations in their shares. However, this objection, though valid, did not carry weight because an alliance of nations, including France, supporting the joint draft resolution and those who wanted to retain the system of automatic allocation outnumbered the critics. Both sets of countries found what they wanted in the draft resolution.

19. E/TAC/L.72.

20. E/TAC/SR.71-75 and E/TAC/40.

Other criticism centred around the role of the resident representatives in the preparation of the country programmes, provision for regional projects, the role of the TAC in approving programmes and the stabilisation of country programmes. Most delegates from the underdeveloped countries objected to the idea of the resident representatives negotiating in the planning process as the responsibility was supposed to rest solely with the recipient governments. They also wanted targets to be set for regional projects in order to ensure stability in the size of the country programmes. Some members expressed apprehensions about the role of the TAC in approving the programmes. They feared that political considerations might influence the process. The sponsors of the draft resolution were quite responsive to these points. These members agreed with the idea of providing targets for regional projects so as to avoid any large and significant fluctuations in the size of the country programmes. They gave an assurance that the resident representatives would function only as coordinators, and that the TAC would not question the priorities reflected in a country programme, but only consider the overall priorities and interrelationships between the programmes. The technical and administrative tasks would be left to the TAB. The draft resolution was subsequently revised and adopted by the TAC, as well as the ECOSOC.[21] Thus, what the ECOSOC ended up doing was, on the one hand, affirming the recipient governments' right to determine their needs and priorities while preparing programmes at the country level, and, on the other hand, protecting the predominant role of the agencies in programme implementation and giving them a considerable degree of financial security. In actual practice, what happened was that while in the past, the agencies prepared parts of the country programmes, now the TAB was to prepare the overall programme in terms of agency shares.

At the time, it was rather surprising to see the French delegation overlooking the contradiction in the draft resolution as its declared purpose had been to eliminate the system of automatic allocation and steer clear of making any prior commitments to the agencies regarding their shares. However, in hindsight, it would appear that the French probably took a practical position, hoping to achieve their ultimate goal in a series of steps. They had managed a partial victory by getting

21. ECOSOC Resolution 542.II. (XVIII).

the Council to accept the recipient countries' right to formulate their own programmes without any pressure or persuasion by the agencies. Having laid this foundation, it would be easier to work towards further improvements in the future.

Six powers tabled a joint draft resolution on the subject of associating non-members with the work of the Expanded Programme. It suggested that two countries which were members of the agencies but non-members of the UN, and two which were members of the UN but not of the ECOSOC, should be added to the TAC. Venezuela questioned the competence of the TAC to decide on this issue and also, mentioned the question of equality in representation. Some members suggested that the TAC should be as large as the ECOSOC, while some wanted to first see how the body would function under the new procedures before enlarging it. However, Venezuela moved an adjournment motion, which was carried, and the decision was deferred. At the following (9th) session of the General Assembly, there was general support for an enlargement of the TAC, but the Assembly, too, failed to take a decision. Later, during its 11th session, it agreed to add six members.[22] which were subsequently decided by the ECOSOC at its 23rd session.

The year 1956 was the first one for which the work programme was to be prepared on the basis of the principles and procedures adopted by the ECOSOC on country programming and agency shares. However, the process used by the TAB to prepare the 1956 programme did not differ much from that of the past.[23] As a first step, the TAB determined a global planning target for the programme. The TAB claimed that while deciding on the country target figures, it had considered size, per capita income, health and educational needs, as well as some indicators of absorptive capacity, such as lack of transport, secretarial assistance, provision of counterpart personnel, housing for experts, and so on.[24] If continuing projects took a large share, target figures were cut to take account of that. The country programmes actually emerged from negotiations between the agencies and the government departments concerned with developmental projects. The country programmes were submitted to the agencies,

---

22. GA Resolution 1036 (XI).

23. E/TAC/L86 and E/TAC/SR.90.

24. A/C.2/SR.358.

which then submitted them, together with regional projects and their own operational costs, to the TAB. The TAB reviewed the programmes, taking into account the geographical distribution and experience of the participating agencies, and then prepared the consolidated programme for 1956. This was no different from the old practice and negated the spirit behind the idea. However, the TAC was quite satisfied with the process and its members' comments were confined to the need for more information and analysis. It was France which, both at the 22nd session of the ECOSOC and the 11th session of General Assembly, expressed disappointment with the lack of any appreciable change in the distribution of funds to the agencies. It emphasised that the prevailing agency sub-totals must be considered as only tentative. Mr. Owen's reply was that since 1956 was the first year when country programmes would come into full force, it was advisable to wait and observe the future trend. At the 12th session of the General Assembly, Iraq observed that sub-agency targets sometimes resulted in failure because a particular agency was neither able to provide experts in its field, nor willing to transfer funds to another agency which could use them effectively. Iraq also asked the TAB to consider a country's population, area and stage of development while allocating resources. Israel, too, expressed its dissatisfaction with agency targets.

In the programme for 1957, the TAB somewhat revised its procedure for fixing country targets. It "sought to give due weight to such factors as the needs of the countries as indicated by governments, the relative urgency of such needs as between different countries, size of population, per capita income, the quantum of assistance received from other sources, levels of programmes in previous years under EPTA, and the extent of commitments for projects already in operation".[25] Both in 1956 and 1957, the country programmes were first reviewed by the agencies from a technical point of view and later consolidated in the TAB secretariat. The TAB had still not provided any conceptual elaboration of indicators, nor was there any information on the relative weights attached to these indicators. Country programming depended very much on negotiations and the discretion and judgement of the TAB. Thus far, no exclusive

25. E/3080, p.9—Annual Report of TAB.

definition of eligibility for assistance had been adopted. In a few cases, in fact, help was being given to countries which were not normally considered economically underdeveloped. The per capita income of the majority of the countries receiving assistance was under US$150.

During 1957, the ACC requested the TAB to undertake a study of the country programming procedure. The TAC was generally happy with the system and did not desire any radical change. However, its members made several suggestions regarding the study to be undertaken by the TAB.[26] These related to "clarification of certain responsibilities of requesting governments and the introduction of some further degree of flexibility in the execution of the Programme." In its resolution, the TAC especially reminded the recipient governments about "progressive assumption of financial responsibility for the administration of projects,"[27] as envisaged under the expanded programme. It also called for clarity and precision in the preparation of country programmes.

In 1958, the TAB suggested that country programming be undertaken on a two-year basis to allow more time for the preparation and execution of projects, and thereby, improve the volume and quality of project delivery.[28] Later, in 1959, the TAB recommended the adoption of a system whereby projects could be approved for their entire duration and cost, but appropriations would be made on an annual basis. As usual, different views were expressed on this matter in the TAC.[29] Some members were concerned about commitment to long-term projects. Some wanted to place an upper limit—say five years—on the duration of a project, while some were in favour of placing a limit on the total resources to be allocated to a long-term project. However, a US intervention on this subject proved to be decisive.

The US strongly endorsed, in principle, the initiation of project programming while cautioning that this would tend to freeze a large amount of resources for up to five years. More importantly, however, the US seized this opportunity to advocate simplification of the

26. E/375, p.9.

27. ECOSOC Resolution 700 (XXVI).

28. E/TAC/84 and ECOSOC Resolution 735 (XXVIII).

29. E/3419.

country programming mechanics and procedures, which it found too complex and unsatisfactory. It felt that given the current country programming procedures, under which the agencies had planning shares in the total programme and subtotals in each country's planning target, any effort by a recipient country to shift assistance to another field "faced risk of having its total aid reduced." According to the US, this weakened a country's negotiating position and inhibited the optimal use of resources. Therefore, to give the recipient countries greater freedom of choice, the US sought the abolition of agency planning shares and agency subtotals. It was confident that this would improve country programming since the recipient countries had by now gained sufficient experience in planning and articulating their priorities and needs.[30]

Commenting on the behalf of all the agencies on the remarks and suggestions of the US, the Executive Chairman of the TAB pointed out that after the introduction of country programming, "agency planning shares and subtotals constituted compromise reflecting interest of the agencies in some degree of stability in planning their operations without fear of sharp reduction."[31] The governments were told that they were not bound by agency subtotals. He opined that a recipient country's "freedom of choice was based on considered suggestions." Project programming, he believed, would be useful to the agencies in the maintenance of long-term projects. He expressed his willingness to work out the programmes of newly independent countries, irrespective of the agency subtotals.

Together with four other countries, the US introduced a draft resolution which was adopted unanimously, with a few comments by the ECOSOC.[32] The resolution affirmed that the simplification of procedures could be promoted by eliminating the agency subtotals and planning shares. It approved project programming in principle and asked the TAB to submit a report on the simplification of procedures in 1961, on the basis of the abolition of agency subtotals and planning shares.

In 1961, the TAB submitted a detailed report[33] on the subject and suggested that project programming be introduced from 1963. To

30. For US Statement see *ibid.*, p.73.

31. *ibid.*

32. ECOSOC Resolution 786 (XXX).

33. E/TAC/L250/Add.3 and E/TAC/105.

begin with, it provided definitions of short-term and long-term projects. "Any project planned to be started and completed within 24 months will be considered a short-term project," it said, "and projects of longer duration would be considered long-term projects." On the question of finding the right balance between long-term and short-term projects, the TAB advised against fixing some flexible percentages and suggested that a decision could be taken later on the basis of experience. While preparing country programmes, the TAB would review long-term projects for their entire duration and approve their total costs. It suggested that the TAC should authorise a project for a maximum period of six years at a time, even if the duration of the project exceeded six years. Projects of a duration of more than six years were to be resubmitted for approval at the end of six years.

The TAC agreed with the TAB's definitions of long- and short-term projects. Though it would have preferred to fix the proportion of long-term to short-term projects, it agreed to review the situation after another year of experience. The TAC also decided that long-term projects should be approved for four years rather than six, and that they should be allowed to continue further only under exceptional circumstances. The system envisaged had one defect: it would pose serious difficulties if the resources in a particular year fell short of the sum of all the continuing commitments.

While accepting the elimination of agency subtotals and planning shares in country programming, the TAB said, "The continuing commitments of projects (long-term) already authorised must, however, be treated as the minimum level of an agency's activities in a given country." It added, "The aggregate of commitments of all participating organisations will thus set the floor below which the target of that country should not be allowed to fall. This will have to be treated as the most important element in fixing individual country targets."[34] The TAB also invoked a provision in the ECOSOC resolution 542B(XVIII) which, with a view to avoiding substantial fluctuations in the agencies' shares, provided that the amount allocated to each agency for the coming year "shall not be less than 85 per cent of the amount allocated to them under the current year's programme..." The TAB thus assumed that this provision would not

34. E/TAC/L250/Add.3 p.7.

be affected by the elimination of agency subtotals and planning shares in country programming. The TAB was essentially protecting the interests of agencies.

The TAC felt that the provision for 85 per cent was not compatible with the revised procedures for country programming. In defence, the TAB argued that whereas the agency shares and subtotals related to the planning stage, the 85 per cent rule applied to the operational stage, after the programme had been finally approved and thus, did not interfere with the freedom of the recipient countries. According to the TAB, the rule had not been invoked in the past because the programme was growing in those years. The TAC, however, believed that the rule had now lost its relevance and hence decided to cancel it. It recommended that the ECOSOC make the requisite amendments to the legislation.[35] Finally, the ECOSOC adopted a resolution[36] which made the 85 per cent rule inoperative.

In the light of the revised procedures for country programming, the TAB stressed the need for improved coordination at the country level. It also emphasised the roles of the resident representatives and agency representatives in providing greater and coordinated assistance to the recipient governments in the preparation of the country programmes.

The US raised a broader question in the context of coordination. The US delegate felt that it was essential to ensure coordination between the pre-investment assistance provided by the Special Fund and the technical cooperation from the EPTA. He said, "The basic issues to be considered whether EPTA and Special Fund should be more closely integrated, or even merged, and how technical assistance activities could be more closely related to overall development plans."[37] Some members of the TAC, especially from the developing countries, feared that the US was pushing for a merger of the Special Fund and the EPTA. But after some discussion, the ECOSOC decided to establish a committee of eight from among the members of the TAC and the Governing Council of the Special Fund to study all matters relating to coordination. The resolution adopted by the

35. TAC Report, E/3547.

36. ECOSOC Resolution 854 (XXXII).

37. See fn 35, p.61.

ECOSOC made no reference to the likely merger of the EPTA and the Special Fund.[38]

Over the years, several members of the TAC had frequently expressed concern over the fact that the resources available were thinly spread over a wide range of projects. These members had sought the concentration of resources in a few areas of priority. However, the TAC had also given the recipient countries the freedom to determine their own priorities and needs. In 1961, several members urged the TAC to provide some guidance to the recipient countries. As a first step in this direction, the ECOSOC asked the agencies to indicate, in a concise manner, the effective assistance they could provide to the recipient governments. It also decided to prepare "an indication of the most important principles for the guidance of Governments wishing to establish priorities for assistance under the Expanded Programme" in 1962.

The TAB submitted a report[39] on guidelines in 1962. It mentioned two overriding factors which had influenced their formulation. First, providing guidelines on priorities would be incompatible with giving the recipient countries the freedom to determine their priorities. Second, no guidelines could be universally applicable over the wide spectrum of countries. Therefore, with the aim of not impinging on the freedom of the countries concerned, the TAB suggested only some general guidelines. These related to the relationship of projects to national development plans, the feasibility of following up the experts' recommendations, projects likely to lead to pre-investment or investment work, and so on. The members of the TAC were divided in the debate on this subject: Some opposed such guidelines, while some sought their application to groups of countries at various stages of development. The TAC, however, could not reach any decision.

In 1962, the Ad Hoc Committee of Eight, set up to review coordination procedures and mechanisms in the UN system also submitted its interim report.[40] One of its important observations was: "Financial control is a vital element in coordination procedures. Under most systems of programming, the allocation of funds should normally

---

38. See ECOSOC Resolution 851(XXXII).

39. E/TAC/114.

40. E/3639.

follow and not precede the formulation of programmes."[41] Therefore, it said, "There should be no automatic recommendation and approval of projects." The programming authorities were to develop their own system of project appraisal and "all projects should be scrutinised carefully ... to determine that they will yield the best results expected from such projects in the context of the country's overall development objectives".[42] This essentially implied the abolition of country targets. However, as several members in the TAC insisted on continuing the practice of country targets, this recommendation of the Committee was put aside. The Ad Hoc Committee also considered several issues in the sphere of coordination, for example, at the headquarters level, at the national levels and in the field. Its recommendations were mostly a repetition of the exhortations made in earlier years. In the meantime, however, the ACC agreed on certain principles of cooperation between the representatives in the field and the resident representatives.[43]

The Ad Hoc Committee was later expanded to 10 members and it submitted a considerably detailed report[44] on substantive, organisational and operational aspects of coordination. This, however, was not a collective report of the Committee as such and merely presented the views of different members. Naturally, these views were widely divergent, both in terms of substance and suggestions. Some suggested the merger of the EPTA, Special Fund and UN Regular Programme, while others suggested the merger of only the EPTA and UN Regular Programme. Some even went to the extent of suggesting the merger of the EPTA, Special Fund, UN Regular Programmes and the regular programmes of Technical Assistance of specialised agencies. Similarly, the members' views on organisational matters ranged from complete centralisation and unified management to decentralisation of technical assistance.

However, an important contribution of the Ad Hoc Committee was to invite the attention of the TAC and ECOSOC to a considerable overlap between the activities of the EPTA and Special Fund, and in their criteria for the selection of projects. Sadly, the TAC and ECOSOC did not take any action on this report, other than requesting

41. *ibid.*, p.22.

42. *ibid.*, p.23.

43. E/3625, pp. 10 and 11.

44. E/3750.

the Secretary-General to transmit it to all Member States of the UN and the agencies in order to seek their views. The Ad Hoc Committee, it must be said, at least succeeded in flagging important issues in coordination for discussion and decision.

The French delegation continued to remain sceptical about the distribution of resources among the country programmes.[45] In spite of the deletion of agency subtotals in the preparation of country programmes, there was hardly any change in the agencies' shares. The French also pointed out that in practice, the TAC and General Assembly continued to authorise funds in terms of agencies and not recipient countries. The distribution of funds for the biennium 1965-1966 was almost the same as that for 1963-64. Some members of the TAC suspected that this might be a result of pressure exerted by the agencies at the national level.

Resolution 1090 B of the ECOSOC, adopted at its 34th session, had requested the Secretary-General to report on the arrangements for coordination of the multilateral technical assistance programmes of the UN system. However, at the 41st session, the Secretary-General and other UN organisations suggested that such a report be deferred until some experience was gained under the new UNDP which was established in 1966 by combining EPTA and the Special Fund.[46] At its first meeting, the Consultative Board of the UNDP simply endorsed the principles governing the role of the resident representatives laid down by the ACC in 1961.

At the session of the Governing Council of UNDP in June 1967, the Administrator of the UNDP proposed project budgeting for the technical assistance component of the UNDP, with a view to harmonising the budgetary process and project approval both for the Special Fund and the technical assistance component of the UNDP.

Specifically, the Administrator recommended the following changes in the prevailing procedures for preparing and approving technical assistance projects:[47]

"(a) discontinuation of biennial programming in favour of a system of continuous programming under which requests for

45. E/SR.1325.

46. E/4205.

47. E/4297.

technical assistance projects would be submitted by Governments as and when the need arose;

(b) establishment of annual country target figures by the Governing Council;

(c) review and approval by the Governing Council of individual projects at each session, and a delegation of authority to the Administrator to approve urgent projects between sessions; and

(d) periodic review of project implementation by the participating and executive agencies and surrender of savings accruing through delays in project implementation, which would thus become available for reprogramming by the recipient Governments."

The Administrator's proposal departed from the old system of project programming in one important respect. In the prevailing EPTA budgetary process, long-term projects were approved for their entire agreed duration, but they did constitute an integral part of an approved country programme. The proposed scheme would disband country programming but retain country targets, and each project would be reviewed and approved on its merits, as and when it was submitted. Also, the Administrator ignored the Ad Hoc Committee's recommendation, which would have entailed the elimination of both country programming and country targets. Instead, the proposed project budgeting was to operate within the framework of country targets.

The Administrator's proposal was discussed extensively in the Governing Council. The discussion centred mainly around the respective roles of the Governing Council and the Administrator, and the determination of country targets.[48]

The representatives of India and Yugoslavia suggested that the Administrator be given full authority to approve individual projects within the country targets approved by the Governing Council. Moreover, they observed, "As a practical matter, the task of reviewing thousands of small projects was not one which the Governing Council can effectively accomplish within the limited time available to it."

The Swedish representative, while agreeing with India and Yugoslavia, further suggested that as under the EPTA in the past, the

48. *ibid.*

Administrator should continue to develop and approve country targets and report them "*post facto* to the Council."

Some members were concerned about the criteria for the selection of projects, as well as those for the level of country targets. They felt that "in principle the Council should approve broad policies, guidelines and criteria governing UNDP and that the Administrator should approve projects and programmes within this policy guidance". They believed that giving authority to the Administrator, as proposed by India, Sweden and Yugoslavia, until such policy guidelines were available, "would amount to an act of faith which was difficult for some members".[49] All agreed that the Administrator should study the criteria for the selection of projects, as well as those for the level of country targets. Some members believed that the Administrator's proposal could be accepted in its original form because the suggestions of India, Sweden and Yugoslavia went too far and the Governing Council could not escape its responsibility. These members believed that changes could be introduced later in the light of experience.

Finally, in its decision, the Governing Council expressed full support for continuous programming with project budgeting. It spelt out details regarding procedures for the preparation, approval and implementation of technical assistance projects in an annex to a draft resolution[50] recommended by it for approval by the ECOSOC and General Assembly. These procedures would authorise the Administrator to review and approve projects, and to set country targets. The Governing Council suggested that while preparing country targets, the Administrator should take into account "such factors as the degree of development of the country, per capita income, the size of population, the extent of assistance from other sources and the capacity for absorbing technical assistance." It recommended that in the interest of stability "any sharp reductions in country target figures in any single programming period" be avoided.

The Governing Council kept for itself issues that mostly related to macro management, such as the total resources and their disbursement, country targets, approval of regional projects,

---

49. *ibid.*

50. *ibid.*, Annex IV and ECOSOC Resolution 1250(XLIII).

contingency authorisation to the Administrator, and so on. All these changes were to be effective from 1969 and the subsequent years since the ECOSOC had previously authorised biennial programming until 1967-68. However, these changes did not remain in effect for long as in later years, the UNDP reverted to country programming again.

4

Growth and Structure of EPTA

Introduction

The TAB, the principal operational arm of the EPTA, was established in early 1950, with Mr. Perez-Guerrero as its first Executive Secretary. The heads of all the participating agencies, 6 to begin with, were members of the TAB. By 1958, the number had increased to 9 and by 1961 to 10. In 1952, the TAC established a full-time post of Executive Chairman of the TAB and Mr. David Owen was appointed to this post. He was given wide-ranging powers for the administration of the EPTA. This entailed amendments to the founding Resolution 222 (IX) of the ECOSOC. Decision-making in the TAB was to be by a majority vote of its members, but the majority had to include a consenting vote by the Executive Chairman. Thus, the Executive Chairman had virtually a veto power over any decision.

In the initial stages, the TAB dealt mainly with its own budget and administrative and procedural matters, besides dealing briefly with issues relating to coordination. Following the practice initiated earlier by the Secretary-General for the UN Regular Programme of Technical Assistance, the TAB, too, decided to have resident representatives for technical assistance in a few countries. It made its first appointment in Pakistan. For operational purposes, the first financial year of the TAB covered the period 1 July 1950 to 31 December 1951. Thereafter, it was on a calendar year basis. The TAC, also set up in 1950, made several programme-related suggestions during its first meeting held after the establishment of the TAB. These included, *inter alia*, the development of criteria for the selection of projects and further clarification of which countries should be eligible for assistance under the EPTA.

During the General Assembly's fifth session in 1950, which was also the first after the formal initiation of the EPTA, there was a general sense of satisfaction over the establishment of the EPTA. The members' attitudes were positive and optimistic, notwithstanding some expressions of disappointment. Lord Ogmore of the UK described, "The question of development of underdeveloped countries as probably the next in importance, after the question of aggression in Korea, of all the items before the present Assembly."[1] Recognising that financing of economic development could not be considered in isolation of technical assistance, he announced that the UK Labour Party, in its policy statement 'Labour and the New Society', had proposed the preparation of a new long-term programme—a World Plan for Mutual Aid—to succeed Marshall Aid in 1952. However, not much of this was heard in the halls of the General Assembly. Later on, the Government of the Netherlands announced the establishment of an international academic institute which would promote the study of development in all its aspects, and would train experts and people from the underdeveloped countries. The Dutch delegate said this would help achieve the objectives of UN Technical Assistance.[2] The optimistic mood at the session was somewhat clouded by disappointment over the non-participation of the World Bank, several eastern European countries and the USSR during the inception of the EPTA. In 1953, however, the USSR, Czechoslovakia and Poland joined the Programme.

The discussions at this session also gave rise to several suggestions regarding the implementation of the EPTA. The delegates emphasised the equitable geographical distribution of assistance, as well as the importance of organisational reforms and dynamic civil service. Mention was also made of standards to determine the urgency, priority and amount of assistance for different regions. There was talk of moderating local costs for small countries, and of the need for a broad interpretation of the resolutions, besides flexibility in their implementation.

As the EPTA grew and unfolded over the years, several flaws in its conception, implementation and effectiveness became evident. In

1. A/C.2/SR.119.
2. A/C.2/SR.121.

order to ensure its continuous growth and effectiveness, the UN legislative bodies had to make periodic corrections and adjustments. Later, the General Assembly established the Special Fund to provide pre-investment assistance instead of capital assistance which was sought by the developing countries. As it turned out, however, there was a considerable overlap between the activities of the Special Fund and the EPTA. This called for a major organisational change and accordingly, the Special Fund and the EPTA were merged in 1966 to create the present UNDP.

Resources (Annexure A-4.1)

1950-1951 to 1958

Contributions to the EPTA were made on a voluntary basis. The General Assembly held an annual pledging conference, at which the Member Governments of the UN announced their pledges. The governments could contribute either in fully convertible currencies, or in their national currencies. Besides the US, only a handful of countries made their contributions in US dollars, and these contributions were very small. Most countries contributed in national currencies, which essentially implied tied aid. The TAB had to manage the expanded programme in such a way as to match the specific needs of the developing countries with the goods and services available in the donor countries. Moreover, several countries used different rates of exchange: one for calculating their contributions and another for the expenses incurred in their countries.

Barring a small dip in 1952, resources grew steadily, though at a small pace, from 1950 to 1958. The number of countries contributing increased from 54 in 1950 to 85 in 1958, while the amounts pledged rose from $ 20.04 million to $ 31.31 million in the same period. Despite the substantial increase in the number of contributing countries, the marginal rate of growth in resources decelerated significantly in later years. In 1958, pledges increased by only 1.5 per cent over 1957. The principal reason for this was a substantial fall in the US contribution. In the early years, the US contributed 60 per cent of the EPTA's resources, but it reduced its contribution to 45 per cent in 1958 and 40 per cent in 1959.

Difficulties arose in the utilisation of some restricted currencies, which hindered optimal growth of the programme. For example, the 'special projects' established by the TAB to utilise contributions by the USSR, Czechoslovakia and other Eastern European countries were a source of special concern. These projects were established separately and were not assimilated with the EPTA's resources, nor were they included in the country programme targets. They were additional to the resources in a country programme and represented a 'special bonus' to the countries utilising such resources. The utilisation of currencies in the 'special projects' was sometimes based on direct negotiations between the donor and recipient country. Some members of the TAC feared that this practice might degenerate into bilateral programmes and militate against multilateralism.

To address this concern, the TAB submitted a report[3] on currency utilisation to the TAC in May 1956. According to this report, only two countries, Brazil and Denmark (only part of Danish contribution) "made their contributions in the form of specific services and training facilities, but the majority of contributions have been received in local currencies expendable only in the countries making them. Of present contributors, 16 countries now contribute in unrestricted convertible currencies, 15 in currencies with limited convertibility and over 40 in currencies expendable only within the countries making the contribution".[4]

The TAB did acknowledge the difficulties encountered in the utilisation of currencies in some cases, but stated that "many of these have progressively been overcome as a result of special measures and continuing experience".[5] It viewed the prevailing practice as a temporary expedient and was in favour of waiting until more experience was gained. The TAB hoped that after the transitional period, it would be possible to eliminate all distinctions in programme planning and that the programme for 1957 could be presented in a form which made no distinction between the use of different contributions. The report stated that complete assimilation of the contributions received in different currencies "will present serious difficulties owing to the need to establish a pattern of acceptable

3. E/TAC/50.

4. *ibid.*, Para 1.

5. *ibid.*, Para 2

utilisation in certain cases, and to ensure equitable geographical distribution of the available resources,"[6] given the basic principle of providing assistance in forms acceptable to the recipient countries. The TAB sought a one-year extension of the transition period and hoped that the 1958 programme would see full assimilation, subject to the condition that "continuation of special measures (i.e., special projects) would be permitted to deal with any backlog of unusual currencies presenting utilisation problems at 31 December 1957."

The TAB's report was quite balanced. While it acknowledged the existence of the problem, it was also optimistic about expediting a solution. However, some members in the TAC were not satisfied with it. Canada, Norway and the US introduced a draft resolution,[7] which aimed at defining a 'non-usable currency' and setting criteria for rejecting further contributions from countries whose contributions in previous years had remained uncommitted and unutilised beyond a certain level. A currency was considered "not readily usable" if "an amount greater than the equivalent of US $ 200,000 and greater than the total of the previous year's pledges in any currency remains uncommitted at the time of the Pledging Conferences." The draft resolution requested the Secretary-General not to accept any pledge "in a currency not readily usable until arrangements have been made for the reduction of the uncommitted amount below the limits" set above, or "the contributing governments have agreed to convertibility into readily usable currencies." The draft resolution agreed with the TAB that unused currencies presenting utilisation problems at 31 December, 1957 should be carried over, but stipulated that no special measures (i.e., special projects) be taken for their utilisation. On future contributions, the draft resolution urged governments "to make as far as possible 50 per cent of that portion of their contribution exceeding the equivalent of $ 200,000 in the form of, or convertible into, readily usable currencies."

The sponsors' case rested on three observations, as explained by the US.[8] First, some governments, notably the USSR, fixed percentages to be spent in their countries for engaging experts and

---

6. *ibid.*, Para 9.
7. E/TAC/L.98.
8. E/TAC/SR.107.

placed limitations on the percentage of their contribution to be spent on equipment or for other purposes. Second, some governments placed an absolute embargo on their contributions except for uses exclusively related to their country. Third, the utilisation of their currencies led to direct negotiations between them and the recipient countries, so that the projects resulting from such negotiations (special projects) were kept out of the mainstream of country programming. The sponsors felt that this situation violated the principles of multilateralism and feared that the EPTA would degenerate into bilateral programmes carried out under the auspices of the UN.

This draft resolution provoked considerable criticism from the USSR, Czechoslovakia and Yugoslavia, as well as from a large number of developing countries.[9] The USSR argued that the utilisation of currencies posed no such great problem to the TAB. It contended that rejecting contributions because of a backlog of unused currency and seeking contributions in convertible currencies would deter governments from increasing their contributions. Further, the USSR believed that the draft resolution was motivated by political considerations and would infringe on multilateralism. Yugoslavia believed that the sponsors of the resolution were dramatising the issue and pointed out that there had been no problems with utilisation so far. While supporting multilateralism, Yugoslavia "considered that all countries, with their widely differing economic structures, conditions and needs could not be expected to conform with every detail of the arrangements made." The delegate suggested that the newcomers should be given some time to adjust. He also believed that the limit of $ 200,000 would discourage pledges, and that the suggested changes raised constitutional issues which should be referred to a working group which could advise the General Assembly. Czechoslovakia repeated more or less the same arguments, but made two additional points. First, it disagreed with the sponsors' allegation that a currency was not readily usable just because it was not used. The Czech delegate also pointed out that while his country's contribution for 1954 had not been utilised that year, it was fully utilised in 1955 and would be in 1956. It had not been used in the

---

9. For discussion in TAC on draft Res., see E/TAC/SR.107-111.

early years because the UN agencies did not have an adequate knowledge of Czech resources and had no contacts with the establishment. He advised the TAC to explore other ways of utilisation.

Most of the developing countries that were members of TAC were critical of the draft resolution and saw no need for change. They wanted to refer the matter to a working group and/or the General Assembly. They also suggested that the new members, i.e., the USSR and Czechoslovakia, be given more time. Egypt, in addition, found the draft resolution unbalanced and untimely. As it was aimed at only two countries, it was too discriminatory. In order to strike a compromise, Egypt came up with a number of amendments. Important among these were proposals to raise the bar on 'not readily usable currencies' from $ 200,000 to $ 500,000; to delete the clause on the rejection of contributions; and to refer the matter to the General Assembly for its comments and any action it might want to take.

While responding to various questions raised by the TAC members, Mr. Owen made an important observation, "So far as can be foreseen now, we anticipate that by the end of the current year, 1956, no contribution will show an uncommitted balance in an amount which would bring it within the category of not readily usable as defined in para 3 of the draft resolution."[10] He did not anticipate that the uncommitted balance of any currency would exceed $ 100,000.

The sponsors of the resolution accepted all the amendments proposed by Egypt. The draft resolution, as amended, was adopted by 14 votes to 2, with 2 abstentions. The USSR and Czechoslovakia voted against it, while Indonesia and Yugoslavia abstained.[11]

There was a widespread feeling among the delegates of the developing countries that the original draft resolution was motivated by political considerations. It was actually aimed at only two countries, the USSR and Czechoslovakia. It is true that difficulties had arisen in utilising their currencies and in the case of the USSR, this situation continued until the 1980s. However, the resolution finally adopted lacked teeth. The bar set for a currency to be termed "not readily usable" was far too high to be breached. Further, now there was no

10. E/TAC/L.100, p.2.

11. ECOSOC Resolution 623.B (XXII).

penalty if the uncommitted balance of a currency did exceed $ 500,000; the only resort was to make a plea to bring it down at the next pledging conference. The sponsors probably just succeeded in making a point.

The ECOSOC transmitted its resolution to the 11th session of the Genaral Assembly "for any action it might deem necessary." Czechoslovakia and Rumania unsuccessfully introduced a resolution that attempted to reverse the provisions of the ECOSOC resolution. However, the ECOSOC resolution put the General Assembly in a bind. The Assembly had three options—to reject the resolution, approve it, or adopt its own resolution. It did not want to set a precedent by rejecting it. Finally, a 16-power draft resolution suggested that the General Assembly should simply note (despite the absence of any prior suggestion by the ECOSOC) that the Council had decided to reconsider the entire issue at its 24th session, and refer the records of the Second Committee's discussions to the ECOSOC and TAC. This draft resolution was adopted by the General Assembly,[12] putting the ball back in the Council's court. Operationally, the provisions of the ECOSOC Resolution 623(XXII) could not come into effect until the Council's next session in the summer of 1957. Subsequently, the TAB experienced no difficulties in the utilisation of currency and the issue was simply shelved.

The growing volume of resources and better execution generated considerable optimism in the TAB about the future of the Programme. In its 18th report,[13] the ACC had requested the TAB "to review experience gained thus far and consider plans for the future development of the Programme". The TAC requested the TAB that while meeting this request, it should consider the concentration of resources, recruitment methods used and other relevant issues, and also asked for concrete recommendations.

The TAB completed the review, "A Forward Look", in May 1956.[14] The report reviewed the Programme's activities during the first five years, projected levels of assistance for the next five years and listed a number of areas in which new projects could be developed, given

12. GA Res. 1021(XI) of 21 December 1956.

13. E/2728.

14. The report on "Forward Look", E/2885, May 1956.

the availability of larger resources. The TAB concluded that the needs for technical assistance far exceeded the resources available. It suggested the two approaches to enhance the level of resources: (i) A modest increase to finance limited expansion within the existing framework: For this, the TAB suggested a target of $ 50 million, to be achieved in stages over the next few years, and (ii) Envisaging a much more far-reaching extension of work: The TAB said no target could be set for this. The areas to be considered for the extension of work were equipment and supplies, expert personnel for national and regional training and research centres, demonstration projects, and the basic problems of low productivity, ignorance and disease.

The TAB did not anticipate difficulties in recruiting experts and placing fellows, or in mustering up the administrative and technical capacity for implementation.

The preparation of "A Forward Look" was based neither on any extensive consultations with the governments, nor on the work being done at the ground level, but was the result of the TAB's own assumptions and calculations. It was analogous to the Plan the Secretary-General and the agencies had prepared for the initiation of the EPTA. The TAB's report merely discussed the importance of various fields of development and presumed the need for assistance in these areas.

The report received a rather lukewarm response in the TAC.[15] The developing countries, obviously, pleaded for the adoption of the target of $ 50 million. However, the major donor countries—the US, the UK, France and Canada—announced that they were not yet ready to commit themselves to this target. They recognised that the resources made available for technical assistance so far fell short of the increasing needs of the less developed countries and expressed the hope that the programme could be further expanded in the future. The TAC, therefore, passed a resolution which simply urged the governments to lend greater support to the EPTA and to provide such support, whenever possible, on a long-term basis. It also asked the TAB to send the report to the participating governments for their comments and report on this to the TAC during its next session. Agreeing with the TAC/ECOSOC resolution, the General Assembly

15. For discussion in TAC, see E/TAC/. SR.140-145.

reiterated the plea that the governments should give the EPTA their fullest support to ensure its continued growth.

When the TAB circulated "A Forward Look" to all the governments, it received replies from only 14 governments, 5 of which had no comments. The others' comments related to the shortage of finances, rigidity in allocation, greater provision for equipment, and so on. The TAB recognised that these replies were not very representative and no conclusions could be drawn from them.

During the discussion in the TAC at the 24th session of the ECOSOC, Brazil observed that the prospects of expanding resources were bleak, with the impending cut in the US contribution from 50 per cent to 33 per cent. The Brazilian delegate suggested stabilisation of the programme, rather than efforts to extend it. 10 developing countries introduced a draft resolution, asking the donor governments to increase their contributions. The resolution invited the TAB to propose concrete measures designed to increase the programme's resources so that the projects mentioned in "A Forward Look" could be carried out. The developed countries preferred a limited and gradual expansion of resources. Most of them believed that the level and quality of the programme could be enhanced through more efficient use of resources, improvements in administrative efficiency, concentration of resources on the neediest projects, placing less emphasis on continuing projects, better utilisation of currency and better coordination with bilateral programmes. Finally, in its decision, the TAC requested the TAB and invited the participating governments "to suggest measures which would make it possible to implement a substantially larger programme...for discussion by the Technical Assistance Committee at its 26th Session of the Council."

"A Forward Look" came up for discussion again in the TAC during the 26th session of the ECOSOC as the former had by now received further comments and suggestions from the governments and TAB. With regard to the future growth of EPTA resources, a related and important development took place in December 1957. During its 12th session in December 1957, the General Assembly had adopted a resolution establishing a separate Special Fund for the expansion of the existing technical assistance and development activities of the UN and its specialised agencies, in order to provide "systematic and sustained assistance in fields essential to the integrated technical, economic and social development of the less developed countries."[16] The establishment of the Special Fund, though welcomed by the TAC, did cause some concern among its members, which emphasised that the fund should not adversely affect the financial position of the EPTA. There was also a consensus in the TAC that several of the projects mentioned in "A Forward Look," "might be appropriately undertaken by the Special Fund" so as to release resources for other projects.

In the light of this, the TAB requested the TAC to give the governments some guidance "on the financial requirements of both the EPTA and the Special Fund in the years immediately ahead." There was also much discussion on the relationship between the EPTA and Special Fund. The TAC again reiterated its conviction that the EPTA could be further extended "even within the limits of its funds" if administrative costs were reduced and the funds utilised more effectively. Several members also suggested that the "TAB might examine in due course whether new funds might be forthcoming from non-governmental and other sources as had already been recommended in the case of the Special Fund." But having said all this, the TAC did not really take any concrete action. It merely requested the General Assembly "to encourage governments to continue to contribute to the Expanded Programme in amounts that will provide for gradual expansion of the Programme."

Although a number of countries had increased their pledges in 1956, the resources likely to be available in 1958 appeared to be less than in 1957. Voicing concern over this, the Netherlands, together with three other countries, introduced a draft resolution[17] at the next General Assembly session. They argued that the governments should reconsider their pledges for 1958 and beyond since the contributions needed to be increased by at least 20 per cent to compensate for the reduction in the US contribution. These countries wanted to stabilise the programme at least at the 1956 level of $ 30 million. The Assembly adopted a rather mild resolution, which simply appealed to the governments to examine the consequences of the prevailing

---

16. GA Res. 1219(XII), 14 December 1957. See also Chapters 3 and 7 for further discussion of the Special Fund.

17. A/C.2/L.347.

situation and consider the possibility of increasing the EPTA's financial resources.

Another idea propounded to increase resources was that of funds-in-trust. According to this, the recipient countries would provide their own funds to finance a few of their projects. This idea originated in the United Nations Technical Assistance (UNTA) programme. Burma was the first to request part of the assistance on a payment basis. Under this arrangement, UNTA was asked to secure the required inputs and administer the project according to its rules and regulations.

This idea soon gained currency, with the developed countries emphasising and seeking further growth and extension of funds-in-trust (reimbursable) projects. This had always alarmed the developing countries, which feared that it would affect the character of the EPTA and the future levels of assistance under it. In 1957, the reimbursable projects requested by the governments amounted to a little over $ 0.5 million. During the 24th session of the ECOSOC, the Netherlands and the US introduced a draft resolution[18] requesting the TAB to explore the possibility of further extending the provision of technical assistance on a reimbursable basis, with due regard to the need for maintaining the basic character of the EPTA. Once the fears of the developing countries had been allayed and they had been assured that the proposed draft resolution was not intended to create any precedent, the TAC adopted a revised draft with some amendments. The resolution requested the TAB to examine, in consultation with the recipient governments and the agencies, "the provision of technical assistance under the Expanded Programme on a payment basis, it being understood that such assistance would be in addition to that already provided under the regular and expanded programme of technical assistance."[19]

In 1958, funds-in-trust amounted to $ 1.3 million. Iran and Turkey were the principal countries participating in this arrangement, and the FAO and UNTA were the main operational agencies for such projects.

To help the EPTA increase its volume of assistance, Australia, the Netherlands and Norway offered resources in kind. They decided to

---

18. E/TAC/L.133.
19. TAC Report E/3041, Annex II, p.2.

provide the services of associate experts, who would assist the experts in the field.

1959 to 1966

In 1959, the total amount pledged ($ 29.66 million) was less than that pledged in 1958, in spite of increased contributions by 20 countries. While the US had reduced its contribution, it agreed to include in its pledge the matching of local cost contributions of the recipient countries. The funds-in-trust resources amounted to $ 2.5 million. Concerned about the decline in resources, the General Assembly, during its 15th session, urged the Member States to consider "that the funds available to the Special Fund and EPTA attain, in the immediate future, the sum of $ 150 million."[20] This plea elicited a favourable response in 1960, when the total pledges amounted to $ 34.16 million—the highest so far. Difficulties continued in the utilisation of restricted currencies. To remedy this, the TAB contacted the major donors still contributing in non-convertible currencies and asked them to make at least 25 per cent of their contributions in convertible currencies. The response was quite favourable, with 34 countries paying wholly or partially in convertible currencies in 1960. In 1961, the amount pledged increased substantially, to $ 41.57 million, with contributions from 91 countries. The distribution of currency also improved. Forty-two countries made contributions in fully convertible currencies and 12 contributed partially (ranging from 10 per cent to 50 per cent) in convertible currencies. During the biennium 1961-62, total pledges increased substantially, averaging $ 43.5 million a year.

The Government of Denmark made a very important announcement during the 36th session of the ECOSOC. It pledged to contribute one per cent of its national income for aid to the developing countries. It was not clear whether Denmark envisaged using only multilateral channels for this aid, or whether it intended to include bilateral aid also. In any case, this announcement posed a challenge to the other donors and ended up setting a floor for future aid. Later, at the initiative of the UNCTAD, the General Assembly would adopt a resolution urging all developed countries to contribute

---

20. GA Res. 1529 (XIII).

one per cent of their national income for aid to the developing countries.

During the biennium 1963-64, governments pledged $ 50.10 million in 1963 and $ 51.50 million in 1964. The target for $ 50.0 million, set in the document on "Forward Look", was achieved during this biennium. Resources from fund-in-trust increased significantly from $ 4.0 million in 1961-62 to $ 11.70 million in 1963-64. As a result of this the number of countries assisted under this scheme also rose sharply from 71 during 1961-62 to 121 during the biennium 1963-64. Moreover during the biennium 1963-64 governments made contributions either in convertible currency or facilitated convertibility in other currencies. The total amount thus made available in convertible currencies accounted for 87.5 per cent of the total.

Local Costs

In his first annual report[21] on the UNTA programme, the Secretary-General raised, for the first time, the question of costs to be borne by governments receiving technical assistance. In his communication to the Member Governments, he advised that they should "communicate (with him) or with the Executive Heads of specialised agencies for the purpose of determining the financial and other terms under which the technical assistance would be available."[22]

He raised the financial question because while the GA Resolution 200 (III) had mentioned various forms of technical assistance, it had not provided guidance on the UN share in the total cost of a technical assistance project. Presumably, this was left to the discretion of the Secretary-General. Therefore, in his report to the ECOSOC, the Secretary General referred to the observations made by the Fifth Committee of the Assembly in connection with the GA Resolution 200 (III). The Fifth Committee had said, "...the virtues of self-help should not be lost sight of and that governments, when framing their requests for assistance, should also take due account of the question of sharing costs of services rendered."[23] The Secretary-General,

21. E/1174.
22. *ibid.*, Para 8.
23. *ibid.*, para 12.

therefore, hoped that more could be accomplished if the recipient countries made a greater effort to share costs.

The question of local costs assumed significance after the EPTA became operational. During the ECOSOC's 12th session, the TAB explained its position on the matter in a paper[24] submitted to the TAC. Citing a provision in the ECOSOC Resolution 222A(IX), which called upon the recipient governments to bear a substantial portion of the costs, at least that part which could be paid in their own currencies, the TAB initially decided that the recipient governments should pay the full subsistence cost of the experts and for local travel. However, difficulties cropped up in working this out. The Board then revised the arrangements proposing that short-term experts should receive full subsistence allowance, plus 25 per cent for incidental expenses, from the recipient governments. Experts appointed for more than a year were to be paid allowance for lodging only. Experts appointed for 6/12 months were to receive allowance for food and for lodging beyond 6 months. The TAB suggested two courses to the TAC: (i) The EPTA should pay for everything except local travel; or (ii) the recipient countries should continue to pay subsistence allowances for food and the cost of lodging. It was pointed out that the UN Regular Programme and bilateral programmes paid for everything.

In response to the TAB's paper, the UK moved a draft resolution which would have the underdeveloped countries cover all the local costs, including allowances for subsistence and lodging. This proved to be a nonstarter. Subsequently, India, Iran, the UK and the US submitted another proposal,[25] which excluded subsistence allowances but retained the provision for lodging. However, although there was general agreement on the sharing of costs, no agreement could be reached on the respective proportions. The developed countries supported the four-power proposal, which, however, was withdrawn later as no agreement could be reached. The Chairman of the TAC then submitted his own proposal, based on the four-power draft resolution. The only important difference between the two proposals was that the Chairman's proposal allowed the TAB to waive the

24. E/TAC/R.8 of 25 January 1951.

25. E/TAC/L.5.

lodging expenses by prior agreement with the recipient countries, which were given the option of contributing more if they wished. This proposal was adopted by the TAC and later, by the ECOSOC in its Resolution 361(XII).

The situation, however, remained somewhat fluid and problematic. The main difficulty arose from the agencies' varying interpretations of the original statement on cost-sharing in the ECOSOC Resolution 222(IX), and also, of the proposal adopted by the Council during its 12th session. Methods of calculating local costs varied from agency to agency. Some agencies expected the recipient governments to make greater contributions, especially for subsistence and lodging allowances and the internal travel expenses of the experts. The provision for lodging proved to be a major obstacle to negotiating agreements on local costs. In a few cases, the TAB used its authority to exempt governments from the payment of lodging costs for a limited period of time. As a result, some recipient countries found the local expenses too high and this limited their use of the EPTA.

The question of local costs was taken up for a detailed review during the ECOSOC's 14th session. The Chairman of the TAB submitted a memorandum on the matter for the TAC's consideration. The memorandum described the variations in the local costs charged by the participating agencies for different types of projects. The agencies used divergent practices even with regard to the travel expenses of fellowship holders headed abroad. The cost was always to be paid in foreign exchange. Some agencies required the recipient governments to pay the full cost, while others expected them to bear half the cost. Though the Chairman of the TAB did not submit any specific proposal, he stressed the need to establish uniform standards for similar projects. He also sought the TAC's guidance.

The Chairman's memorandum was studied by the Working Party earlier appointed by the TAC to review the TAB's fourth report. Unable to agree on a concrete proposal on uniform standards, the Working Party submitted a draft resolution[26] on local costs for the consideration of the TAC. The draft resolution reasserted the idea that the recipient countries should make a substantial contribution, specifically with regard to costs in local currency or in kind. The draft

26. E/2304, Annex II.

resolution suggested that governments which provided substantial staff and other resources could be exempted from paying the cost of lodging. As for local transportation, it allowed exemption "when this requirement would impede the carrying out of a project on account of special circumstances within the recipient countries." The draft resolution also suggested that fellowship holders be exempted from bearing the cost of external travel. Nonetheless, the draft resolution did not provide a clear interpretation of the suggestions and left that task to the TAB and participating agencies.

The TAC did discuss certain alternative arrangements. It was suggested, for example, that the recipient governments should initially contribute a fixed percentage of the estimated costs, agency by agency. The agencies could furnish an account of the detailed disbursements at a later date. The TAB was asked for its opinion on this. However, no agreement could be reached on any specific proposal. The TAC, therefore, simply endorsed the draft resolution submitted by the Working Party. It asked the TAB in consultation with the participating agencies, to ensure uniform application of the Working Party's suggestions in similar projects. However, as mentioned before, these suggestions would be subject to varying interpretations.

In 1953, the TAC again reviewed, this time more extensively, the question of local costs.[27] It focused mainly on subsistence and other allowances due to the experts, or in other words, their living costs. In principle, the TAC did not recommend any change in the responsibilities of the recipient governments with respect to local costs as laid down in the previous resolutions of the TAC and ECOSOC. The only change it suggested pertained to the method of calculation and payment of the recipient countries' obligation. The arrangements prevailing with regard to other living costs would remain unchanged.

The TAC recognised certain outstanding drawbacks in the prevailing arrangements regarding the experts' living costs. First, there was a lack of uniformity in the governments' rates of payment towards living costs. This was due mainly to varying interpretations of the resolutions and decisions of the TAC and TAB, both by the recipient governments and the participating agencies. Second, the position with

27. For discussion on local costs, see TAC Report on Local Costs, E/2395.

respect to government payments had deteriorated owing to lack of standards. This trend was expected to continue. The third drawback was in the method of payments. A part of the living costs was paid directly by the governments to the experts and a part was paid by the participating agencies. Since continuation of the prevailing arrangements "can only lead to further misunderstandings and fiction," the TAC decided to "establish more precise standards for determining the rate to be paid by governments towards living costs, while providing greater flexibility in the method of payment" than proposed previously by the TAB.

The scheme discussed and approved by TAC would require all cash payments due to experts to be paid directly either by the employing organisation or by an agent of TAB out of programme funds. The amount due from each government in respect of each expert man-day provided was assed at 50 per cent of the TAB subsistence rate for the country covered. The governments were given two options for paying the total amount thus calculated. They could either "make payments towards these costs, programme by programme" or alternatively "make such payments inrespect of all experts employed under all programmes in that country, as a lump sum." The TAC provided for general waivers in cases of extreme hardship. The whole scheme was to come into force not later than 1 January 1954. According to a statement prepared by the TAB on the scheme's impact, it was estimated that the new arrangement would have no effect on the total living costs and that the slight reduction in the costs to be borne by the governments would be offset by a corresponding increase in the costs to be borne by the agencies. The new arrangements were approved by the ECOSOC.[28]

The question of granting general waivers proved to be rather troublesome. At the 19th session of the ECOSOC, the TAB reported[29] that it had tried to give relief to some seven countries, but such waivers tended to continue, and that it was finding it difficult to define 'hardship'. Foreign exchange was not a consideration because the living costs (50%) of the experts were to be paid in the local currency. The TAB wondered that if countries could not raise the needed local resources how would they raise resources for economic

28. ECOSOC Res. 470(XV).

29. E/TAC/45.

development. TAB recognised that in times of war, civil strife or natural calamities countries might find it difficult to raise adequate local resources and believed that that cases might deserve consideration for limited periods. In view of this experience, the TAB suggested that no project waivers should be granted in the future, proposed that general waivers be granted only if a country's budgetary situation was adversely affected by war, natural calamities, etc. and or if a country's share of the local costs formed a significant proportion of its current budgetary resources.

Of the participating agencies, only the WHO disagreed with this recommendation and supported the TAC's present policy on general waivers. On the basis of its experience, the WHO believed that the recipient countries spent a substantially greater amount in additional terms than the amount that the WHO contributed to the health projects assisted by it. Moreover, since 1955, the WHO had been paying the full cost of experts under its regular technical assistance programme. Developing countries, such as Egypt and Pakistan, were quite sympathetic with the WHO's position. However, developed countries like the Netherlands, the UK and the US were against it. The TAB's Executive Chairman, too, was quite apprehensive since he feared that accepting the WHO's proposal would end up curtailing field programmes. So the ECOSOC, at its 24th session, simply deferred a decision until the matter could be studied in depth.

Even by 1958, the ECOSOC had not managed to take a decision on local costs. It did consider that "a simplification of the present arrangements might best be obtained if each government were assessed for its local cost obligation on the basis of a percentage of the total cost of experts' services provided to it under the Expanded Programme". However, it did not take a decision on this approach. Instead, it stipulated that for 1960, the percentage figure for a country would be the ratio of its actual local costs to the total costs of the provision of experts by an agency in 1958.[30] Thus, it temporarily accepted the principle of a fixed percentage contribution, but deferred a final decision until 1960 or thereafter.

Having tried the interim arrangements for a year, the TAB reported certain flaws. It pointed out that these arrangements preserved

30. ECOSOC Res.736(XXVIII) of 30 June 1959.

whatever accidental differences that appeared in 1958 among the recipient countries, imposed an unequal burden and, if continued, were likely to result in a decline in revenue. In order to correct these inequities and simplify the procedure, the TAB recommended a single uniform percentage rate—12.5 per cent—of the total cost of experts provided to a country, and the elimination of the obligation to provide lodging. The TAC and ECOSOC accepted this recommendation and the scheme became operational in 1963. In each of the years from 1963 to 1966, the local cost revenue was $ 3.4 million.[31]

Project Expenditure and Administrative Costs—(Annexure A-4.1)

1950-1958

The operational activities of the EPTA took some time to gain momentum. The programme's first financial period—1 July 1950 to 31 December 1951—was essentially a period of transition, during which the TAB was occupied with issues relating to its own organisation and with policies and procedures concerning various aspects of its operational activities. The TAB received 265 requests for assistance. It approved 145 requests from a total of 38 countries. These requests entailed, among others things, the provision of 513 experts. The total cost of this assistance was estimated at $ 2.1 million. Nearly 150 more requests were under negotiation and their conclusion "appeared reasonably assured". However, the total project outlay for the approved and assured projects was only $ 4.52 million out of a total expenditure of $ 6.44 million, as against the $ 20.1 million pledged for this period at the first international conference on technical assistance. The TAB assigned $ 3 million to the reserves and the balance remained unobligated.[32]

The slow pace of implementation during the first financial period was due to several reasons.[33] The actual payments of pledged contributions were slow in coming. By 31 December 1950, only $ 7.5 million of the $ 20.1 million pledged had been received. By the end

---

31. ECOSOC Res. 787(XXX), 3 August 1960.

32. TAB's Second Annual Report to TAC, E/1911, 24 January 1951.

33. Third Report of TAB to TAC, E2054, July 1951.

of June 1951, the amount was $ 11.4 million and even at the end of the period, $ 2.7 million remained unpaid. Due to the snail's pace at which payments were coming in, the TAB found it difficult to estimate the availability of funds and approve government requests accordingly. In order to secure all the inputs for the projects on time, the TAB and specialised agencies needed to have an idea of the flow of funds at least 3/6 months in advance. The initial difficulties were compounded by the shortage of some currencies and the non-convertibility of several others. The shortage of currencies also affected the recruitment of experts. Among the other factors retarding progress was the fact that some of the recipient governments' understanding of the policies and procedures of the programme were still inadequate. Many failed to clarify their needs precisely, as a result of which it took a considerably long time to formulate programmes at the country level and reach agreement. There was a lack of coordination mechanisms at the national levels and further, some of the participating agencies were yet to modify their organisation in order to suit it to the requirements of the EPTA and TAB. There was also some disagreement over the use of supplies and equipment. While the TAB had decided to provide these only as an integral part of a project and not independently, the developing countries saw other opportunities for their use including in pilot projects and demonstration centres. The TAC finally responded to this by requesting the TAB to be more flexible in providing supplies and equipment. In the beginning, TAB also experienced difficulties in finding qualified experts with a knowledge of conditions in the developing countries. This difficulty arose partly because of the different rates of compensation prevailing in the bilateral and EPTA programmes.

Expecting higher contributions for 1952 and with a carry-over of unobligated funds from the previous period, the TAB prepared a budget of $ 38.2 million for 1952. However, though a large number of governments (65) had pledged contributions in 1952, the total amount pledged was only $ 18.8 million, less than that in the first financial period. As a result of this, the actual project delivery during 1952 was $ 18.80 million out of a total expenditure of $ 22.97 million. However, the total obligations incurred by the TAB by the end of the year were far in excess of the total resources available. To enable the TAB to make an accurate assessment of the resources available and to prepare realistic programme budgets, a working group of the TAC recommended that pledging conferences be held well in advance of the year concerned. It also recommended a target of $ 25 million for 1953.[34]

The financial crisis which was brewing owing to the gap between the resources available and the assistance promised by the TAB came to a head in the beginning of 1953. The crisis, in the opinion of the Executive Chairman of the TAB, was due to several reasons. By now the programme had gathered sufficient momentum. The participating agencies had obligated $ 23 million in 1952, compared to $ 6.5 million during the first financial period. At the beginning of 1953, the unpaid balance of pledges of prior years was only $ 1.75 million. The pledges in 1952 fell short of the target fixed earlier at $ 25 millon.[35]

The crisis stimulated lot of discussion during the 15th session of the ECOSOC in 1953.[36] In the TAC, France observed that the crisis was due to the absence of specific rules for project selection from the very outset, as well as inadequate compliance by the agencies with the Council's directives. Australia also attributed the crisis to free play by the agencies and a serious lack of coordination in the preparation of plans at the national level. The US was equally critical and moved a draft resolution, which was subsequently adopted by the TAC.[37] The draft resolution called for closer coordination and consultations at the national level among all parties concerned, and further, asked the TAB to submit a report on the mechanism of coordination.

During the 16th session of the ECOSOC, in 1953, the TAB again highlighted the gathering financial clouds which were casting a shadow on the programme for 1953 and 1954.[38] Though the amount pledged for 1954, $ 25.02 million, was higher than that for 1953 $ 22.32 million, the obligations incurred were still outrunning the pledges. So the outlook for 1954 looked rather grim. As before, the criticism in the TAC focused on the procedures for incurring obligations, high cost of overheads and unsatisfactory evaluation of

---

34. TAB's fourth report, E/2213, May 1952.
35. Fifth Report of TAB, E/2433, June 1953.
36. E/SR.687.
37. E/TAC/L.33.
38. For discussion in TAC, see E/TAC/SR.38,39,42, and 46-57 and ECOSOC Res.492(XVI).

results. Australia argued that financial difficulties arose because the agencies earmarked funds for 'obligations' at the approval stage of a project which restricted flexibility in implementation and contributed to overcommitting. Several delegates also thought that the administrative costs of the TAB, including its support services, were rather high and on the rise, consequently reducing the resources available for country projects. The cost of overheads for 1953 was estimated at more than 25 per cent of the available resources. This was considered high in relation to the level of pledges. The ACC also found the prevailing level of administrative costs unsustainable, considering the low level of pledges.

Members of the TAC believed that besides the TAB's financial procedures, a lack of coordination between the departments of the recipient governments, between the participating agencies and governments, and between the participating agencies and TAB was the principle cause of the ongoing financial crisis. According to the TAC, this situation led to delays in the preparation of programmes at country level, lack of clarity about priorities and incoherence in such programmes, overenthusiasm of agencies, preparation of unrealistic budgets by TAB and eventually to overcommitment and poor delivery.

Initially, the TAB adopted the practice of appointing resident representatives for technical assistance in a few countries—a practice which had been initiated earlier by the Secretary-General for the UN programme of technical assistance. This practice was later expanded, though gradually, to cover a large number of countries in order to ensure better planning and coordination at the country level. In later years, a number of problems cropped up in the relationships and interaction between the recipient governments, agencies' representatives in the field and TAB's resident representatives. In the beginning, the TAB, together with the participating organisations, did not really recognise these problems. The TAC, however, perceived that the agencies, representatives in the field were acting independently and not fully cooperating with the resident representatives. The Committee wanted to affirm the pre-eminent role of the resident representatives in country planning and coordination. This debate continued over quite a few years, during which the TAC attempted to clearly define the functions of the resident representatives, as well as the relationship between them and the agencies' representatives. It also encouraged the governments to set up central coordinating agencies. The relationship between the resident representatives and agencies' representatives, however, continued to be a source of anxiety.

Several members of the TAC did not agree with the TAB's diagnosis of the situation and its explanation regarding the financial crisis. Australia denied the presence of any such crisis and instead, gave figures to demonstrate that the programme and its resources had been growing. It blamed the TAB for adopting flawed budgetary practices, whereby it committed more funds than were actually available or could be foreseen to be available. The Australian delegate suggested that in the future, the allocation of finances for the programme for a given year should be tailored to account for normal delays in the payment of contributions, difficulties in the use of restricted currencies and any other foreseeable difficulties. He sought to cut the programme for 1953, but this was opposed by some recipient countries that were members of the TAC. However, the TAC accepted Australia's recommendation for a comprehensive review of the TAB's financial procedures.

The total amount pledged for 1953 was $ 22.32 million, still short of the target. The estimates submitted by the participating agencies for 1953 amounted to $ 43 million. Expecting delays in the payment of contributions during the year and difficulties in using certain restricted currencies, the TAB pruned it down to $ 25.3 million. However, the total expenditure for 1953 turned out to be lower than that for 1952. It came to $ 22.81 million, $ 17.82 million of which was spent on projects. Downward adjustments were made, especially under the heads of fellowships and equipment. The number of countries receiving assistance also declined from 97 in 1952 to 86 in 1953. In spite of the low level of the programme in 1953, the cost of overheads were higher than in 1952.

The financial procedures of the TAB were the subject of extensive discussion during the 16th session of the ECOSOC in 1953. In its report[39] to the Working Party appointed by the TAC, the TAB continued to underline the late payment of pledges as the principal cause of the crisis. It recommended the adoption of one of two

39. E/TAC/L.51.

specific courses of action: The first option was to extend the period of completion of the projects that had already been approved and not have them reapproved at the year-end. This would allow for the carry-over of 'earmarkings', making it possible to retain earmarked but unobligated funds for projects beyond the end of the financial period. The second option was to earmark funds, closely monitor progress in the execution of projects and make continuous adjustments on the basis of the estimated income and need for reserves.

Australia, too, submitted detailed proposals on the subject to the Working Party.[40] Its contention was that the TAB started preparing the programme for the forthcoming year very late in the preceding year, only after the level of pledges for the ensuing year was known. The TAB approved projects on the basis of the anticipated income, but made obligations only for the curent year, irrespective of the total cost of a programme and its duration. Therefore, Australia argued, though a commitment was made for costs occurring in future years, such commitment was not backed by any guarantee of the availability of funds till the completion of a project. Consequently, if the future pledges and the pace of payment of contributions did not match the pace at which expenditures were incurred for the programme, then the approved projects had to be cut or postponed. Australia recommended a modified version of the 'cash-in-hand' approach followed by UNICEF and some other agencies. Its basic thrust was that a project would not be approved unless the resources corresponding to its total cost were in sight. Australia recognised that the adoption of its proposals would call for some adjustments, necessitating a transition period, during which programmes might have to be cut to match with the current pledges and their fulfilment. However, it felt that the programmes would be restored to their normal levels after the transition period. Among the specialised agencies, the ILO, WHO and FAO supported this proposal as, in their view, it would lend financial certainty to the negotiation and approval of projects. Mr. Owen argued against it, stating that it would cause a sudden contraction in the operating rate and create disruptions in the present policy of country programming, as well as in the inter-agency ratios. He defended the TAB's procedures of programming, and of earmarking and allocating of funds.

---

40. E/TAC/l.53.

The Australian proposal would have made sense if one were to adopt a short-term planning and budgeting cycle because given the annual voluntary pledges, the TAB or, for that matter, even the ECOSOC and General Assembly, could not have foreseen the future levels of pledges. The TAB, on the other hand, as pointed out by Australia, did commit itself to the total cost of a project, irrespective of its duration and the availability of resources when it approved a project. A commitment to total costs, in itself, was not reason enough to cause a crisis in the short-term because the TAB never promised to implement a project over a specific time-period. However, the TAB's practice did have undesirable long-term consequences. Those portions of projects that had not been implemented had to be carried forward and constituted the first claim on future resources. The cumulative effect of this procedure was that the continuing projects kept absorbing a swelling share of the future resources, not leaving much for new projects. Though the TAB continued to blame the crisis on late payment of pledges, it can be said that the TAB's flawed financial procedures and weaknesses in project execution were the main culprits. Indeed, the resources continued to increase, whereas the TAB's project outlays steadily moved in the opposite direction from 1952 to 1954. Moreover, the payment of pledges had stabilised by this time and the amount of unpaid funds for a year was very small.

The TAC tried to remedy the problem caused by late payments by advancing pledges for the ensuing year to the last quarter of the preceding year. To lend further stability to programme implementation, it decided to increase the Special Reserve Fund by adding an additional amount of $ 3 million from the contributions made in 1954. The TAC also recommended to the ECOSOC that this fund be reconstituted as a Working Capital and Reserve Fund, and that its level be raised to $ 12 million by 1956—a recommendation with which the Council agreed.

During the following session of the General Assembly in 1953, Mr. Owen, while addressing the financial crisis, suggested that the pledges for 1954 be increased by 20 per cent of the 1953 level. The good news now was that Poland and the USSR had announced their willingness to make contributions to the EPTA. Several governments reiterated their concern about the TAB's spending on overheads, financial procedures, lack of focus on economic development while planning projects, and high levels of local costs. The topics of efficient use of resources and evaluation of results were also raised. In its resolution 722(VIII) of 23 October 1953, the General Assembly urged the governments, *inter alia,* to make for 1954 contributions that would suffice to at least meet the needs of the programme for that year, and to ensure prompt payment of pledges. In the same resolution, the Assembly also requested the ACABQ to review the administrative procedures of the TAB and the participating agencies, as well as their administrative expenditures so far as those were financed from EPTA funds.

In response, the ACABQ submitted a report[41] to the ninth session of the General Assembly. The former had earlier drawn the Assembly's attention to the fact that the joint costs of the TAB and offices of the resident representatives were not submitted to any legislative body for review. Also, in the previous session of the ECOSOC, some TAC members had suggested bringing the administrative costs of the TAB under the purview of the ACABQ. While the ACABQ's report focused mainly on administrative issues, it also highlighted some constitutional issues. Its main findings on administrative issues were as follows:

(a) The distinction between 'central administrative cost' and 'indirect operational cost' was artificial, and the determination of the two was characterised by confusion and inconsistency. Moreover, these costs did not fully represent the total cost of operating the EPTA as the agencies and recipient governments bore certain additional costs. In spite of this, the TAB's administrative costs appeared to be high. (such costs were 21 per cent and 20.7 per cent of total EPTA projects in 1953 and 1954 respectively). An administrative cost of less than 12 per cent was considered reasonable.

(b) The management of multiple currencies increased administrative costs.

(c) In the field, all administrative work should be centralised in the resident representative's office and the agencies should

41. A/2661.

make full use of the resident representatives. There was no need for the agencies to employ Chiefs of Mission.

(d) The agencies should fully integrate their EPTA activities and regular technical assistance activities with their normal work.

The TAC, which discussed the ACABQ's report during the 20th session of the ECOSOC, responded quite positively to all the findings and observations. It agreed with the limit of 12 per cent set by the ACABQ on the expenditure on overheads. Further, it re-emphasised the need to make the fullest use of the existing administrative and other services of the UN and participating agencies in order to release more resources for operational purposes.

The TAC and the Council also considered the TAB's seventh report,[42] for 1954. The Chairman of the TAB described the year as "another year of paradox" since there was more money than in 1953, but the expenditure incurred on operating the programme had fallen from $ 17.8 million in 1953 to $ 15.1 million in 1954. The total pledges and collections in 1954 amounted to $ 25.3 million and $ 24.4 million, respectively. The TAB attributed the low level of the programme in 1954 to a conservative approach in earmarking funds, and inherent delays in the formulation and execution of programmes.

In 1955, the total expenditure reached a peak of $ 25.8 million. Of this, $ 21.31 million was spent on projects and $ 4.49 million on overheads. Continuing projects took up almost 80 per cent of the resources, leaving only 20 per cent for new projects and assistance to newly independent countries. The rising cost of overheads and increasing proportion of funds claimed by the continuing projects caused much concern in the TAC. The TAB had, moreover, also slightly exceeded the target of 10 per cent set for regional projects by the TAC. In the latter's view, regional projects not only reduced the resources available for country projects, but also posed greater difficulties in evaluation.

In 1956, the Working Capital and Reserve Fund reached its target level of $12 million. In its Resolution 623(XXII) of 9 August 1956, the ECOSOC laid down detailed rules for the fund's administration. Its principal purposes were: (i) to make advances against firm pledges of

42. Seventh Report of TAB, E/2714.

contributions to finance technical assistance programmes as approved by the TAC; (ii) to improve and facilitate currency management; (iii) to provide working balances to the agencies; and (iv) to make advances to finance commitments authorised by the Executive Chairman to meet urgent needs that may arise during the annual programme year. The advances made from the fund were to be reimbursed as soon as contributions were received from the governments for this purpose.

Meanwhile, TAB's overhead costs—indirect operational and administrative costs of TAB—which rose from 1952 to 1954 declined to nearly 17 per cent in 1955. However, even this was considered rather high by the TAC. It concluded that a detailed central review of these expenses was essential to ensure that the maximum proportion of the programme's resources was used for project assistance. Therefore, in mid-1956, it established an administrative review group "to examine and report to the TAC ... on the budgetary provisions for overhead costs proposed to be financed from EPTA for ensuing year," and requested its Chairman to consult the ACABQ on how the latter could effectively assist the TAC in this sphere. This group, which submitted its report[43] in November 1956, did not achieve much. It agreed that there was a "necessity for the greatest economy in operating the Programme" and hoped for a reduction in the proportion of overhead costs in the future. Making recommendations for the 1957 programme, the group "felt that the ratio of operational services to total programme costs proposed for 1957 should not be exceeded in subsequent years". The ratio of overhead costs to total expenditure was 13.34 in the proposed programme for 1957.

The optimal growth of the EPTA was hindered also by difficulties arising in the utilisation of restricted currencies. The 'Special Projects', established by the TAB to utilise contributions by the USSR, Czechoslovakia and other Eastern European countries, were another cause of continuing concern. Established separately, these projects were neither assimilated with the programme's resources, nor included in the country programme targets. The utilisation of currencies in the 'Special Projects' was sometimes based on direct negotiations between the donor and the recipient country. Some

43. E/TAC/54,55,58.

members of the TAC feared that this practice would encourage bilateral programmes and violate the spirit of multilateralism.

The programme for 1956 was the first to be prepared in accordance with country programming procedures. The total expenditure, of $ 30.48 million, was the largest since 1950. The expenditure on projects amounted to $ 25.32 million. The TAB managed to deliver 93 per cent of the approved programme, providing assistance to 56 independent countries and 47 dependent territories. It also faced no difficulty in currency utilisation and the issue was simply shelved. However, the proportion of continuing projects amounted to 85 per cent in terms of money. Some governments did take over a few projects, but this released only a fraction of the resources needed to finance new activities.[44] In the TAC, the US expressed great dissatisfaction with the high proportion of continuing projects. The French observed that it was essential to define 'project' precisely and suggested that the duration of a project be fixed in advance. The TAC requested the TAB to further study this matter, "including such questions as a definition of the term 'project' and 'continuing projects'".

In 1956, 30 countries increased their contributions, whereas the US reduced its own from 60 per cent to 50 per cent. It had decided to reduce its contribution further in future years, and had earmarked a little less for 1957, 45 per cent for 1958, 38 per cent for 1959 and 33 per cent for 1960. With the US determined to pursue this course, the prospects of future increases in resources looked rather grim. Several delegates from the developing countries were disappointed with the US decision.

The level of the programme implemented in 1957[45] surpassed the levels of previous years, amounting to $ 31.5 million. This was close to the approved programme of $ 31.95 million, though the project costs of $ 25.79 million were slightly less than the $ 26.11 million programmed for the purpose. The total amount pledged for 1957, $ 30.84 million, was also the highest till now. The success of the programme in 1957 could be attributed to the reallocation of prior commitments, a higher rate of implementation and timely payment of

44. Ninth Report of TAB for 1956, E/2965.

45. TAB's Annual Report for 1957, E/3080.

pledges. The high level of the programme was accompanied by higher costs of operational services and administration, which together accounted for 18.2 per cent of the total expenditure. When consulted by the TAC on the matter, the ACABQ recommended that a flat rate of 12 per cent of an agency's share in execution be given to it as compensation for administrative and operational costs. The TAC also appointed a working group to examine the issue. The Committee adopted a comprehensive resolution,[46] requesting the participating organisations to consolidate all expenses incurred on administration and operational services in their regular budgets. Further, it asked the TAB to develop a formula for preparing "lump-sum amounts for allocation to the participating organisations in 1959, which shall not exceed and shall preferably be less than the amounts allocated for 1958 towards meeting the Expanded Programme's administrative and operational service costs". The TAC also expressed its wish that in subsequent years, too, such expenses should not exceed the 1959 ceilings for lump-sum payments. The agencies submitted their own estimates for lump-sum payments which, except for ICAO and ITO, corresponded to their compensation in 1958. The Working Group accepted these estimates and TAC agreed to use them for 1959. The Working Group or TAB did not provide any specific formula. The only change was that compensation for administrative and operational services of agencies was now paid on a lump sum basis and not on the basis of actual expenditures reported by them as in the past.

Aware of the TAC's concern about continuing projects, the TAB examined[47] the matter more closely in 1957 "in order to obtain a better idea about the actual situation," which, it concluded, "is not as simple as it might seem at first sight". It observed that the word 'continuing' was used somewhat loosely. It pointed out that whereas a project starting late in a programming year and lasting only a couple of months after the 31 December boundary-line was considered a continuing one, a 12-month project completed during a calendar programming year was not termed as such. The TAB thought that "such a definition of continuing projects is much too mechanical to be meaningful". According to the TAB what really mattered most was the length of time for which a project was in existence. On the basis

46. ECOSOC Res. 702(XXVI).

47. See fn. 44.

of this criterion, the TAB prepared an analysis of 1958 Category I projects.[48] This revealed that in the programme for 1958, 25 per cent of the projects were new and 75 per cent were old, or pre-1958, projects. Of the total number of pre-1958 projects, over 50 per cent had been in existence for less than three years, 38 per cent for less than two and 6 per cent for three to four years. The TAB further argued, "It is essential to differentiate between the title of a project and its substance. A project may continue for a number of years under the same broad title, and consequently be classified as a continuing project, yet its scope and content may be changing at the same time."[49] The analysis of pre-1958 projects in terms of the duration of their existence, though instructive, was not very useful. The TAC was concerned more with the amount of resources being absorbed by the continuing projects in a programming year, as not much was left over for the initiation of new projects.

The TAB, of course, did not feel that the continuing projects were a source of worry and surprisingly, the TAC also seemed to be somewhat reassured by the TAB's detailed analysis. However, with a view to ensuring greater resources for new projects, the TAC suggested[50] that governments should indicate tentative dates for the completion of projects. It also requested the TAB to provide information on the duration of all projects in its Projects Handbook.

The entire concern and debate over continuing projects appeared to be somewhat tragic-comic. On the one hand, TAC and ECOSOC had always reaffirmed the right of recipient countries in determining their priorities and needs. On the other hand, TAC expressed considerable concern over long-term projects. If a country decided to lock up a substantial part of the resources allotted to it in long-term projects then it would not have much flexibility in introducing new projects. But then it would be the country's responsibility under the rules of the game. However, TAC's concern was also legitimate. If all currently recipient countries were to tie up a large part of the given resources in long-term projects then not much additional resources would be available to the system as a whole to accommodate a growing number of newly independent countries and to respond to emergencies.

---

48. *ibid.*

49. *ibid.*

50. Report of TAC on its November 1965 session to the 39th Session of, ECOSOC 51. TAC Report, E/3041, p.7.

The expenditure on projects further increased to $ 27.71 million in 1958. But the slow growth in resources during the latter period, accompanied by the rising costs of assistance, considerably reduced the real value of project outlays. However, assistance to newly independent countries, such as Ghana, Morocco, Sudan and Tunisia, grew significantly over the period 1952-1958.

During 1950-1958, a total of $ 203.05 million had been contributed to the EPTA. The programme's total expenditure over this period was $ 193.39 million, less than the available resources. Expenditure on projects amounted to $ 156.38 million and $ 37 million was spent on overheads, which accounted for 19 per cent of the total expenditure. This was well above the 12 per cent ceiling suggested by the TAC in later years. Part of the increase in the cost of overheads was justified by the appointment of resident representatives in a growing number of recipient countries. Moreover, the overall underperformance of the TAB could not be blamed solely on inadequate coordination mechanisms at the national level because all said and done, the participating agencies had their predetermined shares and it was essentially they who developed projects at the national level in their respective fields. The main weakness lay not so much in the preparation as in the execution of the projects. The TAB always implemented less than it had programmed for.

This was, and has since been, due both to bureaucratic delays in the UN and at the national levels. It has rarely been possible to provide project inputs on time, especially in the case of large projects. It takes the UN a long time to identify, recommend and recruit experts, and the recipient countries to take timely decisions. Similar delays occur in the nomination and placement of fellows. Such delays in execution also partly contributed to the existence of 'continuing' projects, regardless of their defence by the TAB.

In 1958, with a view to improving the volume and quality of its project delivery, the TAB proposed country programming on a two-year instead of annual basis. It argued that annual programming did not allow sufficient time for project preparation, the recruitment of experts and timely completion of projects. Two-year programming would allow more time for securing project inputs, preparing long-term projects and country programming. Pledges and earmarking would still be on an annual basis, but the agencies would retain unobligated funds at the year-end. The TAC felt that two-year programming and annual pledging were not necessarily incompatible. As a first step, it asked the TAB to seek the views of the governments and also consider 'project programming', in which projects would be planned for their entire duration, but financial provision would be made only on an annual basis. The TAC decided to try two-year programming on an experimental basis for the period 1961-62 and to authorise allocation of funds on an annual basis. It agreed with the idea that a government could approve a long-term project for its full duration when it was first included in the recipient country's programme.

1959-1966

The International Atomic Energy Agency (IAEA) joined the EPTA in 1959. A fall in pledges in 1959 led to a decline in the programme. The incidence fell mainly on project expenditures because the total cost of administrative and operational services was actually slightly higher in 1959 than in 1958. Restricted currencies continued to pose difficulties, so the TAB decided that from 1960, it would take currency distribution into account while earmarking funds for the agencies. The Special Fund picked up some projects originally financed by the EPTA, and the EPTA also transferred some projects to the Special Fund. Their jurisdictions overlapped to some extent because certain fields, such as resource surveys and training, were common to both. A committee appointed to study coordination between these two agencies could not reach any conclusions.

In 1960, the expenditures on projects fell further to $ 27.91 million. The reasons cited for this were difficulties in the utilisation of currency and a lower level of delivery of equipment. However, Africa received more aid, while Chile was given special assistance for the devastation caused by an earthquake. In 1960, 16 African countries gained independence and the total assistance given to them amounted to $ 0.56 million, as against $ 0.36 million in 1959, when they were still dependent territories. There was to be a spectacular increase for them in the biennium 1961-62, for which the TAC had approved total assistance of $ 9.31 million. To solve the problem with currency utilisation, the TAB put into effect a new earmarking procedure from 1 January 1960. Earmarking to the agencies was subdivided into six major currency groups and was deemed non-transferrable. Failure to obligate the funds earmarked under each subhead entailed the surrender of the unobligated earmarking. This procedure worked reasonably well but was not entirely, successful. It ended up affecting the flexibility of the agencies in the recruitment of experts and placement of fellows.

As recommended by the TAB, the TAC agreed to extend the two-year programming cycle for another biennium. The TAB had also sought a raise in the ceiling on regional and inter-regional projects from 12 per cent to 16 per cent. The TAC agreed to raise it to 14 per cent but kept an additional margin of 2 per cent for exceptionally worthy projects, which would require its prior approval.

The big jump in resources in 1961 led to a similar increase in project expenditure, which rose from $ 27.91 million in 1960 to $ 31.3 million in 1961. Africa accounted for most of the increase in expenditure. The assistance to Africa grew both in relative and absolute terms. In relative terms, the aid to Africa increased from 15 per cent of the total assistance in 1960 to 20 per cent in 1961, and the total expenditure in Africa in 1961 was 47 per cent higher than the 1960 level. Importantly, the TAB achieved this without necessitating any significant decrease in other regions.

The first cycle of two-year programming (1961-62) proved to be helpful. Essentially, the arrangement afforded more time for the preparation of projects, especially in the newly independent countries of Africa. This, however, led to uneven distribution of project expenditure, substantially more so in 1962 than 1961.

Though the level of pledges crossed the $ 50 million mark both in 1963 and 1964, the pace of implementation during the biennium 1963-64 was just as uneven as in the previous one. The expenditure on projects was $ 39.5 million in 1963 and $ 51.8 million in 1964. The TAB attributed this to the longer time taken by the recipient governments to finalise their programmes and the frequent changes made by them to the approved country programmes. This delayed the implementation of several projects to the second year of the biennium.

The biennium 1963-64 saw the introduction of project programming. Long-term projects in 1963-64 amounted to 32.7 per cent of the Programme but this level was expected to be lower in

1965-66. The TAB felt that the introduction of project programming might render two-year programming superfluous and that the discontinuation of the latter would eliminate the unevenness in programme implementation. Though the TAC was equally disturbed about the imbalance in implementation, it approved the continuation of the two-year budget cycle for the biennium 1965-66.

The TAC met for the last time in November 1965. Before it dissolved itself, after the Governing Council of UNDP came into being, it took decisions on two issues. It worked out a formula for the provision of compensation to the participating agencies for the costs incurred by them on administration and support services. It was agreed that for 1965, "the allocation from the Special Account towards the administrative and operational services costs of the participating organisations shall be made in the form of a lump-sum amount, which shall represent 13 per cent of one half of the approved field (Category I) programme for the previous biennium and of the amount approved by the Technical Assistance Committee for continuing authorisations during that previous biennium; that for 1966 and thereafter, allocation shall be at the rate of 14 per cent of such costs; and that the distribution of the allocations among participating organisations shall be determined on the basis of each organisation's allocation for Category I projects." The compensation was to be based on the actual proportion of the programme implemented by the agencies. The TAC provided for flexibility in the application of this arrangement in respect of small agencies, like the ICAO, UPU, ITU, WMO, IMCO and IAEA. The UPU and IMCO had joined the EPTA earlier in the biennium.

Secondly, the TAC submitted its recommendation for the allocation of funds to the agencies for 1966. Some doubts were raised about the legitimacy of this recommendation since a few members believed that this task was now more the responsibility of the Governing Council to be set up by the UNDP. However, the recommendation was approved in the TAC while still leaving some flexibility for the Governing Council.

The total expenditure during the biennium 1965-66 amounted to $ 122.57 million, $ 101.4 million of which was spent on projects. As in the previous bienniums, the level of project delivery in the first year of the biennium (1965) was lower than that in the second year.

This was attributed mainly to certain changes made to 256 projects owing to difficulties in the recruitment of experts. The level of project delivery in 1966 was substantially higher, at $ 58.9 million.

Since its inception to the end of 1966, the EPTA had incurred a total expenditure of $ 581.4 million. This included direct project assistance of $ 490 million. The administrative overheads and the compensation paid to the agencies for their services averaged 18.7 per cent of the total expenditure incurred over the entire period.

Structure

The structure of the EPTA can be viewed in terms of allocations made to the participating agencies, expenditure by major fields of activity, the geographical distribution of assistance, and project inputs.

1950-1958

Until country programming was introduced in 1956, the shares of the agencies were predetermined by the ECOSOC. The agencies prepared projects at the country level, within the limits of their allocation, and submitted their programmes to the TAB. The summation of the agency programmes formed the global programme of the EPTA. The relative shares of the participating organisations in 1958 and earlier years are given in Annexure A-4.2. Of the 8 participating agencies, the IAEA joined in 1958, the FAO, UN (as a participating agency) and WHO accounted for nearly two-thirds of the total allocable resources, followed by UNESCO and the ILO. While the shares of the UN and WHO declined somewhat over the period, the FAO remained the one with the largest single programme.

The allocations to the agencies were naturally reflected in the composition of the expenditure in major fields of activity. The largest single field of expenditure was agriculture. In the early years of the EPTA, considerable emphasis was laid on assistance for developmental planning. Since the programme was intended to contribute to economic development, it was believed that its projects could be better integrated with developmental activities if the countries concerned had good developmental plans. The EPTA, therefore, offered considerable assistance in the areas of carrying out surveys of resources and in the formulation and implementation of developmental plans. During the discussions in the ECOSOC, several developing countries continued to seek greater assistance for industrial production. Such assistance increased somewhat, from 7.8 per cent in 1954 to 9.5 per cent in 1956 (it was much less before 1954), but the recipient countries were not satisfied. The TAB used to combine this aid with the assistance granted for public utilities and auxiliary services to industry, and pointed out that the total expenditure on industrial production was much greater than what was visible.

With regard to geographical or regional distribution (Annexure A-4.3), the share of Africa was small in the beginning and remained stagnant until almost 1956. The continent had very few independent countries at that time and the assistance was given to a large number of dependent territories of the metropolitan powers. Therefore, although the total number of countries and territories assisted in Africa and Latin America was the same during 1950-1955 (39), Africa's share was less than one-third of Latin America's. Assistance to Africa increased in the 1960s, when more countries became independent. Asia and the Far East remained the largest single beneficiary over this period, while the share of the Middle East declined. Europe's share had dramatically increased in 1952 and remained at quite a high level until 1955. A rather interesting feature of the assistance given during this period was the increase in the number of dependent territories receiving aid. Their number went up from 21 in 1952 to 39 in 1956. The assistance given to them rose from $ 0.3 million in 1952 to $ 1.4 million in 1956, when it constituted 5.5 per cent of the total assistance. The assistance given by the EPTA was spread rather thinly over the period, but politically, there was no alternative except to provide it to those countries which asked for it. Over the period 1950-1956, the EPTA provided assistance to 131 countries in five regions. Interestingly, the assistance granted per country, as a proportion of the total assistance, was the highest in the Middle East and the lowest in Africa.

The EPTA provided basically three inputs in a project: expert personnel, fellowships for studies abroad, and equipment and supplies. After a modest beginning in 1950-51, the number of experts provided doubled in 1952 (Annexure A-4.1) and increased steadily thereafter, barring a drop in 1954. In 1950-51, more than half of the experts came from the US, the UK and France. Responding to persistent pleas from the developing countries, the TAB made efforts to make recruitment more broad-based. The result was that by 1958, the share of these three countries fell to 36 per cent and the number of countries from which experts were recruited increased from 61 in 1950-51 to 77 in 1958.

The growth in the award of fellowships was somewhat erratic. It reached a peak in 1955, but declined continuously till 1958. The TAC was quite concerned about recipient countries' priorities. There was, however, a considerable rise in the number of countries acting as hosts to trainees. The number of host countries increased from 45 in 1950-51 to 107 in 1958. This whole experience in widening the partnership in the EPTA prompted the Executive Chairman to say, in 1958, that UN Technical Assistance had truly been transformed into UN technical cooperation. Indeed, the EPTA was later renamed the UN Technical Cooperation Programme.

The TAC was quite concerned about the fluctuating levels of the fellowships awarded. A majority of the members felt that the officials going abroad for training were expected to eventually take over the functions performed by the EPTA experts; this would reduce the number of experts provided by the EPTA and the duration of their stay. The TAC, therefore, emphasised greater assistance for fellowships, as well as for training of counterparts and national training institutions. However, the TAC was not in a position to do much more than express its concern and make a plea to the recipient countries, since the latter had the right to determine their own priorities for assistance.

The proportions of total assistance provided for equipment and supplies, respectively, fell "considerably short of the 'rule of thumb' limit of 25 per cent suggested by TAC some years ago in the interests of a balanced Programme." In its application, the TAB followed the injunction in the ECOSOC resolution 222(IX), according to which assistance for equipment was to be given if it was an integral part of a project of EPTA assistance. However, in spite of the decision of the TAC and ECOSOC to interprete that injunction flexibly the quantum of assistance for equipment and supplies remained rather small.

When submitting its annual report to the 24th session of the ECOSOC in 1956, the TAB suggested that considering the anticipated absence of large resources in 1958 (owing to the US decision to reduce its contribution), the TAC might concentrate on the really needy countries. The TAB suggested that the new countries in Europe, which were not actually underdeveloped, did not require assistance that urgently. The TAB informed the TAC of its provisional decision that "the question of expansion of activities under the Programme in Europe should be further considered before any new programmes for European countries which had not received assistance in 1957 could be recommended for 1958, and that similarly any substantial increase in the existing programmes in European countries should be avoided."[51] It asked the TAC to review this provisional decision and provide guidance. The TAB further pointed out that "due to the limited resources estimated for 1958, it had been necessary also to reduce the 1958 targets of a number of non-European countries whose continued needs for technical assistance were unquestionable."[52]

In the discussions in the TAC, differences of opinion cropped up as to how to effect the proposed restriction on the 1958 programme. Some members—the USSR, Czechoslovakia and Poland—said the restriction should not be decided upon on a geographical basis, but that assistance should be related to the degree of need. They held that such needs existed in European countries as well. France observed that the programme should not formally exclude any country requesting assistance since the definition of the neediest countries might turn out to be subjective in the absence of any specific criteria of eligibility for EPTA assistance. It suggested that the TAC's decision on the matter should not make any reference to European countries, but should provide for an exception in favour of countries at a very early stage of development. France also said the TAC should keep in mind that countries attaining independence were likely to require greater assistance. Some members were supportive of the TAB's provisional decision as they believed that "the needs of the various European countries were not as acute as those of some other countries". The TAC did accept the suggestions made by France, and its decision endorsed the efforts made by the TAB "to make the most efficient use of resources of the Expanded Programme by giving

51. TAC Report, E/3041, p.7.

52. *ibid.*

priority to most urgent requirements."[53] It accepted the TAB's provisional decision concerning the programme for 1958.

The question of regional and inter-regional projects also came up for serious discussion at the 24th session of the ECOSOC. The main areas covered by the regional projects were the control of diseases and pests, regional training centres, study tours and seminars, area development programmes, and regional surveys and research. The TAC was always somewhat concerned about regional projects, as these were not part of the country programming exercise and hence not subject to the same degree of scrutiny. They were not requested directly by the governments, but were developed and prepared by the participating agencies, which alone indicated that they had the support of the governments. The question of the obligations both of the host and participating countries remained a moot one since the arrangements varied from project to project. Moreover, several members of the TAC felt that expenditure on regional projects subtracted from the resources available for country projects. As the expenditure on regional projects was growing, the TAC prescribed that not more than 10 per cent of the resources be spent on such projects. This ceiling was rarely observed by the TAB, with the actual expenditure rising from 14.3 per cent in 1954 to 16.5 per cent in 1957.

At the 24th session of the ECOSOC, the TAB requested that the ceiling be raised to 12 per cent. All the participating agencies, except the UNTAA, were also in favour of raising the ceiling. In the TAC, some members opposed the idea, while some agreed to support it, provided there were clear indications that the governments concerned had made requests for such projects and supported them; firm arrangements were made for the sharing of local costs; and a rigid adherence to the ceiling of 12 per cent was ensured. Some members suggested differentiating within 12 per cent by observing the existing 10 per cent ceiling and using 2 per cent for extra allocation for very good regional projects. The debate in the TAC centred around this last suggestion. For 1959, the TAC made the proposed distinction between 10 per cent and 2 per cent. The latter amount was to be used "to meet the need for additional projects considered to be specially

53. *ibid.*, Annex II.

promising by the governments concerned". All agencies were given the 12 per cent target and the unspent funds were to be available for planning country programmes.

1959-1966

Several members of the TAC continued to emphasise the importance of fellowships and of practical and theoretical training, both in the national and regional training programmes. They also felt that there was a need for the provision of related equipment. The rationale underlying these views was that as the recipient nations gained greater competence, they could save the money spent on foreign experts and use it to meet other needs. The TAC's exhortations did have some effect. The share of fellowships in the programme increased from 16 per cent in 1959 to 19.2 per cent in the biennium 1961-62. The number of fellowships increased steadily until 1964, and then declined to 18.3 per cent in 1965-66. The share of expenditure on experts in the total expenditure, as well as the number of experts, rose steadily. An important development was the substantially greater utilisation of associate experts, who numbered 146 in 1964; the Netherlands was the largest provider and the FAO the largest user.

As for regional distribution, the share of Africa in the total programme surged ahead during the1960s. It grew dramatically from 14 per cent in 1959 to 35.2 per cent in the biennium 1963-64. This was accompanied by significant declines in the shares of Asia, the Far East and the Middle East. During the bienniums 1963-64 and 1965-66, expenditure on regional and inter-regional projects also registered a substantial growth. In fact, the share of regional projects in the total programme during the bienniums 1963-64 and 1965-66 was higher than the 12 per cent deemed desirable by the TAC. This inevitably drew criticism from the TAC.

The distribution of funds among the agencies during the 1960s remained the same as in the previous years and, therefore, the proportion of funds going into different fields of activity did not change much. Agriculture continued to be the sector receiving the single largest share of funds, followed by basic surveys, health and education. Year after year, the members of the TAC pressed for greater allocation for industry, but it was only in the biennium

1965-66 that industry received about 13 per cent of the total project expenditure.

In the earlier years, the TAB had resisted demands for technical assistance in the field of international law on the ground that such assistance did not contribute to economic and social development. Moreover, it pointed out that the ECOSOC's founding resolution [222(IX)] and the subsequent amendments to it did not provide for assistance in the areas of international law, human rights and the status of women. Finally, during the 20th session of the General Assembly, the Second Committee agreed to extend assistance in these fields if it related to economic and social development. With a view to overcoming this restrictive provision, the UAR suggested that the recipient governments need not qualify their requests for assistance in international law only in terms of their relevance to economic and social development. The chairman of the Second Committee agreed with this position and the EPTA began providing assistance in this field.

Annexure A-4.1

EPTA: Resources and Expenditure

Amount in US $ Million

Year	*No. of Countries Pledging Assistance*	*Amount Pledged*	*Project Expenditure*	*Admin. and Operational Service Cost*	*TAB Cost*	*Total Expenditure*	*Overhead Cost % of Total Expenditure*
	(1)	*(2)*	*(3)*	*(4)*	*(5)*	*(6)*	*(4) + (5) % of (6)*
1950-51	54	20.04	4.52	0.97	0.95	6.44	29.81
1952	65	18.80	18.80	2.10	2.07	22.97	18.15
1953	69	22.32	17.82	3.02	1.97	22.81	21.88
1954	71	25.02	15.11	2.63	1.72	19.47	22.34
1955	71	27.88	21.31	2.74	1.83	25.88	17.66
1956	77	28.84	25.32	3.14	2.02	30.48	16.93
1957	84	30.84	25.79	3.55	2.18	31.52	18.20
1958	85	31.31	27.71	3.88	2.23	33.82	18.07
1959	83	29.66	26.54	4.40	1.90	32.84	19.18
1960	85	34.16	27.91	4.40	2.10	34.41	18.90
1961	91	42.41	31.28	4.12	2.70	38.11	17.90
1962	90	45.44	44.64	3.54	3.40	51.58	13.45
1963	105	50.10	39.50	4.50	3.90	48.00	17.50
1964	109	51.50	51.80	4.60	4.11	60.50	14.40
1965	107	54.03	42.50	6.30	4.60	53.38	20.40
1966	112	56.30	58.90	5.50	4.79	69.19	14.80

Source: Annual Reports of TAB.

Annexure A-4.2

EPTA: Shares of Participating Organisations (%)

Year	*UNTA*	*ILO*	*FAO*	*UNESCO*	*ICAO*	*WHO*	*ITU*	*WMO*	*IAEA*	*UPU*
1953	22.6	10.9	27.4	12.9	5.1	20.1	0.7	0.3	-	
1954	23.7	11.4	24.7	13.0	4.3	21.2	1.1	0.6	-	
1955	21.4	10.8	31.3	12.7	4.0	17.8	1.0	1.0	-	
1956	24.5	10.5	27.5	13.2	4.1	18.1	1.0	1.1	-	
1957	22.0	10.7	28.9	14.2	4.4	17.6	1.1	1.1	-	

Contd. ...

Contd. ...

Year	*UNTA*	*ILO*	*FAO*	*UNESCO*	*ICAO*	*WHO*	*ITU*	*WMO*	*IAEA*	*UPU*
1958	21.7	10.6	25.8	17.8	4.1	17.6	1.2	1.2	-	
1959	22.0	10.8	25.7	16.3	4.5	16.8	1.6	1.2	1.1	
1960	22.3	9.0	25.5	15.6	4.6	17.3	1.6	1.2	2.1	
1961	19.7	10.0	25.4	18.1	4.5	17.9	1.5	1.5	1.4	
1962	19.8	9.9	23.6	20.0	3.7	16.4	1.9	2.1	2.6	
1963	20.7	9.5	26.4	15.1	4.1	17.9	2.3	2.0	1.7	0.3
1964	20.2	10.4	22.2	19.1	4.3	16.3	2.1	2.7	2.3	0.4
1965	21.2	10.6	24.0	17.0	4.1	16.2	2.4	2.4	1.4	0.7

Source: Annual Reports of TAB.

Note: See 'Acronyms' in the beginning.

Annexure A-4.3

Regional Distribution of Field Programme Costs (%)

Year/Region	*Africa*	*Asia and Far East*	*Europe*	*Latin America*	*Middle East*	*Inter-regional*
1950-51	10.6	34.5	4.0	28.4	22.5	-
1952	7.3	32.1	10.5	26.5	23.6	-
1953	8.4	32.1	8.7	26.9	19.9	4.0
1954	8.5	30.8	9.9	25.9	21.5	3.4
1955		31.1	8.0	26.4	21.9	4.1
1956	8.9	32.5	6.8	28.8	19.6	3.4
1957	11.3	32.6	7.2	28.0	19.2	1.7
1958	12.2	34.8	6.3	27.2	18.0	1.5
1959	14.1	34.6	6.4	26.0	17.5	1.4
1960	15.3	33.3	5.9	25.9	17.8	1.8
1961 a_/	22.2	37.7	4.7	24.2	7.8	3.4
1962	30.9	32.0	5.7	20.4	7.4	3.6
1963-64 b_/	35.2	27.4	4.8	20.1	6.1	6.4
1965-66	35.2	24.7	4.3	20.8	6.1	8.9

Note: a_/ From 1961 onwards, countries were assigned to their regional economic commissions, Iran and Afghanistan in Asia and UAR in Africa.

b_/ EPTA adopted biannual programming and reputed on that basis.

Source: TAB Annual Reports.

Annexure A-4.4

EPTA: Project Inputs as Per Cent of Total Expenditures

Year	*Experts*	*Fellowships*	*Equipment*
1950-51	73	20	7
1952	59	27	14
1953	76	14	10
1954	74	17	9
1955	67	22	11
1956	69	19	12
1957	74	16	10
1958	75	13	12
1959	78	15	7
1960	78	17	5
1961	75	13	12
1962	70	21	9
1963	80	-	-
1964	70	23	7
1965-66	77	18	5

Source: Annual Reports of TAB.

5

Evaluation of EPTA

The *raison d'être* for the establishment of the EPTA was that shortage of skilled manpower was one of the serious constraints in faster economic and social development of underdeveloped countries. The UN legislative bodies were keen to ensure that the technical assistance provided under EPTA—experts, fellowships and equipment—did contribute to economic development through sustained growth of skilled manpower in the recipient countries. From the beginning of EPTA activities, there was a growing demand by the legislative bodies for an appraisal of effectiveness of the technical assistance activities and an assessment of results achieved. The ECOSOC Resolution 222(IX), which established EPTA, placed the responsibility for evaluation on its TAC.

At its first meeting in August 1950, TAC asked TAB to provide, *inter alia,* on a regular basis full information for evaluation of actual results.[1] In its subsequent sessions, TAC discussed extensively the periodicity, structure, and substance of TAB reporting system and made several suggestions to develop a reporting system which would provide all relevant data for evaluation. In 1951, TAC appointed a sub-committee to look into standards for reporting and make recommendations on form and content of future reports of TAB. The Sub-Committee recommended[2] detailed information on financial, administrative and managerial aspects of all country and regional projects financed from EPTA as well as in Regular Programmes of participating agencies. It also recommended that TAB should provide information on contribution of technical assistance activities to economic development in each recipient country. During the

1. Report of TAC, E/1833.
2. Document E/TAC/L.6.

discussion[3] of Sub-Committee's report, France suggested to separate information on Regular Programmes and EPTA activities. Iran asked to publish conclusions and recommendations of experts together with steps taken by governments to implement them. The USA welcomed explanation of contribution to economic development but wondered if TAB could do it. India suggested to shift this burden to recipient countries arguing that contribution to economic development should be considered as a pre-assistance cost and recipient countries should explain the impact. TAB was asked to follow the recommendations of the Sub-Committee and comments made in TAC but TAC did not provide any guidelines for evaluation of contribution to economic development.

The annual reports submitted by TAB in the following years were considered by TAC as rather bulky, unduly detailed, excessively statistical, and lacking information on evaluation of results. As previously requested by TAC, the Executive Chairman of TAB submitted at the 16th session of ECOSOC, some proposals[4] on a future reporting system. However, these proposals did not include any suggestions on evaluation. France, therefore, suggested appointment of a working party to undertake comprehensive evaluation of results achieved in a sample of recipient countries. At the request of TAC, Secretary-General undertook this task and later submitted a report on evaluation of activities in six countries. The Secretary-General's report concluded that though programmes in the six countries encountered some difficulties, their governments were satisfied with EPTA assistance. However, TAC was not completely satisfied and wanted to develop a systematic method for evaluation of all technical assistance activities. It requested the Executive Chairman of TAB "To appraise the effectiveness of the activities of the participating organisations financed from the Special Account and the results achieved."[5] The TAC also requested TAB to make suggestions on the best methods of evaluation. In response to this, TAB submitted a first report on the techniques of evaluation used by the participating organisations.[6]

3. E/TAC/SR.8-10.

4. E/TAC/9.

5. E/2238, Annex II.

6. E/TAC/41.

The report drew attention to possibilities of evaluation at different levels: individual project level, country programme level, and for the Programme as a whole. The participating organisations by and large focused on evaluation at project level as this helped to improve the quality of existing projects, to draw lessons for modifications to them, to improve selection of new projects and "to measure the success of the project in terms of specific tangible and intangible accomplishments."[7] The TAB would assume the overall responsibility "to undertake the evaluation of the impact of the Programme as a whole on the economic and social development of the assisted countries."[8]

The participating organisations used different methods of evaluating projects in their respective fields. In spite of this diversity, a common approach was said to be gradually emerging. Generally speaking, the procedure of evaluation involved "a careful scrutiny of the requests to ensure that the governments are prepared to take necessary counterpart action and that these requests are related to the basic problems which the governments are tackling under national programmes or plans of development."[9] This was followed by a "careful definition of the work plan of each expert ... together with a clear definition of the specific goals to be achieved over a period of time." The expert's job description and the defined goals served as benchmarks for evaluation. The field and the technical staff obtained periodic reports on the progress of work which provided basic data for judging the success or failure of individual projects. A final report was submitted to the governments. Quantitative measurements of the specific accomplishments were not always possible and hence in most cases results were described in general terms. The TAB, however, considered that "an elaborate and costly system of project evaluation would not be justified in relation to the possible benefits to be derived."[10]

So far TAB had not been able to undertake evaluation of the Programme as a whole. It believed that Programme evaluation must

7. *ibid.*, p.2.
8. *ibid.*
9. *ibid.*, p.3.
10. *ibid.*, p.4.

be approached on an experimental basis because the size of the existing EPTA represented "only a fraction of the funds which would be required to meet the urgent priority requests of the recipient countries. It would, therefore, be unwise at this time in the life of the Programme to embark on a costly and ambitious experiment of evaluating the results, many of which cannot, in the nature of things, yet be determined."[11] TAB's explanation on Programme evaluation was incorrect. What mattered in evaluation was not as much the size of the Programme in relation to needs, as the nature of the Programme and its constituent elements and consideration of methods that may be best suited to assess effectiveness and accomplishments. But TAB had always taken the position that evaluation would not yield results commensurate with their costs.

During the 18th session of ECOSOC, Pakistan observed that except participating agencies nobody undertook evaluation. Agencies' evaluation, Pakistan believed, and rightly so, was not objective since they performed both the tasks of preparing and executing projects. The Pakistani delegate thought that there was need for an independent evaluation by TAC and that such evaluation should focus on effects on economic development, on integration with development plans and on whether assistance was compatible with stage of development.[12] Pakistan, therefore, introduced a draft resolution asking for the establishment of a Working Group of TAC to evaluate the results and effectiveness of the Programme. In an amendment, China suggested that the Working Group should prepare a questionnaire which should be sent to governments of recipient countries for their response and the Working Group should prepare the report on the basis of such replies. While all members of TAC agreed in principle on the importance of evaluation there were differences on the details. Pakistan as well as other underdeveloped countries considered that the Working Group should visit a few countries at least to fill the gaps in the available material. Most of the developed countries were against any additional expenditure. They believed that sufficient material was available with agencies for the Working Group to prepare a report. A few developed countries advised caution and not to rush with the complicated task of evaluation.

11. *ibid.*, p.5.

12. E/TAC/SR.75.

France was sympathetic with the view that without country visits evaluation may not be useful in the long-run. However, France did not envisage travel at least during the first year because the Working Group would need time to work out its procedures, collect material and interview agencies and TAB. As most of the developed countries were ready to accept a ban on travel at least during the first year, Pakistan agreed with France and the draft resolution was adopted by TAC.[13]

The Working Group submitted its first report[14] at the 20th session of ECOSOC. In preparing this report the Working Group had two documents before it: (i) a review of EPTA activities in six countries during 1951-1954 prepared by TAB, and (ii) the report previously prepared by TAB on techniques of evaluation of EPTA. The Working Group did not receive the first document in time to examine it. Moreover, the Group preferred to have views of the recipient countries and hence decided to send the document for review to the six countries.

The Group's report essentially included a questionnaire on evaluation. On its distribution to governments, there were different views. Some thought that it should be sent to all participating countries. Some suggested that it should be sent only to recipient countries while some thought that it should be sent only to those recipient countries having resident representatives. Finally, it was decided to send it to all governments participating in EPTA though all questions were addressed only to recipient countries.

The questionnaire covered a wide range of issues. There were questions on relation of EPTA to national development activities, coordination, administration of EPTA, performance of experts, efficacy of fellowship, the role played by equipment in projects, on the actual results achieved, follow-up on EPTA financed activities, and on internal national arrangements for evaluation. The questionnaire was sent only to countries with resident representatives (23 countries). Fifteen countries replied[15] and this represented 50 per cent of annual field operations. All these countries testified that EPTA was useful

---

13. E/TAC/L.75/Rev.2.

14. E/TAC/46.

15. Report of the Working Group on Evaluation of EPTA, E/TAC/48.

and beneficial to their economic development. However, these countries remarked that assistance from EPTA was small and only a part of their wider national development programme. It was not, therefore, possible, the countries replied, to isolate the impact of EPTA assistance on their economic development or to measure it in precise statistical terms.

The Working Group also concluded[16] that an academic and scientific approach to evaluation of programme activities would be impractical. It therefore, provided certain objectives of evaluation such as contribution of activities to Programme objectives, extent to which goals were being realised, and whether experience in implementation contributed to better design and effectiveness of programmes and activities. Also, on the basis of conclusions drawn from the evaluation reports before it the Group made several recommendations for future evaluation of the Programme. These included strengthening coordination at national level, role of resident representatives, provision of counterpart personnel, selection of good experts including a Chapter on evaluation in TAB annual reports, etc.[17] Most of these suggestions were more in the nature of improving effectiveness of the Programme rather than guidance on evaluation of completed projects.

At the 20th session of ECOSOC, there was a four power draft resolution on evaluation which included Group's recommendations as its annex. Several members found Group's recommendations too detailed and time-consuming so TAC agreed that they should serve only as a guide. The draft resolution, which was later adopted,[18] requested TAB to prepare a minimum framework for coordination, and include evaluation in its annual reports and also requested participating agencies to provide information on evaluation in their annual reports to the Council.

In its report for 1956,[19] TAB included for the first time a separate chapter on evaluation. TAB prefaced its report by several cautionary observations. It referred to the large number of countries and projects, to the diversity in socio-economic conditions and to lack of

---

16. *ibid.*
17. *ibid.*
18. E/TAC/L.96/Rev.1.
19. Annual Report of TAB, 1956, CH V, E/2965.

standardised data. TAB further observed that EPTA activities were only a fraction of national development activities and constituted one element and not necessarily the most important. Agencies provided only technical advice and guidance and had no control on policy decisions and administrative actions of recipient countries. Some processes and interactions were, and still remain, intangible and eluded measurement. All these observations were rather off the mark because what mattered was not the cross-sectional analysis of the impact requiring standardised data but evaluation of the results achieved under individual projects.

TAB carried out the evaluation exercise only in countries with resident representatives expecting to receive better cooperation and data in these countries. TAB's comments on evaluation were in terms of national planning and coordination machinery, integration of EPTA activities into national development plans, provision made for counterpart personnel and administrative facilities, value of assistance received, and fellows and their performance. TAB covered both successes and failures in the implementation of projects. The failures were attributed largely to lack of adequate national and technical services and of counterpart personnel and facilities.

The report was viewed as favourable and objective by TAC considering difficulties encountered in evaluation. It observed that further emphasis should be given to the importance of the views of recipient governments, the strengthening of national planning and coordination machinery and to the provision of national services and counterpart personnel. TAC suggested that future evaluation should include regional projects, especially training centres.

The Chapter on evaluation in TAB's annual report for 1957[20] marked a breakthrough in its approach to evaluation. Besides all the cautionary observations and limitations it spelled out in 1956, TAB for the first time defined the objectives of evaluation. TAB's perception of evaluation was "not so much to evaluate the actual results of individual projects as to evaluate how favourable or otherwise have been the conditions for the Expanded Programme to produce good results".[21]

---

20. E/3080.

21. *ibid.*, p.66.

TAB's analysis, based on replies from resident representatives in 38 countries, was presented in terms of: (i) country programme procedure, (ii) planning and coordination machinery at national level, (iii) coordination of EPTA assistance with other programmes of technical assistance, (iv) integration of EPTA projects into national development plans, (v) provision made for counterpart personnel, (vi) administrative support and (vii) value and type of assistance.

In each of these categories, while TAB reported considerable progress, it also emphasised need for further improvement. Particularly, it suggested further strengthening of national planning and coordination machinery and provision of more and qualitatively better counterpart personnel. Taking into account the seven conditions conducive to the attainment of 'good results', TAB provided the following rating of individual country projects based on its subjective judgement.

	No. of Projects	*Per Cent*
Excellent	635	74
Too Early to Say	133	16
Below Expectation	57	7
Ended Before Completion	22	3
	847	100

This showed that conditions in vast number (74 per cent) of projects were 'excellent' for achieving 'good results'. Only in 7 per cent of projects, conditions were 'below expectation'. TAB, however, did not provide any benchmark of 'expectation'. In 19 per cent of the projects, TAB supposedly lacked any basis for judgement.

TAB also included 78 regional and 9 inter-regional projects. Half of them were in Latin America and 57 per cent were for training, seminars and study groups. According to TAB, counterpart expenditure by participating countries was substantial. On the whole, TAB was quite pleased with the results achieved in these projects.

In TAC, some members considered TAB's approach to evaluation too narrow and emphasised the need for concrete evaluation of individual projects and especially for information on experts' recommendation. TAB observed that it was difficult to select projects and to evaluate contribution of EPTA experts in the context of much larger efforts made by governments. TAB, however, agreed to try to get information on experts' recommendations while cautioning of the difficulties encountered in the process.

However, TAC as a whole found the Chapter on evaluation as "a balanced and realistic assessment of the strength and weaknesses of the Programme"[22] and viewed TAB's approach to evaluation "as the most practicable one in assessing a programme containing so many projects and covering so many countries and fields of activity."[23] It also appreciated TAB's difficulties in providing intensive evaluation of individual projects. TAC did request TAB to pay greater attention to the implementation of experts' recommendations.

TAB's approach to evaluation was only circumstantial. It is true that a favourable environment is essential for the successful implementation of a project. But that is not the end of evaluation. It is only a starting point. It could not be assumed that the 'favourable' environment for an EPTA project would have necessarily produced good results. TAB should have looked into the design of a project, the relevance and quality of the type of its assistance and at least in a narrow sense whether its assistance met the immediate objective. TAB adopted a passive approach which made it easy to place the responsibility on recipient governments or extraneous factors. TAC, as on many occasions, did not have the time and the scientific nerve to probe into it.

In 1958, TAB did admit candidly that its "evaluation is essentially not of the performance of individual projects, but of the general framework of the programme as a whole, not of the actual results achieved through EPTA activities, but of those basic factors that make for sound programming and effective implementation, and thereby also for good end-results."[24]

In its 1958 report, TAB did describe a few projects where significant results had been achieved. TAC's reaction was predictable. It usually complained about what was not there instead of probing

22. TAC Report, E/3175, p.6.

23. *ibid.*, p.4.

24. Annual Report of TAB, E/3226, p.58.

deeply in what it had in a broader analytical framework. It functioned more reactively than positively. So now, in 1958, TAC remarked that evaluation should devote more attention to causes of failure and observed that the type of evaluation undertaken during the last three years was becoming repetitive with the same conclusions. Further that "it had reached a point of diminishing return and needed new direction and orientation to bring it within more manageable proportions".[25] It was then agreed that TAB in its future reports would retain the Chapter on individual projects but provide brief comments on general evaluation while concentrating on one or two subjects.

In its report[26] on activities in 1959, TAB reported further improvement in national planning and coordination machinery, in coordination with other programmes of technical assistance and in counterpart personnel and administrative support. TAB selected national and regional training institutions for detailed study. It did not include short-term training as a result of which there was thin coverage of training in agriculture. On the whole, TAB found some gaps in government expenditure and concluded that local training was cheaper than training abroad. This was also the view of TAC for a long time because it was more economical.

In 1960, TAB reported[27] more improvements in national planning and coordination and in counterpart support. Apart from these general comments, TAB provided a comprehensive evaluation of training institutes and centres; both regional and national. Data covered 119 long-term and 22 short-term training institutes and centres. The long-term institutes consisted of 95 national and 24 regional and inter-regional institutes. TAB estimated that cumulative expenditure on long-term national institutes was $ 49.36 million and $ 15.66 million on regional and inter-regional institutes. To this total expenditure of over $ 65 million, EPTA contributed $ 21.1 million, governments $ 40.4 million and $ 3.5 million came from other sources. Over the entire period, 30443 trainees were reported to have been trained. All these figures must be taken with a pinch of salt. EPTA records in the early years were not very extensive and contributions by governments

25. Report of TAC, E/3298.

26. E/3337.

27. E/3471.

were and continued to be always inflated. Moreover, this extensive reporting was mainly in statistical terms and there was no qualitative evaluation of the results.

While TAC appreciated these efforts by TAB, it was still not very satisfied. TAC needed a new approach to identify shortcomings and successes but it did not come up with any new ideas or specific suggestions. So in 1961, it again asked TAB "to consider possible improved methods for helping the Committee evaluate the work of the Programme in recipient countries."[28]

During the 1961-62 biennium, TAB prepared a special study[29] of fellowships granted in 1958 and 1959. The study covered 82 countries and 1850 fellows. Of these, 1187 fellows replied. TAB found that 90 per cent of them were still working in their fields. TAB concluded that this evaluation reaffirmed the basic effectiveness of the fellowship programme and also highlighted familiar operational problems.

In 1963, TAB presented an evaluation of regional and inter-regional projects.[30] This study described different sources of financing such projects such as contributions by governments in a region, EPTA contribution, funds provided by agencies, etc; methods of operation; and the part played by host countries. It also explained the process of consultation, selection of candidates and seminar subjects and the procedures followed. TAB provided data on expenditure by regions and by agencies and on advisory and training experts serving under regional projects. TAB had given the agencies responsibility for formulating regional projects. Allocations to agencies for regional projects were in proportion to their share in country programmes. Therefore, the functional distribution of expenditure on regional projects matched the relative shares of agencies in the total EPTA Programme. But all this was purely descriptive and assuring of the compliance of procedures. As usual, this evaluation also did not present an analysis of impact. Evidently, TAC was not satisfied and several members continued to doubt if regional projects truly reflected wishes of governments.

---

28. TAC Report, E/3680, Annex III.

29. E/3739.

30. E/3871.

As a result of this growing frustration in TAC, ECOSOC, at the initiative of TAC, adopted resolution 991(XXXVI) at its 36th session in which it identified certain problems relating to evaluation. These were: (a) efficiency of operations, (b) technical soundness of programmes, and (c) overall development impact on a given country. ECOSOC expected participating agencies to ensure efficiency in operations and technical soundness of projects and programmes. It asked ACC to address itself to the question of evaluating the overall development impact of EPTA assistance in a given country. TAC was always concerned about knowing the contribution of EPTA assistance to economic and social development in recipient countries and was never satisfied with the descriptive text provided by TAB on specific areas or inputs of assistance. Development impact was the *raison d'être* for the creation of EPTA and so TAC continued to insist year after year for evidence for the fulfilment of the primary objective of assistance.

ACC prepared a detailed analysis of the development impact question and submitted its report[31] to the 37th session of ECOSOC. ACC first discussed various difficulties encountered in impact evaluation. It observed that:

(i) The main responsibility for impact evaluation should rest with recipient countries because all of them have to and do make some probable value of each project. However, very few have undertaken any systematic efforts.

(ii) Facilities available to governments for impact evaluation vary greatly. There were serious shortages of manpower and relevant statistics.

(iii) The proposed impact evaluation would be time consuming, and costly and may require recipient countries to divest resources to this exercise from other priorities. So UN will have to provide considerable additional assistance for this purpose.

(iv) It is difficult to obtain any financial or statistical measure of impact.

(v) It is difficult to isolate the impact of UN Programme from other influences, e.g. bilateral and other multilateral assistance, national effort, expert advice to prevent mistakes and thus enhance impact.

(vi) UN assistance is a miniscule of national effort. UN aid is estimated at only one-third of one per cent of the total resources of assisted countries.

(vii) Evaluation of assistance to financial agencies is difficult owing to confidentiality of their transactions.

(viii) There are serious difficulties in evaluation of assistance in social sectors, e.g. community development, population control measures, nutrition, etc.

In the light of these difficulties encountered in an assessment of the impact of UN assistance on overall development, ACC argued for a search for more practical and useful approaches to evaluation pending increase in the volume of pertinent information, its quality, capacity to handle it and availability and use of up-to-date techniques.

ACC recommended a two-part approach to evaluation. First, it suggested that an assessment of total progress in a specific sphere in a country should be undertaken in a certain period of time. By 'specific sphere', ACC did not mean a sector such as health or education but a major project or a cluster of closely related projects in a sector such as eradication of malaria, literacy campaigns, etc.

Secondly, ACC suggested to evaluate the degree to which the international programmes contributed to the final result "upon the basis of human judgement resting on the widest possible knowledge of all the relevant facts."[32] ACC recognised that accuracy of such an exercise will vary according to circumstances prevailing in different countries. So what the ACC basically recommended was carrying out of a few pilot studies instead of an ambitious evaluation at the national level.

---

32. *ibid.*, p.23.

ACC also suggested certain procedures for undertaking pilot studies. These were:

(i) The exercise should be flexible according to circumstances.

(ii) Select those aspects of national life which have received substantial assistance under any of the programmes of the UN family.

(iii) Recipient governments should assess total progress made in the selected sphere in a given time. Governments should also assess the value of UN contribution.

(iv) UN should not undertake evaluation itself but could provide expert assistance on methodology, information, techniques, analysis, etc.

(v) The resident representatives should not do this since they are generalists.

(vi) Participating agencies should be consulted in the selection of experts.

(vii) Develop few pilot projects preferably in small countries.

(viii) Defer establishments of 'permanent evaluation machinery' pending experience in pilot studies.

ACC's analysis of impact evaluation and its suggestions for a more useful and practical approach to evaluation were indeed sound. It had, however, one procedural flaw. The suggestion that UN could recruit and provide expert assistance and that agencies were to be consulted in the selection of experts could not have been conducive to independence in evaluation. Experts would be keenly aware of their patronage and allegiance. A correct procedure would have been to let countries identify and recruit experts, financed by the UN, and UN could have retained the right to check the technical competence of experts recommended by a country for this purpose. Governments would then have total responsibility for evaluation of pilot studies.

However, ACC did make a significant contribution. It succeeded in dispelling, for a time, TAC's obsession with overall development impact without dismissing it for ever. ECOSOC, at its 37th session, adopted a resolution (1042 (XXXVII), which fully endorsed ACC's recommendations and requested the Secretary-General to initiate appropriate measures for undertaking some pilot studies.

At the 39th session of ECOSOC, the Secretary-General reported[33] on the proposals made on pilot studies. Terms of Reference for the studies were prepared. Thailand and Chile were selected for pilot studies, evaluation teams were set up, studies were to be completed by September 1965, and Pakistan and Tunisia were to be taken up in the next round of studies. As feared, the UN involvement was much too heavy to safeguard independence and objectivity in pilot studies.

At the 41st session of ECOSOC, the Secretary-General reported[34] on three completed pilot studies in Chile, Thailand and Tunisia and also submitted his own observations and recommendations. A summary of the main observations contained in the three pilot studies dealt with (i) scope and methods, and (ii) findings and observations of the country teams.

With regard to scope and method, the country teams pointed to the same difficulties which ACC had detailed in its report on impact evaluation earlier. The teams, therefore, proposed that consideration should be given to other methods to judge impact and effectiveness of programmes. The teams suggested, in particular, taking into account government aims and standards as expressed in policy documents, development plans, and judgement of officials. Quoting an observation from the Tunisian study that "evaluation is not an end in itself or an academic exercise," the summary stated that the ultimate purpose of evaluation was three-fold: (i) contribute to the increased effectiveness of future programmes, (ii) gain insights for future from past experience, and (iii) formulate methods and standards to lay down good foundations for future.

The teams adopted a sectoral approach and examined projects and programmes mainly in terms of the broad sectors and where possible in relation to development plans. The overall conclusion of the pilot studies was that "in most cases UN programmes made considerable and constructive impact and were well integrated" with development plans. The general consensus was that improvements could be made in programme formulation, implementation, follow-up and evaluation. The pilot studies made several suggestions for improvement in each of these areas. But all these suggestions covered ground which was

---

33. E/4064.

34. E/4151.

treaded many times before. The teams made familiar observations on principal responsibility of recipient governments, role of resident representatives, coordination at national levels, role of agencies and the UN, etc. Nothing was new. The only remarks on post-project evaluation were that UN should include and strengthen 'built-in' evaluation and agencies should develop improved methodology and objectives.

Having completed the three pilot studies, the Secretary-General presented his own observations and recommendations for action to be taken in a variety of directions to improve further the effectiveness of the programmes in the long run. He proposed detailed measures to improve effectiveness of the programmes at the international and national levels and offered suggestions for future work on evaluation.

At the international level, the Secretary-General proposed the following measures:

(a) A review of the methods of assigning experts with a view to reduce the time lag in recruitment and acceptance. Some stop-gap measures such as 'staff experts' should be considered where experts are not immediately available.

(b) Consideration should be given to the adoption of 'project budgeting' for technical assistance projects.

(c) Examination of the "possibilities for strengthening coordination between the United Nations family and the sources of bilateral assistance."

(d) Strengthening of inter-agency cooperation at all levels and at the various stages to "facilitate the creation of an articulated overall programme in each country."

(e) The establishment of an inter-agency study group to "examine all points of inter-agency concerns raised in (pilot studies) and to propose practical steps where these would seem required for rendering more effective the operation of technical cooperation programmes."

At the national level, the Secretary-General proposed granting increased assistance to governments. Under the existing technical cooperation programmes, in planning suitable machinery for evaluation in order to ensure optimal relation of its needs to its economic and social priorities.

With regard to future work on evaluation, the Secretary-General observed that it was important "to develop gradually a system of evaluation as an integral part of the operational activities of the United Nations family". The Secretary-General pointed out that "persons qualified to undertake an evaluation of the impact of United Nations technical cooperation programmes are few and far between "and this factor has been of decisive importance in determining both the size and the duration of the (evaluation) missions."[35]

The Secretary-General suggested that for the immediate future a further limited number of impact evaluation projects should be initiated and for this purpose made the following observations:

(a) One or two projects of at least three months duration.

(b) One or two of these projects might be undertaken in countries at an early stage in development.

(c) Greater attention to the role of UN technical cooperation programmes in the overall context of assistance being made available from both multilateral and bilateral sources.

(d) Close and continuous assistance of agencies with the organisation and conduct of evaluation missions.

(e) Provision of a few qualified professional officers to assist evaluation activities in the field and to develop methodology and standards on evaluation.

Despite all these recommendations and observations, the Secretary-General felt that "it would be premature to try to reach definitive decisions at this stage as to the exact form of future evaluation techniques and machinery."[36] He believed that "such a decision should only be taken in the light of experience gained as a result of the further evaluation projects and research work suggested above". He offered to report again on these and other aspects of evaluation.

The Economic and Social Council welcomed the Secretary-General's report and practically endorsed all his suggestions for future work.[37] ECOSOC decided to "continue and develop its systematic

---

35. *ibid.*, pp.13 and 14.

36. *ibid.*, p.16.

37. ECOSOC Res. 1151 (XLI).

evaluation of the overall and the specific impact and effectiveness of the operational programmes of the United Nations family of organisations," while, "concerned that further experience is required in ascertaining the appropriate techniques for evaluating the impact of international programmes of economic and social development".

In the immediate future, more pilot studies were to be undertaken. ACC would submit its observations on pilot studies and a report on current evaluation practices of agencies. ECOSOC would continue to express its appreciation and continue work in the field. A striking feature of this history of evaluation was that although EPTA, agencies, most professionals in recipient countries and outside, and even some members of TAC and ECOSOC gradually became aware of the conceptual and statistical difficulties encountered and recognised the limitations of impact evaluation in view of the nature and relatively small amount of UN assistance the legislative bodies wasted so much time, money and energy in pursuing this mirage and not come to terms with peculiar difficulties encountered in evaluating impact of UN technical cooperation programmes. ECOSOC could have adopted a simple approach of ensuring that the assistance was used for the purpose for which it was intended and further that the money was used efficiently. This called for in depth follow-up of project results and not for continued obsession with contribution of individual projects to economic development.

6

United Nations Regular Programme Technical Assistance: Growth and Structure

Introduction

During its first session in 1946, the General Assembly considered the question of providing expert advice to Member States when it adopted a resolution[1] requesting the ECOSOC to study "effective ways and means for furnishing...expert advice in the economic, social and cultural fields to member nations who desire this assistance." Subsequently, commenting on this resolution during the fourth session of the ECOSOC in 1947, the Secretary-General drew the Council's attention to the technical assistance provided by the League of Nations in the past. He also referred to the assistance being then provided by the ILO, WHO, FAO and other specialised agencies from their regular budgets, and drew attention to the fact that all the functional commissions of the ECOSOC had made recommendations for technical assistance. While expressing his readiness to arrange for the provision of expert advice and related services to governments, he suggested that the matter be studied fully by the Coordination Committee of the ACC, which could submit its report to the fifth session of the ECOSOC.

Venezuela and a number of other delegates, however, wanted such a programme to be initiated immediately. They introduced a joint draft resolution, which was agreed to by the ECOSOC.[2] According to this resolution, the UN would simply collect information on the availability of experts and would help the governments seeking assistance to secure the experts' services on mutually agreed terms. The Secretary-General first asked for some financial appropriation to

---

1. GA Res. 52(I) of 14 December 1946.
2. ECOSOC Res. 51 (IV).

carry out this programme, but later agreed to accommodate it within the existing budget. Thus, the UN simply performed the function of a clearing house.

It was only during the third session of the General Assembly that substantial steps were taken in this area. A vigorous debate on technical assistance produced a resolution,[3] which not only provided a sound and comprehensive basis for the UN Regular Programme of Technical Assistance, but also authorised funds in the regular budget for that purpose. The programme for technical assistance in economic and social development became operational in 1949. Prior to this, the General Assembly had authorised technical assistance in social welfare and advisory services, and for training in public administration. In 1951, these three programmes were brought under one umbrella for operational purposes. Initially, the UN experienced some difficulties in the recruitment of experts. In order to assist the UN in this task, several developed countries established national coordination committees, which would locate suitable personnel in their respective countries to serve as UN experts.

When the EPTA was initiated in 1950, the UN also became a participating agency in the execution of the Programme's projects in the fields of its competence. To coordinate all the technical assistance activities of the UN, the Secretary-General established the Department of Technical Assistance Administration (TAA) on 1 August 1950. Besides serving as the principal arm of UN operational activities, this Department also undertook substantive as well as operational activities in public administration. The UN Regular Programme differed in some important respects from the EPTA. Firstly, it was financed from the UN budget and not from voluntary contributions. Secondly, unlike the EPTA, it did not function under a framework of country planning figures or country targets. This feature accorded the UN considerable flexibility in responding to requests for assistance under each of the Regular Programme's three categories. In later years, there was also difference in the nature of projects financed by the UN and EPTA. From its own budget, the Regular Programme focused essentially on short-term and emergency assistance, while the

3. GA Res. 200 (III) of 4 December 1948.

EPTA financed mostly long-term projects in addition to those that could not be accommodated within the limits of the UN budget.

In 1954, the UN adopted the so-called 'Burma Plan'. Under this, the Government of Burma had requested technical assistance and provided funds to finance it, and had asked the UN to execute this arrangement according to its procedures. The 'Burma Plan' became the forerunner of the funds-in-trust programmes, or technical assistance on a reimbursible basis, undertaken in later years. In 1959, the Special Fund was established to provide pre-investment assistance. The UN also became one of its participating agency. In 1959, the TAA was merged in the Department of Economic and Social Affairs (DESA) and a new unit, Office of Technical Cooperation, was created in DESA. In the early 1960s, the General Assembly called for decentralisation of the economic social activities of the UN and strengthening of the regional commissions. As a result, the UN Regular Programme created several posts of regional advisers and devoted more resources to regional programmes of technical assistance. When the UNDP was established in 1966, it had two components—the Special Fund and technical assistance. Later, these two components were also integrated and UNDP became responsible for financing of all technical assistance projects. The UN Regular Programme ceased to provide experts, fellowships and equipment for projects. Its scope and size were substantially reduced to the provision of only regional and inter-regional advisers, and financing of a few inter-regional seminars and training activities.

Evolution of the Programme

The Regular Programme was founded in 1948, with a modest budget of $ 288,000 for 1949. It did not become operational until late 1949. The first year was spent on informing all the Member Governments about the nature and scope of the programme, the facilities available under it, and the terms and conditions of assistance. Also during this year, procedures were devised, and project and fellowship request forms framed.

By mid-1949, the Secretary-General informed the ECOSOC about a few steps that had been taken on specific components of the overall programme. Four governments had made requests for comprehensive missions. These missions were intended to survey governmental plans and programmes for economic and social development in specific fields, and to identify technical assistance needs. Even before the adoption of the GA resolution 200(III), the first comprehensive mission involving some of the specialised agencies, besides the UN, had been sent to Haiti. This idea became quite popular with the requesting governments and gained currency in subsequent years. By the end of June 1949, 152 applications were received for fellowships and 38 were awarded. Assistance in local training focused on organising population censuses. The Statistical Office of the UN prepared population census methods, as well as methods of obtaining national income statistics. The Statistical Office made substantial contributions in these areas and its activities proved to be of great value. In later years, too, it continued to provide leadership in these fields. Two technical handbooks were also being prepared. One was on small-scale iron foundries suitable for small agricultural communities for the production of agricultural implements. The second one, being prepared in consultation with the FAO, was on the operation and maintenance of small plants for the preparation of anti-malarial insecticides. In addition to these activities, the Secretary-General mentioned his intention to prepare periodical bulletins on economic development; set up a clearing house in the Secretariat for technical services and equipment; and prepare bibliographies, and so on.

The total cost of the programme proposals submitted by the Secretary-General for 1950 was estimated at $ 676,000. The principal elements of the programme remained the same. The budget reflected an increase in several activities. All the activities proposed by the Secretary-General were also included in the first year of the EPTA, which was then under discussion, and the activities approved in the latter were to be deducted from the regular budget for 1950. The inclusion in the EPTA of activities eligible under the GA resolution 200(III) was quite logical because the EPTA would be simply an extension of that resolution and would have the same structure of assistance. However, in the Economic Committee of the ECOSOC, several countries questioned the accuracy of the financial estimates of the programme for 1950, arguing that they were arbitrary and not based on experience.

Meanwhile, Chile had introduced a draft resolution[4] which not only sought an approval of the Secretary-General's enlarged programme for 1950 but, more importantly, aimed at continued provision for technical assistance activities in the regular budget of the UN in future years. While the US was in favour of keeping something in the UN budget, several other delegates—Australia, India, the UK and the USSR—were strongly against providing for technical assistance activities in the regular budget beyond 1950. These countries argued that all such activities should be financed from voluntary contributions and, therefore, wanted the technical assistance activities of the regular budget to be fully integrated with the EPTA. However, as the EPTA was not yet operational, these countries agreed, rather reluctantly, to include provision for technical assistance activities to be undertaken in 1950 in the UN regular budget. In the face of this opposition to placing technical assistance under the regular budget on a permanent basis, Chile dropped all references to it from its draft resolution. The resolution adopted by the Economic Committee provided only for provision in 1950. However, subsequent discussions in the ECOSOC resulted in the adoption of resolution[5] by the Council. By this resolution, the members not only agreed on an enlarged programme for 1950, but also recommended continued provision in future years for activities authorised under the GA Resolution 200(III). Later, the General Assembly, too, approved the ECOSOC's recommendation.[6]

In his third report[7] on the Regular Programme, the Secretary-General gave an account of all the activities undertaken in 1949, the first year of the programme, under the GA Resolution 200(III). The programme had naturally created a lot of interest and enthusiasm among the underdeveloped countries, as a result of which the demand for assistance was much greater than the resources available in 1949. The Secretary-General estimated the cost of the requests received (though not documented) for assistance at $ 501,500, whereas the budget for 1949 was only $ 307,750 on a gross basis. At the same time, owing to the initial difficulties of launching a new programme,

4. E/1448.

5. ECOSOC Res. 222.C. (IX) of 14 August 1949.

6. GA Res. 305 (IV).

7. E/1576.

the pace of implementation in the first year was rather slow. The total expenditure that year came to only $ 225,000, compared to the Secretary-General's estimate of $ 345,000 and the 1949 appropriation of $ 307,750. As the unused amount lapsed at the end of the fiscal year, the slow pace of execution meant that an additional amount would be needed in 1950 to catch up with the balance of requests received, but not met, in 1949. This provided another justification for enlarging the programme in 1950. That the demand for assistance exceeded the resources available was demonstrated by the fact that the funds available in 1950 for executing the GA Resolution 200(III) were fully committed by June 1950 and no new projects could be initiated after that.

The launching of the technical assistance programme under the GA Resolution 200(III) stirred up enthusiasm in the regional commissions as well. During its fifth session in 1950, the Economic Commission for Asia and the Far East (ECAFE) discussed the question of technical assistance, among other issues. In its resolutions E/CN.11/226 and E/CN.11/231, it requested the ECOSOC to consider: (i) enhanced participation of the ECAFE in the execution of the technical assistance programme; and (ii) development of such services by the ECAFE to assist its members and associate members, especially in the appraisal and presentation of their needs prior to making formal applications for assistance.

In the Economic Committee, Brazil, Chile and India strongly supported the ECAFE's request for greater participation in the technical assistance programme. This cross-sectional support was perhaps aimed at preparing the ground for increased participation by all the regional commissions in the execution of the programme. However, most developed countries and the Secretary-General favoured centralisation of the administration of technical assistance at that stage, in order to avoid overlap, duplication and delay. Australia felt that the assistance to be given by the Member Governments would be more useful at the headquarters than at the regional level; the commissions could obtain information and give advice on the distribution of technical assistance. The US argued that the regional commissions should function as judgement groups and not as operating groups for the execution of technical assistance projects. It was best not to involve too many parties. The UK, too, was in favour of initial centralisation of technical assistance. The Secretary-General preferred centralisation of all technical assistance arrangements and felt that the commissions could play a supporting role. In the end, the ECOSOC did not support the ECAFE's request but simply asked the Secretary-General to transmit the records of its discussions on this issue to ECAFE.[8]

The ECAFE was also the first to flag the question of providing technical assistance to non-member governments. (The ECAFE's Associate Members were not members of the UN.) In a resolution adopted during its fifth session, the ECAFE requested the ECOSOC to consider the eligibility of its Associate Members to receive technical assistance.

During the 10th session of the ECOSOC, the developing countries in the Economic Committee—notably Brazil, Chile and India—supported the ECAFE's request. Chile even went to the extent of suggesting an amendment to the GA resolution 200(III). Again, the developed countries expressed reservations. The arguments advanced by the US summarised their opposition to extending technical assistance to non-members under the regular budget. The US argued that the EPTA was available to members of the UN and of the specialised agencies, which contributed to the Special Account set up for that purpose. Those who wanted technical assistance could become members of the specialised agencies. However, at the request of Australia, the debate on this question was postponed to the 11th session of the ECOSOC.

During the Council's 11th session, the French delegate expressed the view that since the only difference between the EPTA and the Regular Programme lay in the origin of the funds, the non-member countries could receive assistance under both programmes. On the other hand, India argued that since the Regular Programme was open to all countries—developed and underdeveloped—and considering that acquiring membership of the specialised agencies was not entirely up to them, the non-member countries should receive assistance only under the Regular Programme. Mr. David Owen, Assistant Secretary-General for Economic and Social Affairs, pointed out that while both programmes were designed to help the underdeveloped countries, no

8. ECOSOC Res. 270.B.(X) of 13 February 1950.

definition of 'underdeveloped' had been provided. The Secretariat, he said, depended on a country's own perception of its state of development and hence, provided assistance if a request was made and if its content was perceived of as contributing to the country's economic development.

The confusion arose from the fact that until then, neither the Secretariat, nor the ECOSOC had made an attempt to formulate at least a workable definition of 'underdeveloped'. Several developed countries continued to receive technical assistance from the Regular Programme, especially in the field of social welfare advisory services. Between 1 January 1951 and 31 March 1952, such assistance was given to 14 developed countries, mainly in the form of fellowships. Mr. Owen also said that assistance under the GA resolution 200(III) and the EPTA would be unified. Later, Saudi Arabia again sought a definition of 'underdeveloped' in the General Assembly, but it did not stimulate any discussion.

In the light of Mr. Owen's comments, there was general agreement that non-members should be eligible for technical assistance under the Regular Programme. However, the Secretary-General had suggested that requests which could not be met under the Regular Programme could be met under the EPTA. There was unanimous agreement on this suggestion, which was then approved both by the ECOSOC[9] and the General Assembly.[10] This also meant that non-members could receive assistance under both programmes.

In his fourth report[11] to the ECOSOC, the Secretary-General drew the Council's attention to a mechanism which was currently being tested and which was designed "to assist a Government requesting technical assistance in a number of fields and from a number of agencies to achieve coordinated action both in relation to its own economic development activities and *vis-à-vis* the several outside agencies that are assisting it."

Later he informed the Council that discussions were under way with the Governments of Haiti on "the desirability of stationing within Haiti for an extended period of time a highly qualified person

9. ECOSOC Res. 291.A. (XI) of 15 August 1950.

10. A/1540.

11. E/1700.

who could facilitate ... requests of the Haitian Government for further technical assistance by helping the Government to define its needs with sufficient precision to enable the Secretariat of the United Nations and the specialised agencies to respond as promptly as possible with the services of properly qualified technicians." The discussions with Haiti had been successfully completed and a resident technical assistance representative had been stationed there since 5 May 1950. This was the first step in the evolution of the institution of UN resident representatives, now stationed in almost all developing countries. In his fourth report, the Secretary-General also stated that a similar arrangement had been made with the Government of Pakistan. Several other countries, too, had expressed an interest in such arrangements.

At this stage, a resident representative represented only the UN, and not the specialised agencies. The Secretary-General, however, briefed the specialised agencies on the arrangement of stationing such representatives, and invited them to use it to the fullest extent if they wished. This question had also been discussed by the Technical Assistance Board of EPTA which had not taken any decision as yet. The Secretary-General believed that "appointments of this nature can greatly contribute towards the avoidance of confusion which may otherwise arise from a multiplication of channels through which technical assistance would flow, especially after the technical assistance programme is expanded in response to ECOSOC resolution 222A(IX)." The Secretary-General's initiative and vision were quite prophetic. In the years to come, resident representatives would perform wider functions and take on greater responsibilities in the coordination of multilateral technical assistance programmes at the country level.

With the start of operations under the EPTA, the issue of resident representatives assumed greater significance and the TAB was given the responsibility of dealing with this question. By the end of 1950, the TAB had not yet evolved a uniform policy with respect to resident representatives. They were appointed by a participating agency, though it was the TAB that decided which agency should make the appointment. All agencies submitted their list of candidates and agreed on the final choice. The resident representatives were now assisting a growing number of agencies. In administrative matters, they were responsible to the agency appointing them and for operational matters to the agency seeking their assistance. They were paid by the appointing agency, while the requesting governments paid for their subsistence and travel.

By May 1952, there were resident representatives in 15 countries. The ECOSOC was now convinced of their usefulness and wanted them to effectively help the recipient governments to clarify their requests and develop their programmes, to coordinate the assistance rendered by the UN agencies and others at the national level, and to develop a unified system of reporting. At its 14th session, the ECOSOC took measures[12] to systematise the institution of resident representatives by giving the TAB full responsibility in this area. Resident representatives could no longer be employees of the agencies. When the Council decided to appoint a full-time chairman of the TAB, it authorised him to appoint resident representatives in consultation with the Board, and to supervise their work and receive their reports. The Council also requested the participating agencies to give effective support to the resident representatives. In amending the ECOSOC resolution 222(IX) to incorporate these changes, the TAC also spelled out the functions of the resident representatives. It emphasised their role in assisting the recipient governments with the preparation of country programmes, in coordinating the support given by the agencies at the country level, and in evaluating the results of the programmes.

In his fourth report, the Secretary-General also provided information on implementation of the Regular Programme in 1950 and the proposed budget for 1951. He agreed to keep the budget for 1951 at the same level as that for 1950, *viz.*, $ 508,420. The year 1950 had seen a significant increase in the provision of expert advice and fellowships, the establishment of local training institutes and the number of seminars held. According to the Secretary-General, the total value of technical assistance provided in 1950 was $ 867,587. Of this, $ 507,787 was financed from the UN budget and $ 359,800 was supposed to have been borne as local costs by the recipient governments. The estimates of the local costs were rather fuzzy and no explanation was given regarding the method of their calculation.

12. E/TAC/L.19, 22 May 1952.

The information in the Secretary-General's reports on the activities completed in 1949 and 1950 was very vague, incomplete and imprecise. There were no data on the number of experts provided. The number of fellowship awards reported did not tally with the actual number of placements in the given year. The figures on budgetary appropriations varied from one report to another. The figures in the text did not match with those in the annexes. The first five reports were rather disappointing as they did not provide useful material for analysis and evaluation of progress.

The operations of the Regular Programme were encountering a few difficulties. Among the more outstanding problems were the recruitment of qualified experts, a lack of clarity in defining the requests made by the recipient governments, inability to simplify and properly coordinate the reporting system, and the absence of suitable methods of evaluating the impact of the programme's activities. While both the developed and underdeveloped countries extended full cooperation in the recruitment of experts, there were still no national coordinating agencies. The reporting system of the UN programme, and for that matter, of the EPTA as well, was too detailed and complicated. It provided information on each project in every country, together with summarised information on all aspects of the provision of experts and award of fellowships, but this was not useful for comparative analysis. This did not make it any easier for the legislative bodies to focus on policy issues. Several delegates in the legislative bodies voiced concern about how to evaluate the results, but a general approach and framework did not emerge in either the ECOSOC or the Secretariat.

In August 1950, the Secretary-General established the Department of Technical Assistance Administration (TAA) to administer the UN programme of technical assistance, and to ensure its effective coordination with the technical assistance programmes of the specialised agencies and with bilateral assistance. Mr. Keenleyside was appointed Director-General of the TAA. The establishment of this department also brought under one umbrella the activities in public administration [GA Resolution 246(III)], social welfare advisory services [GA Resolution 58(II)], and the activities under the GA Resolution 200(III). As the EPTA became operational in 1951, the TAA was also responsible for the execution of projects assigned to the

UN by EPTA. The department decided to appoint representatives who would be posted at the headquarters of the regional commissions. This arrangement was to become somewhat controversial in later years.

With all the UN Regular Programme activities being brought under one umbrella and after becoming a participating agency of EPTA, the scope of the UNTA activities was becoming increasingly clear. The major fields of activity of the UN included general economic development, transport and communication, public finance, statistics, population, public administration and social development. These were essentially areas not covered by the specialised agencies. Thus, the UN area of competence was defined on a residual basis.

During the 13th[13] session of the ECOSOC, Mr. Keenleyside, as well as several members of the ECOSOC, stressed the importance of public administration in economic development and asked for continued assistance in this field. As there was near unanimous agreement on this, the ECOSOC recommended [14] to the General Assembly that the Secretary-General be authorised "to place on a continuing basis the programme in public administration authorised by GA Resolution 246(III) and to include an amount for these services in the United Nations budget in the future." The Council also recommended that additional assistance be made available under the EPTA for technical assistance in economic development, public administration and social welfare advisory services when additional programmes could not be financed from the UN budget. Later, during its 6th session, the General Assembly approved these recommendations.[15]

From 1951 onwards, the UN programme included the three components financed from the UN budget and projects funded from the Special Account of the EPTA. The financial data from 1951 to 1954 were mixed. They referred, as before, to either budgetary appropriations or to estimated expenditures and in a few cases, to actual expenditure. The appropriations from the UN budget remained

13. Report by the Secretary-General, E/2001, 6 June 1951.

14. ECOSOC Res. 399(XIII), 1 September 1951.

15. GA Res. 518(VI).

at a constant level of $ 1.4 million through 1954. During the first financial year of the EPTA, the UN received an allocation of $ 4.4 million, but the estimated expenditure was going to be only $ 2.8 million. During 1952, it had been decided to spend $ 7.7 million of EPTA funds. As for the next year, the total estimated expenditure, including EPTA funds, was placed at $ 7.1 million. This was less than the estimated expenditure for 1952 owing to a reduction in the funds coming from the EPTA. The project costs in 1954 amounted to $ 5.2 million, of which $ 3.8 million came from the EPTA and $ 1.4 million from the UN regular budget. Some of the old constraints in implementation continued to pose a problem. In the meantime, there was concern in the ECOSOC about the rising levels of overhead costs which, in 1953, amounted to 19 per cent of the estimated total expenditure.

During this period, there was a noticeable shift in emphasis in the requests received from governments—a shift from general surveys to specific projects, especially in planning and plan implementation. Greater emphasis was also laid on supplies and equipment, and there were increasing requests that the experts assume executive functions. As it had done in the case of the EPTA programme, the ECOSOC emphasised the importance of evaluating the achievements of the Regular Programme. The UNTAA had completed a five-year assessment of the social welfare advisory services, but Mr. Keenleyside observed that an evaluation of the "achievements of technical assistance programmes in both economic and social fields can best be made by an organisation responsible for all aspects of the programme." He, of course, meant that the TAB should be given the responsibility. The subsequent reports of the UN programme did not contain much on evaluation. The ECOSOC, however, continued to emphasise the evaluation of results and was especially insistent on the assessment of the contribution of the projects financed under the EPTA to economic development.

During the 16th session of the ECOSOC, the Secretary-General submitted a report on public administration which was now presented separately on a continuing basis. The USSR argued for a ceiling on the expenditure on public administration, but this was not accepted by the ECOSOC as it was in favour of retaining flexibility in budgeting.

A resolution[16] adopted by the Council placed Technical Assistance in public administration on a permanent footing in the UN budget and raised it to the same status as technical assistance under the GA Resolution 200(III). This widened the UN scope for providing technical assistance services and its projects could now be financed also from EPTA funds.

In his report[17] submitted to the 22nd session of the ECOSOC, the Secretary-General drew the members' attention to the programme's growing emphasis on productivity and public administration. Stressing the importance of public administration in economic development, he asked for a modest increase in resources. He also outlined the need for a new organisational approach at the international level for building up effective national administration in the less developed countries. In response to a request to clarify his approach, the Secretary-General said that in addition to providing experts, it might be worthwhile to consider attaching people to national administrations not as consultants, but as members of the administrations. In support of his suggestion, he provided the following reasons for providing such assistance to the newly independent countries: (i) they needed efficient and mature personnel following the departure of the colonial administrators; (ii) they lacked the social infrastructure to develop a civil service; (iii) they needed people who were not dependent on any country; and (iv) besides an efficient administration, the newly independent countries needed financial assistance to improve their populations' standards of living. The Secretary-General said he was open to different kinds of organisational arrangements, but stressed that greater assistance in public administration was definitely an urgent need.

Several countries in the TAC supported a higher budgetary allocation for public administration. A few, like Canada and the UK, while favouring greater allocation, were against expanding the UN budget for technical assistance. They would rather have any additional assistance to be financed under the EPTA. Canada and the US had reservations about the Secretary-General's approach and preferred the provision of experts on a long-term basis. Finally, both the TAC and

---

16. ECOSOC Res. 492.B. (XVI).
17. E/2856.

ECOSOC agreed that greater importance should be given to public administration in the pursuit of economic development and thus, endorsed the Secretary-General's call for more assistance in this area. However, the ECOSOC requested "the Secretary-General to provide ... a full documentation in support of his request for additional funds," and recommended, "that the General Assembly in the light of such documentation give special attention to the need for sufficient funds for the United Nations programme in public administation."[18] The position taken by the TAC and ECOSOC was somewhat contradictory, as pointed out by the UK, because on the one hand, they clearly recognised the need for greater assistance, while on the other hand, they had passed on the responsibility of taking a decision to the Secretary-General and the General Assembly.

During the same session, the UNTAA's earlier decision to post a few of its personnel in the regional commissions and now to the Economic Commission of Latin America (ECLA), came up for discussion and criticism. The US, the UK and Pakistan, in particular, were against secondment of technical assistance staff to the regional commissions. The US argued that such an arrangement would have substantive and organisational implications, and expressed concern about its effect on the resident representatives, country programming and selection of experts. These countries felt that the arrangement could be extended to the ECLA only on an experimental basis. The General Assembly wanted more time to study the proposal, but agreed to try it on an experimental basis in the ECLA. The issue would be taken up again for detailed discussion and a final decision. Mr. Keenleyside assured the TAC that such secondment was not meant to decentralise operational activities; it was intended only to place staff closer to the countries assisted by TAA and would have no effect on resident representatives and country programming.

Following the discussions in the ECOSOC and General Assembly, the budgetary provision for public administration was increased from $ 145,000 to $ 300,000 in 1957. During the 24th session of the ECOSOC, the Secretary-General submitted a detailed memorandum on "An International Administrative Service",[19] as had been requested

18. ECOSOC Res. 623.II. (XXII), 9 August 1956.

19. E/3017, 10 June 1957.

by Indonesia and endorsed by the ECOSOC in the previous session. In this memorandum, the Secretary-General again highlighted the severe shortage of trained administrators in the less developed countries and underlined the urgent need to provide administrators under the UN framework of assistance. These administrators would assume executive functions and not work as experts, and would also assist nationals with 'in-service training'. He envisaged a scheme in which the UN would help the recipient governments recruit trained administrators for specific executive responsibilities at the national level. With respect to their work, the administrators would be accountable to the government concerned. However, they would be subject to the overall supervision of the UN and would comply with the general principles of UNTA. The UN would be responsible for preparing and monitoring all the contractual arrangements. As for emoluments, the administrators would be treated on par with the UN experts. The recipient government would be expected to pay the salary attached to the post, and also arrange for housing and local transport. The UN would pay the difference between such salary and the total emoluments and other perks normally payable to an expert of equivalent skills and rank.

The Secretary-General asked the Council to authorise the initiation of this scheme on an experimental basis. After a year, future arrangements could be made on the basis of an evaluation of the experience gained during the trial period. Although some members of the Council were prepared to support the scheme on a temporary basis, many were sceptical about establishing an international administrative service. Some members did not see much difference between this scheme and a few of the ongoing projects in public administration. The members also wanted more information on finances, the status of the proposed executive personnel and the size of the programme. Finally, as suggested by France and the US, the TAC agreed that the Secretary-General's proposal be transmitted to the recipient governments for their comments; the Secretary-General could then prepare a comprehensive report for discussion at the 26th session of the ECOSOC.

Accordingly, the Secretary-General submitted a detailed report[20] during the Council's 26th session. He explained the relevance of

20. E/3121.

public administration to economic development and good governance in the light of the critical role played by a government in the process of development. He traced the history of UN legislative actions and assistance in public administration, and recalled the recent significant increase in the UN budget for assistance in public administration. As suggested by the ECOSOC, the Secretary-General had sent a questionnaire to the recipient governments for their comments on the proposal for a one-year trial of the scheme. Seven governments simply acknowledged it, while 56 gave their comments. Of these, 55 endorsed the scheme in principle and agreed to try it out. Sixteen said they would seek assistance under the proposal. The Secretary-General then sought authorisation to provide operational and executive personnel on an experimental basis, on a limited scale, without increasing the level of administrative costs. The intention was to proceed slowly and cautiously, with an initial target of 20 or 30 personnel.

Although a majority of the delegates in the TAC were willing to support the scheme on a temporary and experimental basis, many questions were raised. These related to divided loyalties, disciplinary action, susceptibility of nationals to foreign executives, duration of appointment, adaptability of foreign administrators to national conditions and culture, and so on. The US opined that given the experimental nature of the scheme, the UN should not create a permanent cadre of experts for it. Moreover, it felt that the scheme should be confined to areas of TAA and that the agencies should start playing a role only at a later date. Most delegates were also of the view that the administrative cost of the scheme should be around $ 200,000, though without increasing the total administrative costs of the UNTAA. Finally, the TAC agreed to try out the scheme. It recommended to the General Assembly that "the Secretary-General be authorised, on a limited and experimental basis, and as a supplement to the existing United Nations Programmes of Technical Assistance, but without increase in administrative costs"[21] to have the scheme initiated.

The Secretary-General also submitted a separate[22] report on UNTA in public administration. Several members of the TAC were rather critical of the type of work done in this area, and a majority of them considered it more theoretical than practical. "More than

21. TAC Draft resolutions in E/TAC/L.165/Rev.1 and GA Res. 1256 (XIII), 14 November 1958.
22. E/3085.

dissemination of general principles, methods and techniques," said the Greek delegate, "what was important was their adaptation to local conditions and overcoming psychological resistance to change."[23] These views were widely shared. Many delegates emphasised the need to accord priority to training at the national and regional levels. They felt that training in public administration should be related effectively to a country's requirements of economic and social development.

The year 1957 also witnessed a fall in the EPTA allocations to the UN and especially, a sharp reduction in fellowships. The TAC and ECOSOC were unhappy with the decline in fellowships. The UNTAA attributed it partly to a reduction in TAB support and partly to the transfer of fellowships to the next year in order to balance the programme. The Burma Plan, which, as we have seen, envisaged technical assistance on a reimbursement basis, came on board in 1957. The funds under the plan amounted to $ 91,000 and were expected to reach $ 300,000 in 1958. This plan was to become quite attractive in later years as a means of mobilising supplementary funds for technical assistance.[24]

In 1958, the UN total project expenditure, including EPTA funds, amounted to $ 8.85 million, the highest level reached until then. The UN budgetary appropriation remained unchanged, and the growth in total assistance was due to increased support from the EPTA and the doubling of grants from the Population Council, Ford Foundation and World Veterans Federation. The number of experts increased, but there was a decline in fellowships and a sharp drop in the provision of equipment. This was partly due to inflation as the real value of the fixed amount allocated under the UN budget declined considerably. In 1958, the Secretary-General also changed the UN organisational arrangements for technical assistance. The UNTAA was abolished and the technical assistance work was given to the newly created Bureau of Technical Assistance Operations in DESA.

In 1959, the Secretary-General submitted a second report[25] on technical assistance in public administration. Training projects continued to be an important feature of the UN activities. In 1959,

23. E/TAC/SR.161.
24. E/3081.
25. E/3230.

training institutes in Central America, Cairo and Turkey made considerable progress in the training of government officials and in designing special programmes for senior officials.

The experimental programme for executive personnel, which had been authorised by the General Assembly in 1958, was started in 1959.[26] As of 8 July 1959, 90 requests were received from 28 countries. Since it was a new programme, the progress in its implementation was rather slow. Although a majority of the members in the TAC and ECOSOC supported the experiment, some expressed doubts. On the whole, however, there was general agreement that it was not possible to make an objective evaluation of the programme since sufficient time had not elapsed since its initiation. Therefore, the ECOSOC recommended,[27] and the General Assembly approved,[28] further continuation of the programme, subject to financial constraints. They also asked the Secretary-General to submit a detailed analytical report on the progress and results of the experiment during the 30th session of the ECOSOC and the 15th session of the General Assembly.

1960 was an important landmark in UN history, with 14 African countries gaining independence. All of these were less developed countries, which needed considerable assistance for development and for building up their systems of national administration. Their plight evoked considerable support and sympathy in the UN. The scheme of OPEX[29] also assumed new importance in the light of the new developments. In response to the needs of the newly independent countries, several donor governments, including those of the US, Netherlands, New Zealand, Denmark and the USSR, offered to increase their contribution to the UN Technical Assistance Programme—especially for public administration and OPEX, and to the EPTA and Special Fund[30] with a view to respond promptly to the needs of these countries. The requirements of these countries also galvanised support for the provision of executive personnel. Since the inception of the scheme for the provision of executive personnel in

26. SG's Report, E/3236.
27. ECOSOC Res. 739(XXVIII), 30 July 1959.
28. GA Res. 1384(XIV).
29. An acronym used for the Programme of providing operational and executive personnel to developing countries.
30. Created to provide pre-investment assistance.

1959, the Secretary-General had received an increasing number of requests for assistance in this area—106 from 30 countries in 1959 and 176 from 39 countries in 1960. As a result of this, the ECOSOC recommended to the General Assembly that "the provision of operational, executive and administrative personnel be placed on a continuing basis' and 'the financial resources for this activity be established at a level appropriate to the needs for this assistance." The General Assembly approved this recommendation during its 15th session in 1960.[31]

The emergence of so many independent states, mostly in Africa, had a significant impact on technical assistance activities in 1960.[32] The absence of country quotas under the UN Regular Programme allowed for some diversion of resources to the African countries. Resources also came in from non-recipient governments and non-governmental institutions.The EPTA, too, made additional resources available for assistance to Africa. As far as aid to Africa was concerned, the Secretary-General placed greater emphasis on educational and training programmes. He appointed a special adviser to assist in the formulation of training programmes for civil servants in the African countries' ministries of foreign affairs. The assistance to these countries increased from $ 0.83 million in 1959 to $ 1.10 million in 1960.

The programme as a whole laid much greater emphasis than before on providing assistance to national and regional training centres. Considerable importance was attached to regional projects and to the role of the regional commissions in providing guidance. The TAC and ECOSOC also gave importance to the training of high-level officials in national or regional training programmes, so that these experts could eventually take over from the foreign experts and thus release resources for deployment in the newly independent countries. The Secretary-General initiated a scheme, under which he appointed regional advisers in different fields and posted them at the regional commissions to assist in the regional training programmes and in the provision of short-term advisory assistance to the recipient governments.

31. ECOSOC Res. 799(XXX), 3 August 1960.

32. E/3366.

The OPEX operations were in full force by 1960 and continued to grow thereafter. By the end of 1960, 195 requests had been received from 44 countries and 27 appointments made. During the next year, 48 countries sent 214 requests. The progress was satisfactory and the reports coming in from the governments were positive. The General Assembly gave a strong endorsement to these activities and suggested principles for the sharing of costs between the recipient governments and the UN.

The Burma Plan, under which projects were financed by recipient governments but executed by the UN, also gathered significant momentum. The resources available under this programme rose from $ 129,000 in 1959 to $ 233,000 in 1960. In 1961, the total programme executed by the UN, financed from the budgetary and extra-budgetary funds, increased substantially.

The UN Regular Programme continued to place emphasis on training and the establishment of national institutes of training. The General Assembly, too, recommended in its Resolution 1708 (XVI) that regional economic development and planning institutions be established to provide an impetus to training activities. In order to give substance to this resolution, the UN Commissioner for Technical Cooperation suggested strengthening of the regional economic commissions through the provision of regional advisers, setting up of technical cooperation units in the commissions and the provision of more funds for regional seminars. It may be noted that whereas in the case of the EPTA, the TAC had fixed a ceiling of 15 per cent for regional projects, the UN spent nearly 30 per cent of its resources in the regular budget on regional projects.

In 1962, the Commissioner asked for more assistance for industrial development.[33] In fact, during the discussions on assistance under the EPTA, the members of the TAC and ECOSOC had always sought more aid in this area. However, the EPTA officials manipulated the data to show higher levels of assistance for industry. Actually, the amount of direct assistance for industry was always small, but the EPTA showed assistance for infrastructure—power, transportation and communications—as indirect assistance for industry. The need for assistance to industry seemed more urgent now, since the establishment of the Committee for Economic Development by the General Assembly and the setting up of the Center for Industrial

33. E/3680.

Development in the UN Secretariat. One of the problems in this context was that the funds in the UN budget were earmarked for special purposes, e.g., economic development, social welfare and public administration, and could not be transferred for other purposes. This built-in inflexibility made it difficult for the Secretary-General to respond to new and important legislative decisions. Some members in the TAC, therefore, while pleading for greater assistance to industry, "hoped that the financial rules should be so altered as to enable the transfer of funds from one resolution to another if need be to initiate some of the much needed projects."[34]

The Commissioner also drew attention "to the growing volume of requests for OPEX personnel and the inadequacy of funds to meet these requirements." In this connection, he recommended several measures to augment the resources of operational executive and administrative (OPEX) posts. These were as follows:

(a) OPEX should be authorised to use any savings arising in the General Assembly appropriation for public administration.

(b) The specialised agencies should provide greater financial support to the OPEX posts in their areas.

(c) The recipient governments should increase their level of support.

(d) The governments could also supplement OPEX posts through funds-in-trust programmes.

The Commissioner had also requested the EPTA to finance some of the posts. The members of the TAC were quite sympathetic to the Commissioner's plea to ease the financial situation and hoped that some OPEX posts could be financed by the EPTA. In addition, the TAC proposed that the specialised agencies should finance OPEX posts from their regular budgets.

An important issue which came up for discussion in the TAC was that of rationalisation of all technical assistance provided by the UN. In response, the General Assembly, in Resolution 1768(XVII), invited "the Technical Assistance Committee to prepare at its November 1962 session a study of the relationship between the various United Nations programmes of technical assistance under its mandate and

34. TAC Report, E/3704, p.27.

the regular budget programmes with a view to their rationalisation and in order to avoid duplication of activities in future fiscal years". By way of initial preparation, the TAC appointed a working group to study the issue. The Working Group had before it, *inter alia,* a report prepared by the Secretary-General that provided information on the existing relationship between the Regular Programmes and those financed from the EPTA. The Secretary-General had pointed out certain differences between the two types of programmes. First, there were obviously two different sources of funds. EPTA financing of OPEX and human rights activities was still not acceptable. On the other hand, the UN budget provided funds for certain specific activities, most of which were also acceptable for financing under the EPTA. Further, unlike the EPTA, the UN Regular Programme placed no restrictions on expenditure on regional and inter-regional projects. Another difference was that the funds provided under the UN budget had to be used during the given fiscal year and unused funds would lapse at the end of the year.

Once The Working Group had submitted its report, the TAC used it as the basis for preparing and adopting a statement as an interim response to the General Assembly's request. This statement was not particularly useful. It did not address the question in detail and referred the matter further to the ad hoc committee of 10, requesting it to study the long-term aspects of the General Assembly's request. The statement simply concluded that it "is informed that as a consequence of the integrated administration of technical assistance projects by the United Nations, there is no duplication in the use of funds as between the resources the United Nations receives from EPTA and its own budgetary sources."[35]

The UN Regular Programme had been growing rapidly since 1960 owing to the Special Fund projects, the steady growth of the EPTA, an increase in extra-budgetary resources, and the GA resolution 1527(XV) dealing with assistance to newly emerging countries. The total expenditure nearly doubled from $ 10 million in 1960 to $ 19.8 million in 1962. This period was marked by a substantial increase in aid to Africa—the amount doubled from 1960 to 1961 and doubled again from 1961 to 1962. By 1962, Africa was receiving the single

35. For discussion on this issue, see *ibid.*, pp.29-31.

largest share of UN resources (34%). Another area that witnessed growth was that of regional and inter-regional projects. As a result of the UN decision to expand and strengthen decentralisation of technical assistance, the share of such projects in the total expenditure had risen to 32 per cent by 1962, much higher than the 15 per cent allowed under EPTA rules.

As mentioned earlier, the OPEX scheme continued to expand. Between 1961 and 1963, the UN filled 183 posts and there were 200 unfulfilled requests. The Secretary-General received more requests for operational personnel than the limited UN budget could handle. He, therefore, requested the TAB and TAC to consider whether OPEX posts could be financed from EPTA funds. After reviewing the matter in 1963, both the TAB and ACC endorsed the proposal. In view of this and the growing volume of requests for such assistance, the TAC recommended approval of the proposal to the ECOSOC. In its Resolution 951 (XXXVI) of 5 July, the latter authorised, subject to the agreement of the General Assembly, financing of OPEX posts from EPTA funds on an experimental basis for the years 1964-1966. The matter would be reviewed at the end of the period. This authorisation not only covered requests made by the UN, but also extended to all the participating agencies. The recipient governments were to submit requests for operational personnel within the framework of their country programmes. The ECOSOC stipulated two conditions for such assistance. First, the training of national counterparts must form an essential component of such projects, and operational personnel should train national counterparts whenever practicable. Second, the recipient governments were expected to pay at least 12.5 per cent of the total cost of the projects. Later in December 1963, in its resolution 1946(XIII), the General Assembly expressed full agreement with the ECOSOC recommendations. The following year, the EPTA approved 78 OPEX posts. Of these, 52 went to the UN and the rest to the other participating agencies.

By 1963, there was increasing legislative pressure in favour of transferring the activities of the UN Regular Programme to the EPTA. During the 37th session of the ECOSOC, Mr. Phillipe de Seynes, Under-Secretary General for Economic and Social Affairs, made a strong case for the retention of the UN Regular Programme.[36] He

---

36. E/TAC/L.301,20 June 1963.

suggested that instead of being merged with the EPTA, the programme should be reconverted or reclassified. This meant that the UN Regular Programme would focus only on those priority areas which were recommended by the General Assembly, ECOSOC and functional commissions. He elaborated extensively on his suggestion, but it received only a tepid response in the ECOSOC. A few delegates supported it, while others believed that such a classification was impracticable. Those who were in favour of a merger obviously opposed the idea.

Since 1962, the UN programme had remained almost frozen at a level of $ 6.4 million. It did not register any growth in subsequent years. There was, however, a significant improvement in extra-budgetary funds, especially in funds-in-trust programmes, including one for Congo.

However, allocations from the EPTA continued to increase, as a result of which total expenditures kept growing, reaching $ 16.8 million in 1964. Regional and inter-regional activities still constituted a major chunk of the Regular Programme. In 1964, the programme allocated nearly 40 per cent of its resources to such activities. The regional activities were concentrated largely in Africa. The number of regional advisers grew from 65 in 1963 to 83 in 1964.

In 1963 and 1964, the TAC made a few recommendations on the reorganisation of allocations for technical assistance in the UN budget. First, it recommended that the Secretary-General seek authorisation for some flexibility in the transfer of funds of the UN budget, i.e., from one section to another in Part V (the latter concerned technical assistance). He was later authorised to transfer up to five per cent of the resources allocated to a section. Second, the TAC requested the Secretary-General to allocate more to the section on economic development [funds approved under the GA Resolution 200(III)]. Within this section, the TAC wanted a larger allocation for industrial development. For years, the developing countries had been vying for greater support to industrial development, but the actual progress was very slow. In 1964, the Secretary-General allocated $ 555,000 for this purpose—nine per cent of the total resources in the section—and promised to do better in 1965. Thirdly, the TAC suggested that from 1965, the budget in Part V be presented in terms of three broad categories: (i) economic development, social activities and public administration; (ii) human rights; and (iii) narcotics. Finally, though the UN Regular Programme had no country targets and country programming procedures, the TAC recommended that the Secretary-General consult governments on their priorities and from 1965, prepare a budget on the basis of priority programmes.

The UNDP became operational on 1 January 1966 and consisted of the Special Fund and the Technical Assistance component (old EPTA). It was the Governing Council of the UNDP that reviewed the UN programme for 1965. The total expenditure on all UN programmes reached $ 34 million in 1965, owing largely to an increase in the number of Special Fund projects. The authorisation for the UN Regular Programme remained at $ 6.4 million. This amount had not changed since 1962 and was to remain fixed until 1968. The real value of assistance declined considerably due to inflation. Within the activities of the UN Regular Programme, economic development received the largest share. EPTA resources had now stabilised and thus only modest gains were expected in the immediate future. The regional distribution of UN funds remained unchanged. As decided earlier, the Governing Council of the UNDP and the ECOSOC reviewed the OPEX programme in 1966. They recommended that the General Assembly temporarily authorise the continued use of the technical assistance component of UNDP funds for OPEX for 1967-1968, a suggestion which was approved.

During its third session,[37] the Governing Council reviewed the technical assistance programme of the UN. The review provided information on the activities undertaken in1966 and the budget proposals for 1968.

In 1966, the total field expenditure under the UN programmes, financed from all sources, reached a level of $ 40.5 million, compared with $ 34.0 million in 1965 and $ 32.9 million in 1964. The annual rise was due mostly to an increase in the number of Special Fund projects. Of the total field expenditure in 1966, 79 per cent was spent on economic development, 14 per cent on social development, 7 per cent on public administration, and less than 1 per cent on human rights and narcotics. The corresponding percentages for the Regular Programme were 49 per cent, 21 per cent, 16 per cent and 4 per cent.

37. E/T4297.

There were no significant changes in regional distribution. A distinct feature of the allocations made under the UN Regular Programme and the Technical Assistance component of the UNDP was that the former laid a significantly greater emphasis on social development than did the latter. Several members of the Governing Council expressed disappointment with this state of affairs and pleaded for a higher allocation to social development under the technical assistance component.

In view of the UN rising levels of total expenditures on technical assistance, several members of the Governing Council felt that the UN programme deserved greater attention by the Council. They were particularly worried about the constant level of appropriations by the General Assembly for the UN Regular Programme. Since 1962, the budget for the UN Regular Programme had been frozen at $ 6.4 million, and was to remain so for 1967 and 1968 too. In the meantime, the costs incurred on experts, fellowships and equipment had risen considerably. As a result, the real value of assistance had fallen substantially. According to some members of the Governing Council, inflation had reduced the real value of assistance by 20 per cent since 1962. The share of the UNTA had declined from 7.8 per cent of the UN budget in 1962 to 5.3 per cent in 1966. Several members, therefore, suggested that the UN provide a 'constant level' of services in real terms, and not in fixed dollar terms. Some members argued that additional assistance could be considered under the Special Fund and the technical assistance component of the UNDP. There were, of course, a few members who had always been opposed to the provision of technical assistance from the UN budget and preferred all such assistance to be given on a voluntary basis. However, there was no agreement in the Governing Council on the levels of assistance in future years. The Council agreed to discuss the issue again during its fifth session, on the basis of a report to be prepared by the Secretary-General on the relationship of the regular budget activities to other programmes of technical assistance.

During its third session, the Council also considered a recommendation from the Industrial Development Board, the legislative body of UNIDO. The Board recommended that Part V of the UN budget—dealing with technical assistance— should contain a separate section on industrial development, to which commensurate resources should be allotted. The Board would provide policy guidance, besides reviewing and approving all programmes and projects in the sphere. The Council, however, felt that "both the proposed fragmenting of the Regular Programme appropriations and the removal from the jurisdiction of the Governing Council of a portion of the United Nations Regular Programme were undesirable."[38]

38. *ibid.*, p.57.

Annexure A-6.1

UN Regular Programme of Technical Assistance—Total Expenditure (in US $ '000)

	1949 a_/	1950 a_/	1951 b_/ c_/	1952 c_/	1953	1954	1955	1956	1957	1958e_/
I UN Regular Programme										
(i) Project costs	248	508	1417	1393	1393	1393	1393	1624	1704	1750
(ii) Administrative expenses	NA	NA	NA	360	1451 d_/	360	364	409	442	453
(iii) Funds-in-trust	-	-	-	-	-	-	-	-	-	-
(iv) Extra-budgetary	-	-	-	-	-	-	-	-	-	254
Total UN Regular Programme	248	508	1417	1753	NA	1753	1757	2033	2146	2457
II EPTA Programme										
(i) Project costs	-	-	NA	6971	4215	3843	4982	6722	6236	7145
(ii) Indirect operational services costs	-	-	NA	704	NA	837	794	900	918	940
Total EPTA	-	-	2800	7675	NA	4680	5776	7622	7154	8085
III Special Fund	-	-	-	-	-	-	-	-	-	-
IV Total Expenditures (I+II+III)	248	508	4217	9428	7059	6433	7533	9655	9300	10542

Contd. ...

	1959	1960	1961	1962	1963	1964	1965 f_/	1966 f_/
I UN Regular Programme								
(i) Project costs	2331	2339	3529	6024	7242	6400	NA	NA
(ii) Administrative expenses	NA	NA	NA	NA	NA	NA	NA	NA

Contd. ...

...Contd. ...

	1959	*1960*	*1961*	*1962*	*1963*	*1964*	*1965 f_/*	*1966 f_/*
(iii) Funds-in-trust	129	233	382	431	1201	3600	NA	NA
(iv) Extra-budgetary	NA	873	974	396	580	NA	NA	NA
Total UN Regular Programme	NA	NA	NA	NA	NA	NA	NA	NA
II EPTA Programme								
(i) Project costs	6275	6212	6160	8824	8168	10463	NA	NA
(ii) Indirect operational services costs	NA	NA	NA	NA	NA	NA	NA	NA
Total EPTA	NA	NA	NA	NA	NA	NA	NA	NA
III Special Fund	-	906	1710	4092	6657	12313	NA	NA
IV Total Expenditures (I+II+III)	NA	NA	NA	NA	NA	32900	34000	40500

Notes: Extra-budgetary: Contribution from NGOs and non-recipient governments.

a_/ TA under GA Resolution 200 (iii) only. Budget appropriations.

b_/ From 1951, figures include TA under GA Resolution 200 (iii), public administration, social welfare advisory services and the EPTA.

c_/ Budget estimates.

d_/ Includes the UN and EPTA.

e_/ From 1958, includes human rights, narcotics and OPEX.

f_/ Breakdown of total expenditure is not available.

Source: Annual reports of the Secretary-General on UN Regular Programme of Technical Assistance.

Annual reports of the TAB on the EPTA.

Other reports submitted to the ECOSOC and General Assembly.

Annexure A-6.2

UN Programme of Technical Assistance—Experts in the Field and Fellowships Awarded

Year	Experts			Fellowships		
	UN Regular Programme	EPTA-financed	Total	UN Regular Programme	EPTA-financed	Total
1949	NA	-	-	NA	-	-
1950	84	-	84	-	-	-
1951	-	-	-	319	132	451
1952	103	328	431	286	443	729
1953	105	389	494	191	436	627
1954	132	366	498	175	165	340
1955	160	457	617	286	517	803
1956	168	570	678	297	660	957
1957	226	574	800	291	491	782
1958	198	578	776	244	612	856
1959	272	526	798	361	466	827
1960	402	522	924	372	556	928
1961	444	588	1032	601	506	1107
1962 a_/	-	-	1253	846	997	1843
1963 a_/	-	-	1540	864	788	1652
1964 a_/	-	-	1849	827	1492	2319
1965	-	-	2364	-	-	1262
1966	-	-	2577	-	-	1709

Note: a_/ Includes fellowships from extra-budgetary funds.

Source: See Annexure A-4.1 of Chapter 4.

Annexure A-6.3

UN Regular Programme Project Costs by Resolutions (in US $ '000)

Year	GA 200 (III)	GA 418 (V) Social Welfare	GA 723 (VIII) Public Administration	Total UN	EPTA ECOSOC 222 (IX)	Grand Total
1949	308	a_/	a_/	308	-	308
1950	508	a_/	a_/	508	-	508
1951	653	945	168	1766	3990	5756
1952	NA	NA	NA	NA	6971	NA
1953	NA	NA	NA	NA	4215	NA

Contd. ...

...Contd. ...

Year	*GA 200 (III)*	*GA 418 (V) Social Welfare*	*GA 723 (VIII) Public Administration*	*Total UN*	*EPTA ECOSOC 222 (IX)*	*Grand Total*
1954	479	769	145	1393	3843	5236
1955	479	769	145	1393	4982	6375
1956	479	1000	145	1624	6722	8346
1957	479	925	300	1704	6236	7940
1958	479	925	300	1704	7145	8849
1959	480	925	300	1860 b_/	6275	8135
1960	480	1200	300	2339 b_/	6212	8551
1961	1125	1375	542	3529 b_/	6160	9689
1962	2072	2098	922	6003 b_/	8824	14827
1963	2092	2102	1061	6298 b_/	8168	14466
1964	2291	2114	986	6400 b_/	10463	16863

Note: a_/ Separately administered.

b_/ Includes fellowships from extra-budgetary funds.

Source: See Annexure A-6.1.

Annexure A-6.4

UN Regular Programme Regional Distribution (%)

Region	1951 a_/	1952 a_/	1953 a_/	1954 a_/	1955	1956	1957	1958	1959	1960	1961	1962	1963	1964
Africa	-	-	-	-	-	-	-	-	9.6	12.1	23.3	33.8	37.3	35.3
Asia & Far East	23.1	26.2	27.6	32.0	30.6	35.9	36.9	35.4	39.8	42.0	34.6	31.0	27.9	25.5
Latin America	32.7	29.8	39.4	32.7	27.6	30.1	27.0	28.1	27.5	26.1	26.9	20.0	18.7	19.3
Europe, Middle East & Africa	44.2	44.0	33.0	35.3	36.4	29.6	33.0	34.5	20.2 b_/	16.5	12.1	12.1	11.3	12.1
Inter-regional	-	-	-	-	5.4	4.4	3.1	2.1	2.9	3.3	3.1	3.1	4.8	7.8
Total	100.0	100.0	100.0	100.0	100.0	100.0	100.0	100.0	100.0	100.0	100.0	100.0	100.0	100.0

Note: a_/ EPTA finances only.

b_/ Excludes Africa hereafter.

From 1960 onwards, data include Special Fund and extra-budgetary funds.

Source: See Annexure A-6.1.

7

Special Fund

I
ESTABLISHMENT OF THE SPECIAL FUND

From the outset, beginning with the first session of the General Assembly in 1946, while the developed countries were largely preoccupied with the reconstruction and rehabilitation of European economies devastated by the war, the developing countries were emphasising the urgent need for external flows of public and private capital, besides technical assistance, for their economic development. In support of their drive for external assistance, the latter advanced arguments based on their domestic conditions and on the interdependence of the economies of all countries. Low incomes in the poor nations left little for savings and investment, resulting in low rates of growth, which barely kept up with these countries' rates of population growth. Injections of massive doses of external assistance were needed to break this vicious circle of poverty and step up their levels of investment and growth. The developing countries argued that the economic interdependence of all economies warranted simultaneous and integrated efforts to lift up all countries and enhance world prosperity which would also contribute to world peace.

The persistent efforts of the developing countries did finally result in the creation of the EPTA in 1950. On the question of capital assistance, the developed countries unrelentingly advised the developing countries to seek private foreign capital, resisting all pleas for the provision of such assistance by the UN, wholly or partially, on a grant basis. Over the years, there was considerable discussion in the UN legislative bodies on the policies, terms and conditions which the developing countries could adopt to attract private foreign capital. Appeals were made to the World Bank, too, to increase its lending to the developing countries. One of the concrete and positive results of all these discussions was the creation of the International Finance Corporation to stimulate and assist private-sector investment in the developing countries.

During the discussions, the developing countries introduced a third dimension of external assistance, which fell somewhere between traditional UNTA and private capital flows. It could also have been considered as an extended form of technical assistance. These countries asked for UN financing of non-self-liquidating projects. The projects financed under the EPTA were also non-self-liquidating, but now, the developing countries asked for projects such as feasibility studies and technical or engineering studies, which would examine the potential for investment in a specific sector and thereby, attract the attention of both domestic and foreign investors. The EPTA projects differed from such projects in that they were not directly related to investment, and provided only individual experts for policy and institutional reforms, as well as assistance for training of nationals. The developing countries' request for financing of non-self-liquidating projects found much support in the reports of the Economic, Employment and Development Commission,[1] Sub-commission on Economic Development and especially, the Group of Experts on Measures for the Economic Development of Underdeveloped Countries.[2] It was the Group of Experts which identified the needs for financing of non-self-liquidating projects with international aid.

The first significant step in this direction was taken during the fifth session of the General Assembly in 1950. Extensive discussions were held on the question of financing economic development in the underdeveloped countries and the Assembly, in Resolution 400(V), recommended that the "Council, in giving further study to the problem of the financing of economic development, consider practical methods, conditions and policies for achieving the adequate expansion and steadier flow of foreign capital, both public and private, and pay special attention to the financing of non-self-liquidating projects which are basic to economic development." The Council was requested to submit its recommendations to the sixth session of the General Assembly.

In response to the General Assembly resolution, the ECOSOC took up the question of financing economic development during its 13th

1. E/2006.

2. Report of the Group of Experts.

session in 1951. It initially asked its Economic Committee to prepare a set of recommendations. The Committee drafted recommendations[3] on the flows of public and private capital, as well as on "Encouraging the Flow of Capital to Help Finance Non-Self-Liquidating Projects Basic to Economic Development." The Economic Committee recognised that some countries, particularly the least developed, might, under some circumstances, require a measure of external grant assistance "in order to provide an initial impetus to such basic projects." It noted that some grant assistance was already available under various programmes of the UN and specialised agencies. It pointed out that "many countries, which formerly were substantial exporters of capital, are not in a position now to make any appreciable contribution to any International Agency along the lines of recommendation No.14 (Common-Self-Liquidating Projects) of the Report of the Group of Experts."[4] It went on to say, "The improved monetary reserve and balance of payments position at present enjoyed by some underdeveloped countries is expected to enable them to finance their non-self-liquidating projects to a greater extent than heretofore from their own resources or to assume larger debt obligations for such projects."[5] Nevertheless, the Committee believed that "the needs of economic development are so large in relation to funds available that it is desirable to explore the possibilities of increased resources, domestic as well as external, including international." However, it did not make any specific proposals. It merely requested the Secretary-General, in consultation with the World Bank and the specialised agencies concerned, "to keep under active consideration the problem and methods of domestic and external, including international, financing of non-self-liquidating projects in underdeveloped countries and to present to the Council proposals on this subject as soon as practicable."

When the draft resolution of the Economic Committee came up for discussion at the plenary session of the ECOSOC, Chile, which had earlier voted for the draft resolution, now changed its mind and moved a draft resolution seeking the establishment of a fund to provide grant assistance for financing of non-self-liquidating projects.

3. E/2061, Section D.

4. *ibid.*, p.7.

5. *ibid.*

Chile argued that all past efforts for such assistance had been resisted by developed countries and that more and more studies were requested. The GA Resolution 400(V) had asked for concrete recommendations, whereas the Economic Committee's report was dilatory and procrastinating. Chile urged the Council to seek authorisation to set up a fund first, and then work out the details. The Chilean position was supported by the Philippines and Iran.

The developed countries in the ECOSOC supported the original draft resolution of the Economic Committee and opposed the Chilean proposal. They argued that the time was not ripe because their resources were tied up in fulfilling their defence needs and their responsibility to further economic development in the countries dependent on them. They cited the rather weak position of their balance of payments as another reason. It was pointed out that in all likelihood, apart from the US, the other developed countries were in no position to support grant assistance at that stage. The US believed that there was probably general agreement on the issue of external grant assistance, but pointed out that there was disagreement on (a) the type of machinery to be used, and (b) when such international machinery should be established. The US felt that a truly international authority should be supported by a large number of countries and since such support was not forthcoming, the idea of a fund was not practical and feasible at that time. Chile tried to modify its stand by refraining from specifying any particular date for the establishment of a fund, but the opposition was overwhelming.[6]

After extensive discussion, the ECOSOC adopted a comprehensive resolution[7] covering several aspects of public and private flows, and also, the question of financing non-self-liquidating projects. With respect to non-self-liquidating projects and grant assistance in general, the Council made two major recommendations. First, it endorsed the Economic Committee's recommendation that the Secretary-General should keep under active study the methods of financing non-self-liquidating projects. Second, without accepting or rejecting the principle of the establishment of an international fund for financing economic development in the underdeveloped countries, it requested

6. E/SR.498, 502, 504 and 505.

7. ECOSOC Res. 368(XIII), 22 August 1951.

the Secretary-General "to formulate a series of methods which he deems practicable for dealing with the problem of grant assistance" and to submit his proposals to the ECOSOC before the seventh session of the General Assembly. It also requested the Member States to submit any proposals they might have to the 15th session of the Council through the Secretary-General.

The arithmetic of voting in the General Assembly was different from that in the ECOSOC. The General Assembly comprised all Member States, whereas the Council consisted of 18 members. During the Assembly's sixth session, the developing countries mustered enough support to push further their proposal for the establishment of a Special Fund. The General Assembly, in its Resolution 520 (VI), stressed the great urgency and importance of creating new sources of international finance, and recognised that "it is necessary...to give special attention to the solution of this problem through international cooperation within the framework of the United Nations". It believed that, among other sources of finance, grants-in-aid were essential for economic development and that there was an immediate need to prepare a detailed plan of action in this area. Therefore, in Resolution 520(VI), it requested "The Economic and Social Council to submit to the General Assembly at its seventh regular session a detailed plan for establishing, as soon as circumstances permit, a Special Fund for grants-in-aid and for low-interest, long-term loans to under-developed countries for the purpose of helping them, at their request, to accelerate their economic development and to finance non-self-liquidating projects which are basic to their economic development." The General Assembly also told the Council that while preparing the plan, it should make a series of recommendations on the size, composition and administration of the Special Fund; the manner of collecting contributions; the character of the contributions; the policies, conditions and methods to be followed for making grants and loans; and the principles to be observed by the recipient countries. In addition, the Assembly asked the Secretary-General to assist the Council in preparing the detailed plan. It may be noted that a majority of the developed countries voted against this General Assembly resolution.

As requested by the General Assembly, the Secretary-General submitted a working paper,[8] to the 14th session of the ECOSOC, in which he discussed various elements of a detailed plan. He did not discuss the need for a Special Fund, nor the issue of whether the time was ripe for its establishment. The matter was left to the governments to decide. The Secretary-General's working paper was organised into three parts, which dealt with income, operations, administration and inter-governmental control of the fund, respectively. His view was that arrangements for administrative and inter-governmental control should be discussed by the Council only after all other details had been finalised. He presented possible alternatives for each major element of the plan, but none of these was to be understood as his personal recommendation.

The section on income covered the character and composition of contributions. The Secretary-General pointed out that full convertibility of all contributions might not be necessary because in any case, the recipient countries would purchase goods and services in the donor countries. Contributions could be made either by agreement or on a voluntary basis. The initial size of the fund could be based on the amount needed to make it operational, or the availability of contributions from a particular number of countries. In discussing the operations of the fund, the Secretary-General did not provide any clear-cut guidelines or criteria for the selection of projects, except for the suggestion that the assistance should contribute towards promoting the interests of the people, irrespective of the nature and structure of the government. With regard to the question of loans *versus* grants, he suggested that the per capita incomes of the recipient countries should be taken into account and grants be given to those falling in the lowest income categories. The countries wishing to receive assistance were expected to demonstrate that they would use the fund resources appropriately and to identify corresponding domestic efforts.

The Secretary-General's working paper did not help to settle the issue. During the 14th session of the ECOSOC, Cuba,[9] together with other members of the Council, submitted a joint draft resolution,

---

8. E/2224, 27 May 1952.
9. E/SR.608.

seeking the establishment of a preparatory committee for a Special Fund. The Committee, to be appointed by the Secretary-General, would consist of nine experts and would study all the technical aspects discussed in the working paper. It would report to the ECOSOC by 1 March 1953. The issues of inter-governmental control and administration were to be left to the Council. Several developed countries again argued that the present circumstances did not permit the establishment of a Special Fund. However, they agreed to vote for the Cuban joint draft resolution, as amended, without committing themselves to joining the fund, if and when it was established. The resolution was adopted[10] without a negative vote. The USSR, Poland and Czechoslovakia abstained.

During its seventh session in 1952, the General Assembly obviously did not have a detailed plan, which it had requested a year earlier. Most of the developed countries continued to oppose the establishment of a Special Fund. Reiterating their view that the proposal was untimely, the US also said it had reservations on the principle of an international agency providing grants-in-aid. However, while it was opposed to the machinery, it was not opposed to the purpose. A majority of the members appreciated the Secretary-General's working paper, as well as the Council's decision to establish an expert committee to study the issue and prepare a plan, but they preferred to wait till the Committee had completed its work.

The developing countries, notably Chile, were anxious to keep the issue alive. Chile submitted a draft resolution which basically sought to include the item of the Special Fund on the agenda of the Assembly's eighth session. Cuba suggested an amendment to the Chilean draft, requesting the General Assembly to ascertain, during its next session, the desirability of convening a conference of governments to consider practical steps for the establishment of the fund. The amendment was later rejected. The Chilean draft resolution was adopted with minor amendments by the General Assembly in Resolution 622 (VII).

Meanwhile, the Secretary-General had appointed the Committee of Nine Experts, in accordance with Resolution 416 (XIV) of the Council. The Committee submitted its report[11] in March 1953. It did not go

10. ECOSOC Res. 416.A.(XIV), 23 June 1952.

11. Report on a Special UN Fund for Economic Development, E/2381.

into the questions of the justification for, and timeliness and broad purposes of, the fund. Instead, it focused only on the technical aspects involved in the preparation of 'a detailed plan' for the fund's establishment.

An important recommendation of the Committee was that the fund should come into being only "by voluntary pledging of the equivalent of a minimum of $ 250 million by at least 30 countries if and when the GA decides to ascertain whether a sufficient number of governments are willing to pledge sufficient funds for this purpose." In later years, many industrialised countries would camouflage their opposition to the fund by arguing that the resources available and the number of supporting countries were not in sight for the establishment of the fund!

The Committee's other recommendations related to the nature, form and determination of contributions, the principles to be observed by the recipient countries, the operating principles of the fund, disbursement of resources, distribution between grants and loans, and the fund's management structure.

As for the question of distribution between loans and grants, the Committee felt that the test lay in the contribution each would make to economic development. It did not really lay down any criteria and left the matter to the discretion of the fund. The Committee recommended that while making loans, it was predominantly the interests of the borrowers which should be taken into account, and loans should not be based on the commercial approach of balancing the interests of both the lenders and borrowers. Loans were not to be recovered if they imposed a heavy burden on the borrowers and impeded their economic development.

When the Committee's report came before the 16th session of the ECOSOC, the developed countries reiterated that the time was not yet ripe to set up a fund because their resources were fully committed to defence, domestic priorities and bilateral aid. During this session, the US introduced a declaration in the form of a draft resolution. The declaration urged all countries to reduce their expenditure on armaments and stated that when internationally supervised disarmament was in place, then part of the savings from the reduced expenditure on armaments could be diverted to finance the economic development of the developing countries. Most of the developed countries supported the US position and the Council adopted the declaration[12] by 11 votes in favour, with 3 abstentions. This was a major setback to the proponents of the fund because thereafter, its establishment would be linked to internationally supervised disarmament, especially by the US and the UK. Despite the pleas of the developing countries and the Committee's report, no further progress was made during this session. The ECOSOC simply transmitted the Committee's report to the General Assembly without any comments or recommendations.

Three draft resolutions relating to the Fund came up for consideration during the eighth session of the General Assembly. The US submitted a declaration linking the establishment of the fund to savings from disarmament. Greece, Haiti and Pakistan submitted a draft resolution, seeking the circulation of the Committee's report among all governments in order to obtain their comments on the creation of the Fund, as also to know what contribution they could possibly make. The third draft resolution, submitted by 20 developing countries, suggested that in addition to sending the Committee's report to all governments for their comments, the General Assembly should appoint a representative to explain the idea and promote it in different countries. The representative should also ascertain the moral and material support that might be forthcoming for the fund. Later, the 3-power and 20-power draft resolutions were integrated and the Assembly agreed to the proposed measure. It appointed Mr. Raymond Scheyven from Belgium, who was then the President of the ECOSOC, as its representative to undertake the task. A resolution to this effect, Resolution 724 B (VIII), was adopted on 7 December 1953. The US declaration was also adopted by the General Assembly.[13]

Mr. Scheyven submitted an interim report,[14] based on the replies received from 20 countries, to the ECOSOC during its 18th session in June 1954. Since the adoption of Resolution 724 B (VIII), Mr. Scheyven had not had much time to get in touch with all the countries. He had visited 9 developed countries and discussed the

---

12. ECOSOC Res. 482.A.(XVI).

13. GA Res. 724.A.(XIII).

14. E/2599.

problem of financing as a whole. Of the 20 countries that sent replies, 12 were developed and 8 were developing countries.

There was broad agreement on the principle of setting up a fund, but there were wide differences on the practical problems involved in establishing it. Broadly, the countries which had sent replies fell into three groups. The first group, comprising developing countries, held that there was no need to wait for progress in disarmament since the economic conditions in the developed countries were quite favourable. A modest beginning would do. These countries felt that it was time to prepare draft statutes and they would contribute according to their capacity. The second group, comprising some of the developed countries, repeated the earlier arguments, i.e., that this was not the right time to establish the fund owing to lack of progress in disarmament, heavy expenditures on defence, and so on. They also opined that the developing countries would not agree to the diversion of resources from other UN programmes. A few of them said they would contribute only if the US did, knowing full well that the US was leading the opposition.

The third group, which consisted of Denmark, the Netherlands and Norway, was in favour of the immediate establishment of the fund and was willing to contribute without delay. These countries believed that the fund should not be linked to disarmament, and that the proposed $ 250 million for the fund was 'an infinitesimal fraction' of the world's annual defence expenditure. Further, they felt that assistance to the developing countries would contribute to peace. It would also stimulate government and private investment, and fill a gap in the financing of non-self-liquidating projects.

By July 1954, only 36 replies had been received. Most of the industrialised countries had replied, while many developing countries had not. Few had commented on the recommendations of the Committee of Nine. An encouraging sign was that eight developed countries no longer considered disarmament an essential precondition. Mr. Scheyven made a strong case for the fund on moral, economic and institutional grounds. However, not much progress was made at the 18th session of the ECOSOC, which, in its resolution 532(XVIII) of 4 August 1954, simply recommended "that the General Assembly urge governments to review their respective positions with respect to extending their material support to a special United Nations fund for economic development, in accordance with changes in the international situation and other relevant factors." The Council also requested the General Assembly to extend the appointment of Mr. Scheyven so that he could continue his consultations with the governments. The action taken by the ECOSOC thus amounted to nothing more than somehow keeping the issue alive.

Two reports were placed before the General Assembly during its ninth session—a report by the Secretary-General[15] and Mr. Scheyven's final report.[16] The former summarised the governments' comments on the report of the Committee of Nine. It contained replies from 40 governments. Australia, New Zealand, the US, Switzerland, the UK and Sweden were still opposed to the fund. Belgium and Canada expressed restricted support, while 31 countries expressed full support. With regard to material support, only 14 countries answered that they would give support without imposing conditions. There was an even split on the issue of when the fund should be established.

In his final report, Mr. Scheyven described the economic and social conditions in the developing countries, and the prevailing levels of poverty. He drew attention to the lack of complete conviction among certain authoritative circles on the need to finance non-self-liquidating projects through multilateral aid. He traced the genesis of the idea of financing such projects to the past recommendations of various UN commissions and Expert Groups, and called for continued efforts in this direction.

The discussions in the Second Committee of the General Assembly were naturally characterised by divergent views. While a large section of the developing countries were now ready to proceed with the drafting of statutes for the Special Fund, the majority of the developed countries still had serious reservations and, therefore, exercised caution. The US and the UK repeated their now familiar arguments relating to progress in disarmament, the burden of domestic defence expenditures, levels of bilateral aid, and domestic priorities. The US believed that infrastructure should be financed by the governments in collaboration with private enterprise. Belgium felt that the option of making contributions in capital goods could be considered. It also

15. A/2727.

16. A/2728.

expressed the view that the Special Fund should not be established until at least 30 countries were ready to contribute.

The Second Committee (in charge of economic and social issues) had three draft resolutions to consider. The Netherlands introduced a draft resolution,[17] calling for the provision of public capital to the developing countries through multilateral channels. Further, it suggested the setting up of a working group to draft statutes, and proposed that Mr. Scheyven's appointment be extended to allow for continued consultations with the governments. The draft resolution urged the committee to submit a report to the Assembly during its tenth session.

A Belgian draft resolution[18] requested the governments to review their positions regarding the provision of material support to the Special Fund. It, too, suggested extending Mr. Scheyven's appointment. The developing countries introduced a 20-power draft resolution,[19] suggesting the appointment of a committee of seven experts to prepare statutes. It also requested the governments to review their investment priorities, besides proposing an extension of Mr. Scheyven's appointment.

A Working Group was set up to consider the three draft resolutions and prepare a consensus draft. Following a few amendments, a draft was agreed upon. The final result was the adoption of Resolution 822(IX) by the General Assembly. The resolution expressed "the hope that a special United Nations fund for economic development be established as soon as practicable."[20] In addition, it extended Mr. Scheyven's appointment; urged the governments to review their positions with respect to the material support they could provide for the Special Fund; and requested "Mr. Scheyven to prepare, with the assistance of the Secretary-General and of an *ad hoc* group of experts... a further report giving a full and concise picture of the form or forms, functions and responsibilities which such a Special United Nations Fund for economic development might have...."

---

17. A/C.2/L.226 and Corr. 1.

18. A/C.2/L.227.

19. A/C.2/L.228 and Add.1.

20. This resolution used the wording "special united nations fund for economic development" (SUNFED) but later several governments resisted linking Special Fund to SUNFED.

The report of the Experts Group[21] was submitted by Mr. Scheyven in May 1955 and was considered by the ECOSOC during its 20th session. It dealt mainly with the role of the Special Fund in the developing countries, the prospective resources and structure of the fund, and the methods of its operation. The major recommendations of the report were as follows.

(a) Role of Special Fund

- The fund should improve production in the developing countries through the development of skills, technology and equipment.
- It should provide finance for non-self-liquidating investment—roads, schools, hospitals, power and other facilities—which would also induce private investment.
- It should finance only such investment as cannot be financed by private investment, commercial loans, the IBRD or other lending institutions.

(b) Resources

- The governments should make regular and punctual payments, preferably with long-term pledges, subject to national parliamentary approval.
- They could use contributions to the IBRD, IMF, EPTA and UN as guidelines.
- Contributions could be made in the national currency. Subscriptions in kind—capital goods—would create difficulties.
- Owing to the duration of preparatory work needed to formulate good projects and also, varying absorptive capacities, the amount of $ 250 million suggested by the committee of nine was not absolutely essential. The Special Fund could be started with a lower amount.
- The General Assembly should decide on the initial sum and minimum membership of the fund.
- The General Assembly could establish the Special Fund initially for five years, and then review the experiencee.

---

21. E/2757.

(c) Methods of Operation

- The provision of mostly grants would simplify administration and would not reduce the recipients' capacity to repay other loans. The IBRD also recommended grants.
- The IBRD and Special Fund could combine loans and grants.'
- Loans could be made on normal terms, but repaid in local currency. (The report did not clearly explain how accumulated balances of local currency were to be utilised.)
- Governments could specify their contribution in terms of loans and grants.

(d) Structure of the Special Fund

- General Council: This would be in charge of overall policy and the budget. It would review reports from the Executive Board.
- Executive Board: This would be the executive organ, the size of which would be decided by the General Council. There would be equal representation and equal voting rights. Representatives of the Secretary-General, IBRD, IMF and TAB would attend and participate in its meetings, without a vote.
- Director-General: He would be appointed by the Executive Board, in consultation with the Secretary-General and IBRD.
- Joint Committee: This would comprise the Secretary-General, the president of the IBRD and the Director-General of the Special Fund.
- Considerable involvement of the IBRD should be ensured.

During the 20th session of the ECOSOC, some of these recommendations came in for strong criticism, especially by delegates from the developing countries. They did not take to the idea of the Special Fund being closely aligned with the IBRD. Nor did they approve of the large involvement envisaged for the IBRD in the operational activities of the fund; like the loan/grant combination by the IBRD and the fund; and the proposal to set up the fund on an experimental basis for five years. Moreover, with regard to the structure, Mr. Scheyven and the Expert Group had literally borrowed the IBRD model, which was very alien to the UN.

The Expert Group's report, now third in the series, did not substantially alter the respective positions of the governments. The US, the UK and Australia were still firmly against the Special Fund. Some of the European countries, like France, Denmark and Belgium, supported the fund in principle but still saw the need to exercise caution. The Netherlands had been actively and fully supporting the developing countries since the last session of the ECOSOC. On the whole, the developed countries were not yet ready to start the process of drafting statutes. Presumably to defer the decision and gain time, they suggested that to begin with, comments should be received from all the governments, specialised agencies and other organisations concerned, and these should then be analysed by an *ad hoc* committee.

The Economic Committee of the ECOSOC, during its 20th session, had two draft resolutions to consider: a six-power draft resolution[22] sponsored by the Netherlands and developing countries, and a two-power draft resolution[23] sponsored by Norway and France. The former, introduced by the Netherlands, suggested the preparation of statutes, by an *ad hoc* committee once all the governments' views had come in. The Dutch delegate compared the Special Fund with the Marshall Plan. He pointed out that the Marshall Plan was devised to make grants because recovery could not be financed by commercial loans or private capital. He said the Special Fund, too, was intended to finance infrastructure in the developing countries in order to raise their production. This would be beneficial for all.

The two-power draft put forth the opposite view. It argued that most major contributors still disagreed on the basic principles of the fund, the timing of its establishment and the pace of the preparatory work. It concluded, therefore, that appointing an *ad hoc* committee was untimely and would result in failure.

As usual, after mutual consultations, there emerged a text that was agreed upon. The text recommended by the Economic Committee for adoption by the ECOSOC was slightly amended in the Council's

22. E/L. 683.

23. E/AC.6/L.131.

plenary session. On 5 August 1955, the ECOSOC adopted resolution 583 (XX), which requested the General Assembly to ask all governments, specialised agencies and others to send their detailed comments on the Expert Group's report. It also asked the Assembly to appoint an *ad hoc* committee to analyse the comments and submit its report to the 22nd session of the Council. The US, the UK and Australia abstained during the voting on the resolution.

The matter then came up for consideration during the 10th session of the General Assembly, when extensive discussions took place in the Second Committee. The developing countries firmly reiterated their position: the Special Fund must be set up as a separate entity, with its own staff, within the framework of the UN and without any links to the IBRD. They said the establishment of the fund should not be linked to disarmament. Contributions should be in local or convertible currency, and not in kind. The major developed countries—Australia, Canada, the UK and the US—continued to oppose the establishment of the fund, citing the oft-repeated reasons, including the link to disarmament. Belgium would agree only if 30 countries, including the US, joined. The USSR and other Eastern European countries would support the fund, but wanted to make contributions in kind.

Mr. Scheyven took a totally different and unacceptable position, one actually taken by the Expert Group in its report. He said the Special Fund should not undermine the IBRD's work, and that the Great Powers should be convinced and their objections taken care of. He was even ready to give the Great Powers more voting rights on the Executive Board! Further, Mr. Scheyven recommended that the operations of the Special Fund be mainly in the form of grants. He was against long-term interest loans as these would compete with the IBRD's operations and undermine its work. He defended the structure of the Special Fund as recommended in the report of the Expert Group, and wanted the fund and IBRD to be closely linked. Further, he was not opposed to a close association between the fund and private credit institutions. Over the preceding two years, Mr. Scheyven had worked hard and enthusiastically, and been genuinely committed to the idea of a Special Fund. However, in his zeal to establish the fund as soon as possible, he lost sight of the realities at the UN. With regard to the fund's structure, he failed to read or understand the sensitivities of the developing countries.

Some divergent views were expressed on the role of loans *versus* grants in the operations of the Special Fund. The majority of the developing countries were of the view that loans, if at all, should be given for a long-term period at low interest rates and be payable in local currency. Some proposed repayment in convertible currency, while a few preferred loans strictly on commercial terms. The majority of countries, however, were in favour of grants, not because they wanted to protect loans by the IBRD, but because they wanted aid in the form of grants.

On behalf of mostly the developing countries, the Dutch delegate introduced a 32-power draft resolution.[24] The Netherlands argued that there was no need for more experts and it was time to elicit the views of the governments on precise issues listed in the annex to the draft resolution. The governments' replies were to be analysed by a committee of Member States. The next step was to prepare statutes. This would make it easier to consider various aspects of the Special Fund in detail. The Netherlands delegate also made it clear that the adoption of the draft resolution would not bind any member to join.

The US, while reaffirming the link to disarmament, offered an olive branch this time. It said that it might support the draft resolution if agreement could be reached on the amount of detail the governments were expected to give in their comments, and on the nature and functions of the proposed *ad hoc* group. Consequently, the Chairman appointed an informal Working Group to explore the possibility of agreement. The draft prepared by The Working Group was adopted unanimously and the Second Committee decided that the *ad hoc* group would consist of 16 governments.

The GA Resolution 923(X) was very much on the lines of the ECOSOC Resolution 583A(XX). It differed from the latter mainly in two respects: (a) its annex listed specific issues on which the governments' comments were sought, and (b) it established a committee of Member States to analyse the comments, rather than setting up another group of experts. It thus elevated the debate to a higher level. During the 10th session, the President of the General Assembly appointed 16 members to the committee, one of which was the US.

24. A/C.2/L.271.

The *ad hoc* Committee submitted an interim report[25] to the 22nd session of the ECOSOC. It had received and analysed replies from 46 governments, 43 of which had agreed to the establishment of a Special Fund. Only 6 wanted certain conditions to be fulfilled before the fund was established.

The responses to the specific questions in the annex to the GA Resolution 923(X) naturally varied in nuance, scope and substance. The views on the fund's role ranged from financing of non-self-liquidating projects to financing of infrastructure and productive investment. On the question of contributions, a majority of countries was in favour of voluntary contributions in the local currency, renewable every year. A few were for fixed contributions and some for advanced pledges. Five countries, mostly Eastern European, suggested contributions in goods and services. Eighteen countries were willing to start the Special Fund with an amount of less than $ 250 million, whereas 17 wanted to start it with $ 250 million or above. As for the issue of grants *versus* loans, the governments were generally in favour of both, but placed varying emphases on their combination. The majority of the respondents wanted the Special Fund to be an autonomous body within the framework of the UN. Most of them endorsed the Expert Group's recommendations regarding the structure of the fund. There was, however, considerable disagreement on the establishment of a joint committee in which the IBRD was to be involved.

In the ECOSOC, the positions of the major donor countries had not changed. The Netherlands again made a strong case for the Special Fund. The US still linked the whole issue to disarmament and believed that no action was necessary on the interim report, other than sending it to the General Assembly. Canada held that the interim report was not truly representative since many large industrialised countries had not sent in replies. In the end, the ECOSOC unanimously adopted a Resolution 619(XXII), which simply expressed "the hope that, in the meantime, the General Assembly will consider what steps may help to promote the early establishment of a special United Nations Fund for Economic Development." It requested the countries which had not replied to do so as soon as possible. The

25. E/2896.

Netherlands delegate rightly observed that the resolution did not mark any advance. He hoped that the atmosphere in the General Assembly would be more conducive to further action.

That, however, was not to be and nothing changed much in the Assembly. The developing countries continued to press for the preparation of statutes, pointing out that such a step would not commit any country to the Special Fund, but would help to focus the discussion on the specifics. A number of developed countries continued to insist that the preparation of statutes should wait till wide support or major donor support was forthcoming. What they really meant was waiting until the US agreed to join because the US would be the largest single contributor. Norway suggested limiting the scope of the Special Fund in order to garner more support. Among the developed countries, only France and the Netherlands supported the drafting of statutes. France suggested that the *ad hoc* Group should submit its final report to the ECOSOC in April 1957 and the General Assembly should take a final decision during its 12th session. The Netherlands even offered, if the Special Fund proved ineffective, to consider alternatives, so long as these financed infrastructure within a multilateral framework. The US made it clear that it would participate in the exploration of resources and other work, but not in the drafting of statutes. The US again reminded the delegates of its perception of the link between disarmament and resources for the Special Fund. This was countered quite effectively by Iran and India. Citing the defence expenditure of the US, the UK and France, as well as the estimated world expenditure on armaments in 1955, Iran concluded that the amount of $ 250 million proposed for the Special Fund would constitute only 0.25 per cent of the global expenditure on armaments. India commented, "Just as it would be absurd to claim that disarmament should wait until the underdeveloped countries reach the level of developed countries, so it would be also absurd to claim that the Special Fund should wait till disarmament takes place."[26]

Finally, two proposals were put before the Second Committee. Ireland and Denmark proposed, in a draft resolution,[27] that the *ad hoc* Committee should prepare a number of different patterns upon which

26. A/C.2/SR.435.
27. A/C.2/ L.321.

the Special Fund could be based. They saw this as a piece of essential preliminary work required for the drafting of statutes later on. A 41-power draft resolution,[28] sponsored mostly by developing countries, requested the *ad hoc* Committee to prepare the legal structures on the basis of which the fund could be established. This was seen as a step that would immediately precede the final drafting of the statutes. As there was not much difference between the two draft resolutions, a compromise emerged. This was adopted unanimously by the Second Committee and also by the General Assembly. The GA Resolution 1030 (XI) marked some progress over the non-action in the ECOSOC. Firstly, it asked the *ad hoc* Committee "to set forth the different forms of legal framework" on the basis of which a Special Fund could be established and the statutes drafted. Secondly, it requested the *ad hoc* Committee "to indicate the type of projects which might be provided for in programmes of operations of the Special Fund." The final report of the *ad hoc* Committee and the supplementary report sought by the GA Resolution 1030(XI) were to be considered by the ECOSOC at its 24th session and by the Assembly at its 12th session.

The *ad hoc* Committee accordingly submitted its final and supplementary reports[29] to the ECOSOC during its 24th session. The final report covered replies from 57 governments, 11 more than the 46 governments which were included in the interim report submitted earlier. Fifty-four of these clearly supported the establishment of the fund. Only eight governments sought the fulfilment of certain conditions, including conditions pertaining to the participation of a certain minimum number of countries in the fund, initial size of the fund and disarmament. There was considerable commonality of approach among those who supported the establishment of the fund. They wanted the Special Fund to finance economic and social infrastructure, and visualised the initial size of the fund in the range of $ 200 million to $ 250 million. This amount would be supported by voluntary contributions in local currency, convertible at the donor country's convenience. Further, they recommended disbursements both in grants and long-term loans. They wanted the fund to be set up as an autonomous body within the framework of the UN, and

28. A/C.2/L.315.

29. E/2961 of 16 May 1957 in response to GA Res. 923(X) and E/2999 of 27 May 1957 in response to GA Res. 1030(X).

endorsed the structure recommended by the *ad hoc* Committee and the Committee of Nine earlier. All in all, the final report, which included only 11 more countries, was not much of an advance over the interim report.

In preparing a legal framework, the *ad hoc* Committee simply took all the replies from the final report and reclassified them under presumed components of a legal framework. As a result, there were several views under each component. The Committee did not do any fresh thinking, nor did it even make an effort to synthesise the information under each component. The supplementary report thus prepared provided only a pretext of a legal framework, and not a good basis for discussion. The report was also not particularly enlightening on the question of the types of projects that could be considered for financing by the Special Fund. It merely listed various fields of activity, such as agriculture, industry, education, health, social services, transport, power and communications, and gave a few examples of projects in each field. No attempt was made to develop criteria for eligible projects or for the areas in which the fund's resources should be concentrated.

During the 24th session of the ECOSOC, the Netherlands introduced the final and supplementary reports of the *ad hoc* Committee. The Dutch delegate pointed out that the GA resolution 1030(XI) had given no definition of the concept of 'forms of legal framework.' The *ad hoc* Committee had presented the various views expressed, but a draft statute would have to choose one of the alternatives. He further pointed out that certain provisions in the *ad hoc* Committee's report, for example, only grants *versus* only loans, could not be logically combined. The Dutch delegate also drew attention to the fact that the Committee had not indicated priorities under the different types of projects. Since all had agreed on the principle of setting up a Special Fund and a majority had supported its establishment, and since more than enough studies had been done, he believed that it was time to take a firm stand rather than advance further arguments. In his view, agreement on the fund was the most essential and the details could be contemplated later. He also felt that the majority should now go ahead and the others could join later. "Unanimity," he said, "is desirable but no good if it leads to stagnation." Several developing countries, too, had become tired of the idea of conducting more studies and were against further postponement of the issue. They shared the views expressed by the Netherlands.

The developed countries—especially Canada, the UK and the US—while reiterating their familiar positions, now tried to manipulate to their advantage the differences in views reflected in the governments' replies. They argued that given these differences, the establishment of the Special Fund should be deferred until a consensus emerged. Canada even introduced an amendment to this effect to a seven-power draft resolution[30] introduced by the Netherlands. The amendment, however, was soundly rejected by the ECOSOC. This move by the developed countries was certainly most inappropriate. It should have been very obvious to them that while replying to the questions in the annex, each government was totally unaware of the replies given by the other countries. The countries were not expected to coordinate their replies. The task of coordination, synthesis and compromise should have been done by the *ad hoc* Committee or the ECOSOC.

The attitude of the French government was quite positive. It held that the Special Fund should finance projects which could not get finance from the World Bank, IMF, and private foreign and domestic sources. The French also suggested that a modest start could be made with selected projects which would have the potential of attracting private or public investment capital. After a discussion on the seven-power draft resolution, a few amendments were made to it and the ECOSOC adopted the Resolution 662 B (XXIV), with 15 voting in favour and 3 against. The negative votes were cast by the UK, the US and Canada. In its operative paragraph II, this resolution, while citing the fact that all governments agreed on the principle of establishing a Special Fund, urged the General Assembly "at its 12th session, to decide to establish this Fund and to take the steps necessary to this end." It further recommended "to the General Assembly to establish a preparatory commission entrusted with the task of:

(a) Preparing the necessary steps for the establishment of the Fund, as mentioned in operative paragraph II above;

(b) Selecting a number of projects to be financed through voluntary contributions on an experimental basis pending the full operation of the Fund."

---

30. E/L.764.

The 12th General Assembly witnessed a radical change in the approach to the establishment of a Special Fund. The seven powers which had sponsored a joint draft resolution at the Council's 24th session now introduced an 11-power joint draft resolution[31] in the Second Committee, with a view to follow up the measures suggested by the ECOSOC in its Resolution 662B (XXIV). The US also introduced a draft resolution[32] at this session of the Second Committee.

The 11-power joint draft resolution provided for the establishment of the fund, to be known as the Economic Development Fund (EDF). It also mooted the setting up of a preparatory commission, to be appointed by the President of the General Assembly, and the drafting of rules (not statutes) to govern the fund's administration and management, including methods of selecting projects. The rules were to be drafted on the basis of the principles laid down in an annex to the draft resolution. These principles basically stated that the EDF would be a multilateral fund of the UN. It would be financed by voluntary annual contributions in usable currencies, and would provide loans or grants to "projects designed to accelerate the integrated economic development of under-developed countries, principally by strengthening their economic and social infrastructure". The principles also touched upon the management structure of the fund. The draft resolution further proposed that the draft rules be communicated not later than 1 May 1958 to all Member States of the UN and specialised agencies, and to the ECOSOC during its 26th session. The ECOSOC would then refer them, together with its recommendations, to the Assembly's 13th session for action. The draft resolution also expected the EDF "to begin operations by 1 January 1960, at the latest." While introducing the 11-power joint draft resolution, the delegate from the Netherlands pleaded strongly for multilateral assistance, saying that private capital could not satisfy all needs and competitive bilateral assistance would be harmful to the balanced growth of the underdeveloped countries.[33]

The US, which until then, had maintained its solid opposition to the fund, now suggested a totally different approach.[34] It said the existing resources for technical assistance would not suffice and more

31. A/C.2/L.331.
32. A/C.2/L.354.
33. A/C.2/SR.492.
34. *ibid.*

could be spent "in such basic fields as the survey of natural resources, industrial research and the training of manpower and also in public administration and basic statistics." The US would support any move to increase technical assistance from $ 30 million (the level at that time) to $ 100 million. The US delegate said his country was also in favour of "the establishment, as an integral part of the programme in technical assistance, of a Special Projects Fund, earmarked for sustained assistance in the fields" which he had mentioned. He went on to say that even if the Special Fund were established right away, its limited resources would allow the financing of only such projects. The US, therefore, introduced a draft resolution, the main elements of which were as follows:[35]

- The EPTA "cannot now meet certain urgent needs for technical assistance which, if met, would advance the processes of economic and social development and thus contribute to the stability and peace of the world".
- A substantial increase in the resources of the EPTA "would constitute a feasible and constructive advance in the United Nations machinery which would be of immediate significance in accelerating the economic development of less-developed countries".
- A Special Projects Fund should be established within the Programme "to permit systematic and sustained assistance in certain basic fields".
- The "Special Projects Fund may require new administrative and operational machinery".
- A governmental preparatory committee should be established to: (a) define the basic fields of assistance and the types of projects eligible for assistance; (b) define changes which may need to be made to the administration and machinery of the EPTA; and (c) ascertain the extent to which governments would be willing to make additional contributions, over and above the EPTA, to the Special Projects Fund.
- The governments and specialised agencies should be requested to submit their views and suggestions to the preparatory committee.

35. See fn. 32 above.

- The preparatory committee should submit its report and recommendations to the 26th session of the ECOSOC, which would refer these, together with its comments, to the 13th session of the General Assembly.
- The Special Projects Fund should be operative as of 1 January 1959.

The US initiative, the first since the discussion on the Special Fund began in 1951, and its offer to increase financial assistance caused quite a few shifts in the positions of other governments. Perhaps, sustained opposition over the years by the US and its allies, together with the unwillingness of some industrialised countries to support the Special Fund without US sanction, had by now considerably eroded the energy and endurance of the developing countries. A cloud of pessimism had descended upon these countries regarding the future of the Special Fund, and their responses to the draft resolutions were split. The positions of all the countries could be roughly divided into three categories. Nearly all the developed countries, joined by Laos, Iran, Panama and Syria, supported the US proposal. Some developing countries, such as Pakistan, Argentina, Ghana, Peru and Sudan, were in favour of a compromise as they felt that the two draft resolutions complemented each other. They were quite sympathetic to the US proposal and their call for reconciliation perhaps constituted a graceful parting gesture towards the ardent supporters of the Special Fund. The third group comprised several developing countries, such as India, Yugoslavia, Egypt, Indonesia and the Netherlands. This group viewed the US proposal as merely an extension of UNTA, and did not think it would provide finance for economic and social infrastructure. These countries did not see the US proposal as a substitute or an alternative to the Special Fund. They were prepared to make a modest start and accept staggered implementation of the fund only if the US proposal represented a first step towards the establishment of a Special Fund. If the matter could be viewed thus, they would not consider the two draft resolutions as mutually exclusive and would work towards their reconciliation.

The 11 powers revised their joint draft resolution, incorporating the main elements of the US proposal while retaining a link to the Special Fund. The revised draft was, in a sense, a radical departure from the 11 powers' original joint draft resolution. It omitted nearly all references to the Special Fund in the preambular paragraphs, and the operative paragraphs now centred around the expansion of technical assistance rather than the establishment of an Economic Development Fund. The 11 powers gave in probably because they must have concluded that with the defection of several developing countries, the majority would have supported the US proposal. The US, while generally agreeing with the revised draft, said that the fund proposed by it was not a substitute for or an alternative to the Spècial Fund. "It would not," it added, "be a first step towards or involve commitment to establish a capital development fund." The US did not want the proposed fund to provide capital assistance and be viewed in terms of staggered implementation of SUNFED. After a few minor amendments, suggested by the US and Iran, the revised 11-power joint draft resolution became acceptable to all. The US, Canada and France also joined in as cosponsors. The Second Committee unanimously adopted the revised joint draft resolution, as amended, and recommended its adoption to the General Assembly.

In the plenary, the Assembly adopted the resolution unamimously.[36] Several countries offered explanations as to why they had voted as they did in the Second Committee. France said it continued to support the establishment of SUNFED to finance projects that could not be financed by the Bank or IMF. However, France believed that the studies carried out on SUNFED till then were vague, as far as contributions to be made by the countries and the criteria for the selection of projects were concerned. On the whole, France felt that the resolution represented a progressive effort, and was a significant step towards a gradual extension of the UN resources and activities devoted to the economic development of the underdeveloped countries. "Unanimity," France said, "does not ensure success unless there is agreement on the meaning of the task to be implemented and determination to ensure its success. There are different views on the short-term and long-term objectives of the Fund. When resources permit extension of activities, agreement is essential on types of investments to be financed and on respective responsibilities of various international financial agencies to avoid overlapping and duplication."[37] France agreed that the future activities

36. GA Res. 1219 (XII), 14 December 1957.

37. A/PV/730.

of the fund should be devoted to non-self-liquidating projects and urged the governments to participate fully, in spite of their earlier reservations. France called on all members to "improve atmosphere by progress in disarmament and avoid sterile debate over merits of capitalist and Marxist economic systems." The UK was happy with the outcome, but doubted that enough resources would be available in the foreseeable future in the absence of disarmament. The USSR did not think the Special Fund agreed to in the resolution was the fund that the underdeveloped countries wanted. It remarked, "This is an attempt to replace SUNFED by expansion in technical assistance and prevent SUNFED."[38]

The US believed that the resolution achieved two objectives: (a) it created a Special Fund for a new and different approach to technical assistance and technical development to meet basic needs; (b) it recognised the need of the underdeveloped countries for larger amounts of capital investment, and left open the possibility of future action by the UN with respect to capital investment in the less developed countries, as and when resources permitted. The US position was that later the General Assembly might decide to enter the field of capital development but no government was committed to do so at that point in time. "Nothing in the resolution," the US said, "authorises the transformation into a capital development fund of the Special Fund." The US was opposed to a capital development fund until the resources were in sight. It estimated that such a fund might be feasible only when resources worth $ 400 million to $ 500 million were available in usable currencies on an annual basis in addition to the current funds for technical assistance and the new Special Fund. The US further said that it might have to make shifts in its bilateral assistance once a capital development fund was considered, thereby implying cuts in bilateral assistance.[39]

India, speaking on behalf of several developing countries, said the resolution was a compromise that reflected two opposite views. Though unhappy with the outcome, India accepted it because it was a conclusion which had been agreed upon. It felt that the resolution laid the foundation for the establishment of SUNFED, an institution

---

38. *ibid.*
39. *ibid.*

to which the developing countries aspired. The resolution represented a process of staggering operations according to the availability of funds. This understanding, India said, was based on paragraph 1 of Section II that was integrally linked to Section III. Paragraph 1 of Section II of the GA Resolution 1219 (XII) stated, *inter alia,* that "Special Fund—would provide systematic and sustained assistance in fields essential to the integrated technical, economic and social development of the less developed countries". Section III also made reference to "capital development, principally the development of the economic and social infrastructure." According to India, the resolution was not an integral part of the technical assistance programme and the resources prospectively available would not apply to additional resources for technical assistance. The Indian delegate said his country would continue to strive for the future extension of the activities of the Special Fund.[40]

The GA resolution 1219 (XII) attempted to distinguish the proposed Special Fund from the operations of the EPTA. It recognised that EPTA assistance had proved effective "in promoting the economic development of the less developed countries", but concluded that neither the EPTA, nor the other existing programmes of the UN or the specialised agencies "can now meet certain urgent needs which, if met, would advance the process of technical, economic and social development of the less developed countries, and, in particular, facilitate new capital investments of all types—private and public, national and international—by creating conditions which would make such investments either feasible or more effective."[41] Thus, financing projects which would lead to or attract capital investment was claimed to be the defining feature of the proposed Special Fund. The GA resolution,[42] therefore, suggested the financing of intensive surveys on natural resources, "the establishment—including staffing and equipping—of training institutes in public administration, statistics and technology, and of agricultural and industrial research and productivity centres." The preparatory committee was asked to do the following:

(a) "define the basic fields of assistance" and "the types of projects which should be eligible for assistance;"

40. *ibid.*
41. Preambular paragraph 6 of GA Res. 1219(XII).
42. See footnote 36.

(b) "define...the administrative and operational machinery for the Special Fund, including such changes as may be required in the present legislation and procedures of the Expanded Programme of Technical Assistance;" and

(c) "ascertain the extent to which Governments would be willing to contribute to the Special Fund."

The President of the General Assembly appointed 16 Member States to the Preparatory Committee, in accordance with paragraph 5 of Section II of the Resolution 1219 (XII). The Committee completed its report on 15 April 1958.[43] It had received comments and suggestions from the governments, specialised agencies, UN, TAB and UNTAA. Only 26 governments referred to the question of contributions and only three—the Netherlands, Turkey and the US—clearly stated their willingness to contribute. The contributions of the Netherlands and Turkey would be in the same proportion as their contributions to the EPTA. The US would contribute $ 38 million to the Special Fund and EPTA combined. The Committee could not establish a firm total for contributions and asked the Secretary-General to pursue the matter.

The Preparatory Committee made recommendations[44] on (i) the guiding principles of and criteria for the Special Fund; (ii) the basic fields of assistance and types of projects; (iii) participation in the fund; (iv) its organisation and management; (v) procedures for formulation, evaluation, approval and execution of projects; and (vi) finances.

Some of the Committee's recommendations bore evidence of the lessons learnt from the experience of the EPTA. The Special Fund was to be a separate fund. The text on the guiding principles was taken largely from the GA resolution 1219 (XII). It was recommended that, unlike the EPTA, "The Special Fund shall concentrate, as far as practicable, on relatively large projects and avoid allocation of its resources over a great number of small projects." Another recommendation was that projects should be chosen in accordance with their potential to make an early impact, in particular, those "facilitating new capital investment" should be considered.

With regard to the basic fields of assistance and types of projects, the Committee listed practically all major economic and social sectors,

43. E/3098.

44. *ibid.*

as well as human resource development. The assistance was to take the form of surveys, research and training, and demonstration, including pilot projects. In order to facilitate implementation, the requisite staff, experts, equipment, supplies and services were to be provided for. In addition, institutes, demonstration centres and plants or works were to be established to this end. In an annex to its report, the Committee gave an illustrative list of the types of projects which could be undertaken in various sectors.

In the Committee's view, participation in the Special Fund "should be open to Members States of the United Nations or members of the specialised agencies or of the International Atomic Energy Agency." Countries which were members of the regional economic and social commissions, but not of the UN, were thus excluded.

With regard to organisation and management, the ECOSOC was to be "responsible for the formulation of the general rules and principles which will govern the administration and operations of the Special Fund." The ECOSOC would also review the annual reports of the Governing Council, and coordinate the operations of the Special Fund and EPTA. It was expected to establish a committee for this purpose. The Governing Council would exercise "immediate governmental control of the policies and operations of the Special Fund" and "provide general policy guidance on the administration and operations of the Special Fund". It would "have final authority for the approval of the projects and programmes recommended by the Managing Director." The Managing Director was to administer the fund under the policy guidance of the Governing Council. A Consultative Board, comprising the Secretary-General of the UN, Executive Chairman of the TAB and President of the IBRD, was to be set up "to assist the Managing Director in the examination and appraisal of project requests and proposed programmes of the Special Fund."

The composition and functions of the Consultative Board were rather strange. As a member of the Board, the Secretary-General would be subordinate to the Managing Director who was to be appointed by the Secretary-General!

With respect to finances, contributions were to be made voluntarily and in usable currencies. Drawing on the lessons of the

EPTA, the Preparatory Committee recommended that in order to respect the multilateral character of the fund, "no contributing country should receive special treatment with respect to its contribution, nor should negotiations for the use of currencies take place between contributing and receiving countries". In the early years of the EPTA, it had become difficult to use the contribution of the USSR and there had been instances of direct negotiations between the USSR and a recipient country. Another departure from the EPTA was that the Special Fund would steer clear of country programmes. The Committee recommended, "Since programmes shall be developed on a project basis, there should be no *a priori* allocation of funds on a country basis or among basic fields of assistance." An interesting feature was a reversal of the 'Burma Plan', or funds-in-trust. The Committee stated, "The Governing Council shall be authorised to consider allocating part of the resources of the Special Fund for assistance on a refundable basis at the request of Governments for projects within the terms of reference of the Special Fund."

The ECOSOC considered the Preparatory Committee's report and recommendations during its 26th session. As there was general agreement on the recommendations, not much discussion took place. On 31 July 1958, the ECOSOC unanimously adopted Resolution 692 (XXVI), the annex to which contained a "Draft Resolution Recommended for Adoption by the General Assembly". This incorporated literally all the recommendations of the Preparatory Committee on various aspects of the Special Fund.

During the 13th session of the General Assembly, the matter was initially discussed in the Second Committee, as usual. At the outset, the Chairman wanted a decision to be taken before 16 October 1958, when the UN Technical Assistance Conference was to meet, so that pledges to the Special Fund could be made at that time. He, therefore, Requested the members to focus only on the annex to the ECOSOC resolution 692 (XXVI). However, several members were in favour of further discussion. One group of developing countries still wanted to continue its battle to keep the idea of SUNFED alive. Though the resolution in question made a few oblique references to a future review of the scope and activities of the Special Fund, a large group of developing countries was not satisfied with it. Pakistan, as the chairman of the Preparatory Committee, introduced a joint draft resolution[45] on the behalf of 23 countries for the adoption of all provisions relating to the Special Fund in the annex to Resolution 692 (XXVI). However, this joint draft resolution made only a passing reference to a preambular paragraph in Resolution 692 (XXVI), relating to the future activities of the Special Fund. A group of developing countries introduced a 17-power joint draft resolution,[46] which suggested three changes to the ECOSOC draft resolution.

First, it would add a new operative paragraph, whereby the General Assembly "reaffirms the provisions contained in Section III of General Assembly Resolution 1219 (XII), under which the Assembly shall review the scope and future activities of the Special Fund and take such action as it may deem appropriate." Second, the draft resolution would delete the word "possible" in the first paragraph of the annex to Resolution 692 (XXVI) because the use of the word "possible" there was contrary to the language used in GA Resolution 1219 (XII) wherein the GA said in Section III, that it " shall review." Thirdly, the Group wanted the General Assembly, and not the ECOSOC, to elect the members of the Governing Council. So the discussion in the Second Committee centred basically around two issues: the future of SUNFED and the election of the members of the Governing Council.

Introducing the 17-power joint draft resolution, India expressed regret that the unanimity of the delegates who had long been advocating the establishment of SUNFED had now been broken. He said that many countries had temporarily abandoned the idea of SUNFED because of the lack of funds available. They had approved Sections I and II of the GA Resolution 1219 (XII), which provided for the establishment of the Special Fund, on the understanding that its scope and future activities would be reviewed whenever it was possible to establish a fund for the development of infrastructure in the less developed countries. He urged the countries not to take any action in the General Assembly that would hamper the prospective transformation of the Special Fund into SUNFED. The Indian delegate pointed out that the 17-power joint draft resolution simply restated principles which had already been accepted earlier in the

45. A/C.2/L.363.

46. A/C.2/L.362.

GA Resolution 1219 (XII). He could not, therefore, understand the objections being raised now. Saudi Arabia and the United Arab Republic (UAR) supported India's statement. The Netherlands, Poland and Czechoslovakia felt that the Special Fund was the first step towards the establishment of SUNFED. The position of France and Denmark was somewhere in the middle—they said that the idea of SUNFED had not been abandoned and could be revived later on.

The US, on the other hand, reiterated its position that the Special Fund could not finance capital development needs, but could attract investment. Referring to Section III of the GA Resolution 1219 (XII), it said the section provided only for a review of the Special Fund's scope and activities, and did not say that the fund would be transformed into SUNFED. At the time of the review, the General Assembly might decide either on SUNFED or on the International Development Association (IDA) as an affiliate of the World Bank.[47] Sweden, too, had doubts if the Special Fund could serve any purpose for SUNFED. According to Sweden, the difference between the Special Fund and EPTA was very slight, but the General Assembly wanted the former to be a separate body. Sweden would have preferred it if the Special Fund were managed by the TAB and supervised by the TAC.

Opinion was divided also on the election of the members of the Governing Council. The 23 countries which had sponsored a joint draft resolution asking for the adoption of the Preparatory Committee's recommendations were naturally in favour of the ECOSOC electing the members. They did not want to break the tradition and felt reassured that the General Assembly would have the final authority. The other group, mostly sponsors of the 17-power joint resolution, joined by the USSR, Hungary and Czechoslovakia, wanted the General Assembly to elect the members of the Governing Council. Their argument was that the Special Fund should be open to all and that the ECOSOC, being a smaller body than the Governing Council, should not elect the larger body, in which all countries would participate.

At the request of several delegates to strike a compromise, the sponsors of the two joint draft resolutions revised their texts. The texts had much in common, except two points. The sponsors of the

47. A/C.2/SR.519.

17-power draft resolution called for election of the Governing Council by the General Assembly and appealed to the Member States to work for the speedy establishment of the UN Capital Development Fund. At this point, the Chairman offered to submit a draft combining all the points that the two revised drafts had in common, and if disagreement persisted, then the members could amend the Chairman's draft. Pakistan was the only country to say that a reference to SUNFED would be out of place in a text adopted by the Preparatory Committee.

The Chairman's draft had an expanded preamble, which included several expressions from the preambles of the GA Resolution 1219 (XII) and from the two revised texts before the Committee. He deleted the word "possible" from the operative paragraph 1 of the annex to the ECOSOC Resolution 692 (XXVI). However, he dropped the paragraph pertaining to the speedy establishment of SUNFED from the 17-power revised draft. The sponsors of the draft resolution offered to make amendments to restore what the Chairman had deleted or not included. The two original joint draft resolutions were held in abeyance by agreement for the time being.

The amendment in favour of having the General Assembly elect the members of the Governing Council was rejected. Most of the developed countries, in addition to 17 Latin American countries, voted against it.

As for the second amendment regarding speedier establishment of SUNFED, the US and the UK wanted more time to decide. In the meantime, Mexico and Italy had made suggestions to improve the text. The 17 powers agreed to accept the Mexican suggestions and introduced a new text in paragraph C: "...and appeals to Member States to make efforts towards the attainment of these conditions as soon as possible."

According to the US, "Section III of GA Resolution 1219 (XII) was a compromise between those who held that the Special Fund was a step towards SUNFED and those who held that Special Fund in itself was a concrete step forward."[48] The US said that it will not vote for the second amendment and the Special Fund resolution if the second amendment was accepted. Denmark and the Netherlands were in

48. A/C.2/SR.526.

favour of the idea of SUNFED, but said they would support the amendment only if its sponsors took it up separately. They called for the establishment of the Special Fund then itself.

Referring to the comments of the US, Iraq said, "If the Special Fund was going to be the end in itself, it would not have been agreed to unanimously at the last session. There was no need to establish Special Fund and the costly machinery if Special Fund was to be merely an extension of technical assistance. We could have given more money to TAB. US objection means that Special Fund will never exceed $ 100 million. The General Assembly will never review the scope and future activities of Special Fund and that SUNFED would never be set up."[49]

To bring about a compromise, France introduced a five-power draft with a new text. Iraq rejected it and agreed to withdraw the 18-power amendment if France withdrew the five-power draft. Both parties withdrew. Iraq and the others said that they would reopen the subject of a capital development fund in another context. The Chairman's draft was adopted, with everyone voting in favour (barring one abstention). In a plenary meeting on 14 October 1958, the General Assembly adopted the Second Committee's draft as GA Resolution 1240 (XIII). At its 782nd meeting on 5 December 1958, the General Assembly confirmed the nomination by the Secretary-General of Mr. Paul G. Hoffman as the Managing Director of the Special Fund.

It must be said in conclusion that from the beginning, the US was against providing capital finance for the economic development of the developing countries through multilateral channels. It was, in principle, in favour of foreign private capital and continued to advance different reasons for opposing the creation of SUNFED. Initially, it had argued that the time was not ripe for the establishment of SUNFED. Knowing that the US would be the largest single contributor, other developed countries, notably, Canada, Australia, Belgium and the UK, had followed the US lead, or rather, taken shelter behind the US position. They had contended that they were already doing enough through multilateral and bilateral channels, and also, that they had heavy domestic responsibilities. The US then went on to argue that sufficient resources were not in sight. Later, it

---

49. *ibid.*

introduced the condition of verifiable disarmament and some of the other developed countries latched on to this. The developing countries countered this with the convincing argument that the condition of disarmament was neither practical, nor realistic, because just as disarmament could not wait for development, so also development could not wait for disarmament. These countries somehow managed to keep the debate alive over the years. When the US managed to transform the scale and character of the Special Fund, other developed countries suddenly dropped their previous objections and started echoing the US position. The defection of some developing countries, whether out of fatigue, conviction, or practical considerations, effectively killed the establishment of SUNFED as originally conceived.

But all said and done, it must be noted that the US position was consistent from the beginning unlike many other countries. The US always held the view that developing countries should seek capital finance from international lending agencies, private foreign investors, and capital markets. It was against provision of capital finance through the UN. The US believed in multilateral technical assistance and hence launched the creation of EPTA and later of the Special Fund. Many other countries, developed as well as less developed, did not adhere to a defined position. Some developed countries took shelter behind the US position. Some initially and enthusiastically supported the creation of SUNFED but later changed their course and sided with the US. Many developing countries also switched their position on SUNFED when the US proposed the Special Fund. What was always clear to all from the beginning was that no major financial initiative could be launched without the support of the US.

II
OPERATIONS

The Special Fund came into operation on 1 January 1959. The first and second sessions of the Governing Council of the Fund were held on 26-27 January 1959 and 28-29 May 1959, respectively. During the first session, the Managing Director of the Special Fund presented some tentative conclusions with respect to the initial policy to be followed by the Fund. In his view, "The policy should be to put major emphasis on projects which would demonstrate the wealth-producing potential of unsurveyed natural resources in less developed countries, on training and research institutes and on surveys of limited cost which would lead to early investment."[50] Such an approach entailed carrying out preliminary engineering and feasibility studies in areas with possible investment potential. He further stated that the fund's projects would have a terminal point, and subventions to the operating expenditures would be given only for new or experimental programmes. In the ensuing year, the Managing Director suggested additional areas for assistance, such as advisory services for economic planning and programming, manpower surveys, assistance to industrial estates, housing, science and technology, training of secondary school teachers, establishment of planning institutes for regional development, technical education, and so on.

For 1959, the first year of the fund's operation, the Managing Director received 164 project requests, the total cost of which was $ 159 million. He submitted 44 projects for approval, and the Governing Council appropriated $ 31 million for these. The contributions for the year were made by 68 governments and amounted to only $ 25.8 million. At the urging of the US, the General Assembly had aimed at a target of $ 100 million[51] as the combined contribution for the Special Fund and EPTA. However, this target was reached only in 1962.

In 1960, the General Assembly urged the members to increase their contributions to the Special Fund and EPTA so as to take the combined total up to $ 150 million in the immediate future.[52] This target was attained only in 1962, in spite of repeated appeals by the Managing Director.

From the time of the inception of the Special Fund in 1959 until the end of 1965, after which the fund became a part of the UNDP, the total contributions to the fund amounted to $ 422.3 million. Over this seven-year period, the total expenditure of the executive agencies was $ 193.7 million, including the agencies' overheads. The major executive agencies were the FAO, UN, UNESCO and ILO.

The total field costs of the Special Fund over the same period amounted to $ 3.6 million. The Special Fund and EPTA shared

50. Report of the Governing Council of the Special Fund on its first session, January, 1959.

51. E/3401 and SF/L.28/Rev.1.

52. GA Res.1529 (XV).

common administrative arrangements in the field. The share of the Special Fund in the total combined field costs rose from 9 per cent in 1960 to 51 per cent in 1965. Thus, from 1959 to 1965, the total expenditure of the Special Fund, including expenditure by the executive agencies, field costs and headquarters cost, fell substantially short of the total contribution received by the fund over the period.

The Special Fund was chronically plagued by the problems of poor delivery and implementation. The members of the Governing Council continued to draw attention to these problems during every session. They complained about the high cash balances resulting from slow implementation and appealed for liberalisation of the fund's financial policies. The members repeatedly referred to the long gaps between the approval of a project, the signing of the agreement and the commencement of work on the project.[53] The Managing Director and his staff invariably explained the delays in implementation in terms of lack of adequate counterpart personnel, delays by recipient governments in meeting their obligations, difficulties in recruiting suitable experts, non-competitive salaries of the experts, and so on. Frustrated by the poor performance of the executive agencies, the members of the Governing Council proposed that the projects should be executed by the governments and non-UN bodies.[54] They also advocated greater resort to sub-contracting. At one point, the Governing Council suggested the appointment of a working group to review all problems in the sphere of implementation. During its pre-merger life of seven years, the Special Fund did make a valuable contribution by identifying potential areas for investment, but its achievement remained well below its scope.

The Special Fund toyed with the idea of the establishment of an information service, as an ancillary service, on sources of development capital and assistance. The Managing Director sent a questionnaire to the recipient governments, but few replies were forthcoming. In the Governing Council, some members expressed concern about the advisability and cost of setting up such a service but, nonetheless, asked the Managing Director to study the subject further. Later, the Managing Director submitted a note suggesting ways and means of going about it, but the Governing Council could not reach agreement

53. For example, see Report of the Governing Council on its 11th session in 1964.

54. See Governing Council Report on its 10th session.

on the course of action to be adopted. It was, however, agreed that the Special Fund would provide *ad hoc* advisory services at the request of governments.[55]

When the UNDP was established in 1966, the Special Fund became one component of the UNDP and EPTA the other; both with their separate objectives, policies and programmes as before the merger.

Capital Development Fund (UNCDF)

The developing countries had initially aimed at the creation of SUNFED to provide capital finance on concessional terms for the development of infrastructure in the developing countries. They ended up compromising because the developed countries argued that it would not be feasible to muster up the annual resource requirement of $ 500 million, as estimated by the US. They also said that the General Assembly could review the matter at some future point, when the time was ripe. Some developed countries, notably, France, the Netherlands, Belgium and Italy, while sharing the disappointment of the developing countries, indicated that they would continue to work with them towards the establishment of SUNFED in the future.

The process, therefore, continued in the General Assembly. In 1960, the Assembly, in its Resolution 1521(XV) "decided in principle that a United Nations capital development fund should be established." The resolution also appointed a committee to study the subject and make recommendations. The Final Act of UNCTAD (1964), too, contained decisions which lent strong support to the idea of establishing a capital development fund. The Committee, appointed by the General Assembly, did extensive work and, during its third session, it requested the General Assembly to ask the Secretary-General to look into the potentialities that might be opened up through the transformation of the Special Fund into a capital development fund.[56]

In his study,[57] the Secretary-General reviewed the origin and development of the Special Fund. Observing that the resources

55. Governing Council reports on 8th and 9th session.

56. A/5536.

57. E/3947, 15 July 1964.

available to the Special Fund already fell substantially short of the demands made on it, he said the Special Fund would not be able to accommodate the needs of a capital development fund. As to whether the Special Fund could be transformed into a capital development fund, the Secretary-General presented two scenarios. A capital development fund receiving more than $ 200 million to $ 250 million in additional resources could act independently, in collaboration with other financial agencies. If additional resources were not available, or the resources available fell short of the amount envisaged, then the addition or merger of such a fund with the Special Fund would require a number of institutional, legislative, operative and procedural changes.

During the second of its five sessions, the Committee prepared a draft statute of the capital development fund. This was approved by most of its members. During its fifth session,[58] the majority of members "strongly urged that the GA Resolution 1521(XV) should now be finally implemented by the adoption of a statute for the Fund and the institution of its operations."[59]

There were dissenting views,[60] however. Some delegates were opposed to the creation of a capital development fund, whether as a separate entity or through the transformation of the Special Fund in UNDP. These delegates believed that there were sufficient financial institutions outside the UN to serve the purpose. If combined with the UNDP, such a fund "was likely to prejudice its important pre-investment and technical assistance functions." A second group of delegates expressed full agreement with the objectives of a capital development fund and was convinced that various General Assembly resolutions provided enough justification for the establishment of such a fund. They maintained that "the only proper way of establishment of UNCDF was the gradual transformation of the United Nations Special Fund." According to them, "The Administration of UNDP was unwilling to initiate the transformation recommended by the General Assembly and UNCTAD." They "criticised the statement of the Administrator of UNDP that efforts

58. A/6418.

59. *ibid.*, p.3.

60. For discussion during the 5th session, see A/6418.

should be concentrated on further strengthening its pre-investment activities" and were not convinced of the Secretary-General's statement "that UNDP had at present no authority to undertake actual capital investment." Other delegates "felt that the main objective should be to continue the transformation of UNDP as provided for in recommendation A.IV.8 of the United Nations Conference on Trade and Development on an experimental and pragmatic basis". Pending the creation of a new agency, "it would clearly be more efficient to use existing bodies such as UNDP." In their view, the UNDP was already financing projects on the borderline between pre-investment and investment. The delegates who were committed to the establishment of a capital development fund "expressed the opinion that, in the present circumstances, it would be unrealistic to expect that UNDP could be transformed into a development finance agency in the foreseeable future". They decided to make a few changes to the draft statute and take up the matter in the General Assembly.

During the 21st session of the General Assembly, a large number of developing countries sponsored a draft resolution[61] in the Second Committee concerning the establishment of a capital development fund. The draft resolution included the statute prepared by the Committee on the capital development fund (as revised during its fifth session), and wanted the fund's operations to be started. The draft resolution received sufficient support in the Second Committee and was referred to the plenary of the General Assembly for adoption. During its consideration in the plenary, objections were raised by practically all the developed countries, as well as all the socialist countries, to paragraph 2 of Article IV of the statute. This paragraph provided that the administrative expenses of the fund would be met from the UN regular budget. The US considered this an 'important' question and felt that it should be approved by a two-thirds majority. A separate vote was thus taken on this paragraph, which was adopted and retained by a vote of 72 to 31, with 8 abstentions. The draft resolution as a whole was adopted by 76-19-14.[62] This seemed like a triumph for the developing countries, but it proved to be a hollow one. Practically all the major donor countries had either voted against

61. A/6578.

62. GA Res. 2186 (XXI), 13 December 1966

the resolution, or abstained. They did not make any contributions in the ensuing years. The CDF was therefore born with very scant resources. CDF is now a window in UNDP and its limited resources are used to finance some projects in low income countries.

8

Creation of United Nations Development Programme (UNDP)

The Special Fund, all said and done, was an extension of the United Nations Technical Assistance Programme. At the time of its creation, the US tried to distinguish it from the EPTA probably because the US wanted to make it as a proxy for the capital development fund, for which the developing countries were aiming. The US presented it as a compromise between assistance for pure technical assistance and assistance for investment. The only distinguishing features of the Special Fund were its focus on surveys, and on research and training in areas with potential for investment. Another such feature was the size of its projects—the Special Fund financed larger projects. However, with the passage of time, the EPTA transferred to the Special Fund projects which it could not finance. The line of distinction was getting increasingly blurred. Therefore, while speaking on coordination in the TAC during the 32nd session of the ECOSOC, the US delegate raised a broader question. He said, "It was also essential to ensure cooperation between pre-investment activities of the Special Fund and Technical Assistance of EPTA."[1] According to him, "The basic issues to be considered were whether EPTA and the Special Fund should be more clearly integrated or even merged, how technical assistance activities could be more closely related to overall development plans."[2]

During its 32nd session, the ECOSOC appointed an *ad hoc* Committee to consider the question of coordination between the two programmes. The Committee was asked, *inter alia,* to study the question of the merger of the EPTA and Special Fund. No unanimity

1. Report od TAC, E/3547, p.61.
2. *ibid.*

of views was in evidence during the deliberations of the Committee. Some members were against the idea of merger because they feared that it would not only destroy the individual character and identity of the two programmes, but might also imperil the chances of transforming the Special Fund into a capital development fund. Since the Committee could not reach agreement, it found an easy way out. It submitted that in the absence of sufficient evidence, it could not reach any conclusion. Further, it suggested that the Secretary-General, in consultation with the specialised agencies, should study the question and submit a report. The ECOSOC, therefore, requested the Secretary-General to study "the possible advantages and disadvantages of a partial or complete merger in due course, without running counter to the basic objectives of each programme, of some or all of the technical assistance programmes of the United Nations, including that of the Regular Programmes, the EPTA and the Special Fund."[3]

The Secretary-General submitted his report[4] to the 37th session of the ECOSOC. In the light of the past experience of the EPTA and Special Fund, he foresaw that the future range and scope of activities under these programmes "will tend to be substantially larger than at present".[5] He pointed out that "the need for higher levels of pre-investment activities is evidenced by the inadequate rate of progress in many developing countries"[6] and referred to the current volume of requests from governments—amounting to an expenditure of over $ 500 million, "to which the Fund would be expected to contribute $ 200 million if all the projects were approved."[7] This statement was somewhat exaggerated because in the past, the Special Fund did not and could not approve and finance all the projects it had received for assistance. The report also stated, "All indications make it clear that governments urgently require and desire from the United Nations system substantially more assistance of the kinds provided under the expanded programme and the Regular Programmes of Technical Assistance, including OPEX."[8]

3. ECOSOC Res. 900.A. (XXXIV).
4. E/3850.
5. *ibid.*, p.2.
6. *ibid.*
7. *ibid.*
8. *ibid.*

Referring to future assistance in particular directions and the proposals for the creation of new and semi-independent institutions, the Secretary-General felt "strongly that further dispersion through the creation of new agencies should not be decided upon without having thoroughly explored the potentialities of the existing organisations with their funding experience, knowledge and technical skills, as well as the inter-agency coordinating mechanisms that have been built up over the years."[9]

With a view to gearing the UN system "to administer an increased proportion of an increased volume of needed assistance", the Secretary-General came to the conclusion that "certain organisational rearrangements would offer obvious advantages and be entirely feasible. Rather than attempt to set out the possible advantages and disadvantages of the many different forms of rearrangement or merger that might be envisaged ... it will be more useful that we should state clearly the conclusions to which his study has led him."[10]

Having said this, he proceeded straightway to present his proposal for the merger of the EPTA and the Special Fund with a new United Nations Development Programme. He pointed out that the heads of all the specialised agencies and the heads of the Special Fund and TAB were in agreement with his proposal. The UNDP would have a single intergovernmental body, to be known as the Intergovernmental Committee, and an Interagency Board. The Programme would be managed by a head and a co-head, with a single staff. With regard to procedures appropriate to different types and sizes of projects, the Secretary-General recommended the continuation of country programmes in the case of smaller projects, as well as the maintenance of the ongoing procedures being followed by the Special Fund for larger projects. The Intergovernmental Committee would provide "general policy guidance and direction for, as well as the necessary intergovernmental supervision over, the Programme as a whole."[11] He believed that this unified body could be easily established by merging the Governing Council of the Special Fund and the TAC, given a little alteration in their membership. The Interagency

9. *ibid.*

10. *ibid.*, p.3.

11. *ibid.*, p.5.

Board would be established "to provide for the full participation in the process of decision and policy making of the Head of the Programme, the Secretary-General of the United Nations, the executive heads of the specialised agencies and the IAEA or their representatives."[12]

Considering the mandate given by the ECOSOC, the Secretary-General's report was very inadequate. He failed to examine the advantages or disadvantages of a partial or complete merger of the two programmes and did not consider any alternative options for rearrangement. He reached his conclusion solely on the ground that the United Nations system might have to assume greater responsibilities as the future demand for assistance, both in traditional and new directions, was expected to increase. It should be noted that the argument for merger had never surfaced in the past even though the demand for assistance continued to grow and the assistance rendered by the EPTA and Special Fund increased significantly since their establishment. In fact, after the establishment of the Special Fund, the EPTA and the Fund had shared certain facilities, such as field representation and UN support in financial management. The Secretary-General's report failed to prove that the existing arrangements could not cope with further increases in the activities of the two programmes.

However, there was an *a priori* case for merger. The two programmes used the same specialised agencies for the execution of their projects and the same field staff; both received contributions on a voluntary basis, in convertible or national currencies; and both had annual pledging conferences, shared maintenance and management of financial records, and practiced the same (UN) financial management procedures. They provided the same forms of assistance. The Special Fund was, in fact, an extension of UNTA. The only differences were in the allocation procedures and in the type of projects financed. The EPTA had country programmes whereas the Special Fund used project budgeting. It can well be argued that there was no need for a Special Fund in the first place because given additional resources, the EPTA could have undertaken financing of pre-investment projects. The Special Fund was born out of political and ideological conflict as the

12. *ibid.*, p.6.

developed countries were unwilling to provide concessionary capital finance through multilateral channels. At any rate, the Secretary-General could have better justified the case for merger by concentrating on the commonalties between the two programmes rather than on the basis of their possible future levels of growth.

The Secretary-General's report came up before the *ad hoc* Committee on coordination in March 1964. The Committee tried to elicit the views and comments of the governments, but only 20 submitted comments. Most governments were not satisfied with the report. The oral reply given by the Secretary-General's representative was considered inadequate and incomplete.[13] Two distinct views were expressed during the discussion in the *ad hoc* Committee.[14] Some fully supported the proposal for merger, while others had serious reservations about it. The supporters of the proposal felt that a merger would encourage unified purpose and planning, an increase in resources and their efficient use. They believed that it would help the developing countries to prepare unified plans and check the dispersion of resources. According to them, a merger would retain the special qualities and characteristics of the two programmes, while at the same time, help avoid overlap and duplication, thus resulting in better use and eventual growth. The opponents of the merger, on the other hand, believed that the programmes worked satisfactorily, and that the arrangements for joint administration and representation were adequate. They argued that the main problem was that of co-ordination which could be improved further between the two programmes and at the field level. However, there would be no savings on staff in the case of merger. This group also felt that a single governing body would reduce the number of governments participating in policy-making.

The majority of members were in favour of having one inter-governmental body for both programmes. There was disagreement on how to work out the merger at the management level. Some were for centralised management, while some preferred two separate levels of management for the two programmes. There was a suggestion to create one fund, but "it was decided that two funds would be

13. E/TAC/L.333.

14. Report of the Ad Hoc Committee, E/3862, 10 March 1964.

maintained, as well as most EPTA procedures, especially country targets and country programming."

At the end of the discussion, the US submitted a draft resolution[15] for the consideration of the ECOSOC. This was adopted by the *ad hoc* Committee with some amendments. The main thrust of the resolution was to combine the Special Fund and the EPTA in a programme to be known as the UNDP, as suggested by the Secretary-General. However, the structural arrangements envisaged in this resolution differed in important respects from those proposed by the Secretary-General. The resolution recommended that "The special characteristics and operations of the two programmes as well as two separate funds will be maintained, and that contributions may be pledged to the two programmes separately as hitherto, and the principles, procedures and provisions governing EPTA and the Special Fund not inconsistent with this resolution be reaffirmed."[16] There would be a single inter-governmental body, to be known as the Governing Council of UNDP, and also a single advisory committee, to be known as the Interagency Consultative Board for UNDP. With regard to arrangements at the management level, pending a further review within a period of two years, the resolution recommended that "the Managing Director of the Special Fund and the Executive Chairman of the Technical Assistance Board act as joint heads of the Programme, responsible for the Special Fund and the EPTA respectively, and requests them to make common administrative arrangements to ensure overall planning and coordination and maximum efficiency". In conclusion, the resolution suggested that the Secretary-General should prepare "a draft resolution" for the implementation of the above resolution.

The success of the US in getting this resolution adopted was due to various compromises made in the *ad hoc* Committee. The opponents of the merger, mostly developing countries, were concerned about maintaining the special characteristics and identities of the two programmes. They also had apprehensions that the absence of a separate Special Fund would seriously affect their efforts to transform it some day into a capital fund. It is for these reasons that the

15. *ibid.*, p.16.

16. *ibid.*, operative paragraph 1.

resolution provided for two separate programmes with separate funds and separate pledging conferences, as well as for preserving their existing procedures, provisions and separate managements. To assuage the developing countries' sentiments regarding a capital development fund, the following was included in the preamble to the resolution:

"Without prejudice to the study requested from the Secretary-General by the General Assembly in Resolution 1936 (XVIII) of the practical steps to transform the Special Fund into a capital development fund in such a way as to include both pre-investment and investment activities, or the recommendation of the Council and General Assembly thereon..."

In reality, this was not of much help because in his report on the merger, the Secretary-General had not seen the need for any new institutions or entities. The opponents' concern over the size of the new inter-governmental body was addressed by enlarging the size of the Governing Council. In the end, therefore, the *ad hoc* Committee's vision of the UNDP was nothing but placing the two programmes under a common address, so to speak. It is instructive to note that the two-page resolution of the *ad hoc* Committee did not use the word 'merger' anywhere. Merger existed only at the legislative level (the single inter-governmental body), and at the advisory level (the single inter-agency consultative board).

The *ad hoc* Committee's report, including its resolution, was considered by the TAC,[17] which was not required to take any action but was asked by the ECOSOC to give its comments. A considerable majority of its members expressed strong support for the *ad hoc* Committee's proposal. Some reserved their comments, pending discussion in the ECOSOC and General Assembly. Many members, while agreeing to have a single inter-governmental body, were "opposed to or reserved their position as to, a unification at the management level at the present stage."[18] The others "expressed their support of the Secretary-General's position, endorsed by the ACC, that there should be unified management". Several members also stressed "the essential importance of ensuring that the proposed re-organisation would be without prejudice to any action aimed at the

17. TAC report, E/3933.

18. *ibid.*, p.30.

establishment of a United Nations Capital Development Fund."[19] Among those who opposed a merger, some felt that it was necessary to consult a large number of developing countries before taking any action. They believed that both the Secretary-General and the *ad hoc* Committee had not sufficiently explored the advantages and disadvantages of a possible merger.

As requested by the *ad hoc* Committee and ECOSOC, the Secretary-General prepared drafts of two resolutions: one to be adopted by the ECOSOC and the other by the General Assembly.[20] The latter was to be included as an annex to the ECOSOC resolution. These were first reviewed by the *ad hoc* Committee.

The *ad hoc* Committee did not make any significant changes to the draft Council resolution, except to add two paragraphs to the preamble.[21]

The draft General Assembly resolution prepared by the Secretary-General was largely based on the resolution which had been sponsored by the US and previously adopted by the *ad hoc* Committee. The Secretary-General did add certain new elements, of which three were important. These related to the role of the agencies in the Inter-Agency Consultative Board, the principle of representation in the new Governing Council of the proposed UNDP, and unified management. With regard to the second of these, the Secretary-General suggested equal representation of the developed and developing countries. As for the arrangements at the management level, the Secretary-General submitted two options: one was the *ad hoc* Committee's previous recommendation for separate management of the two programmes, while the other proposed unified management.

The *ad hoc* Committee made changes to two of these. It deleted some details regarding the role of the agencies in the Inter-Agency Consultative Board, without affecting the effective participation of the specialised agencies. The committee amended the Secretary-General's proposal regarding the principle(s) of representation, and suggested two options. The first called for "equal representation of the economically more developed countries, on the one hand, having due

---

19. *ibid.* p.31.

20. E/3899.

21. Report of the Coordination Committee, E/3966, p.5.

regard to their contribution to the UNDP, and of the developing countries, on the other hand, taking into account the need for geographical distribution among the latter members."[22] According to the second option, "There shall be equitable geographical representation of all members of the United Nations and of the specialised agencies and the International Atomic Energy Agency." On the subject of management, the *ad hoc* Committee abandoned its original proposal for separate management of the two programmes and embraced the Secretary-General's suggestion for a unified management, according to which the UNDP would have an Administrator and a Co-administrator. The Secretary-General had further suggested that as a transitional measure, the Managing Director of the Special Fund should serve as the Administrator and the Executive Chairman of the TAB as the Co-administrator. Thus, with these modifications, the *ad hoc* Committee submitted a consolidated draft resolution to the ECOSOC.

There was hardly any discussion when the ECOSOC considered the draft resolution during its 37th session. Even if the ECOSOC were to fully support the two texts, it still had to decide on the principle of representation in the new Governing Council, as the *ad hoc* Committee had suggested two alternatives. Practically all the developed countries that were members of the ECOSOC expressed a strong desire for parity in representation. However, no decision was taken in the ECOSOC and the choice was left to the General Assembly. The Council adopted the draft resolution submitted by the *ad hoc* Committee, without any change.[23] Many delegates wanted to resume their positions pending discussions in the General Assembly.

The draft General Assembly resolution, submitted by the ECOSOC, was discussed extensively by the Second Committee during the Assembly's 20th session. The discussion focused mainly on the question of representation in the new Governing Council of the UNDP. The General Assembly had to decide on the size and composition of the Governing Council. The developed countries preferred a small and compact body, whereas the developing countries argued for a larger one to ensure greater participation. Finally, it was

22. *ibid.*, Annex, p.2.

23. ECOSOC Res. 1020 (XXXVII), 11 August 1964.

agreed that the Governing Council should have 36 members. Later, one more seat was created, presumably for Yugoslavia, but this seat was to be rotated among all regional groups over a nine-year cycle. With regard to the composition of the Governing Council, the developed countries argued for equal representation. The developing countries wanted a slight majority, using a rubric of 'equitable and balanced' representation. Jordan, on behalf of a majority of the developing countries, suggested 19 and 17 seats, respectively, for the developing and developed countries. Following a vigorous debate, in which France continued to insist on equal representation, the developed countries accepted Jordan's proposal. The two groups worked further to delineate the seats among different regions. The annex to the resolution[24] which was finally adopted provided 14 seats for the Western European and other countries and 3 seats for the Eastern European countries. It allotted 7 seats to the African countries, 6 to the Asian countries, and 6 to Latin America.

The Second Committee also decided that the UNDP should come into effect on 1 January 1966. Incorporating all these changes, the General Assembly adopted Resolution 2029(XX) on 22 November 1965 which made way for the consolidation of the two programmes. All said and done, the consolidation was more of a union than a merger of the two programmes. True, there was a single intergovernmental body and a single advisory committee, but the two programmes remained separate, with their own funds and own pledging conferences. The management was apparently unified, but in practice, the administrator continued to manage the Special Fund and the Co-administrator retained charge of the EPTA. Of course, this situation did not last long. In a few years, the two programmes were completely merged and fully integrated under an effective unified management.

---

24. *ibid.*

9

Summary and Observations

It is useful to recapitulate major highlights of the past experience, to note what further progress was made after 1966, and to consider areas in which more reforms are needed.

In the first place, despite the proclamations in the UN Charter on eradication of poverty, hunger, malnutrition, illiteracy, disease, etc. throughout the world, it took so long, after the founding of the UN, for the developed countries to agree with the persistent demand of the underdeveloped countries to provide technical assistance through the UN for their economic and social development. Finally, when it was agreed to make a provision in the UN budget in 1948, the amount was too small and fell seriously short of the prevailing demand for technical assistance. Nonetheless, the United Nations Programme of Technical Assistance, set up in 1948, received a very warm welcome because it marked the beginning of unconditional multilateral aid through the UN. The UN did make larger provisions in the subsequent years until financing of all technical assistance was placed on a voluntary basis when the UN ceased to provide project related technical assistance from its budget. The UN Regular Programme was then absorbed by EPTA.

The UN Regular Programme had several drawbacks. It did not have any country targets and hence there was no question of formulating an integrated programme at the country level in accordance with the expressed priorities and needs of governments. While this practice could have been defended on grounds of its small size, it nonetheless did give considerable discretion to the UN officials in the selection of projects for financing. The UN did not give much explanation about projects not approved for financing. Its chief merit was that all its resources were fully convertible and in that sense represented truly untied aid.

EPTA represented quantum jump in the provision of development aid. It raised $ 20 million through voluntary contributions in the first year of its operations, in 1950, compared to a provision of $ 0.25 million in the UN budget in 1948. While this was almost revolutionary in its scope, EPTA also suffered from several drawbacks. For a long time EPTA channeled its resources to the recipient countries through the participating agencies which thus wielded considerable power over the dispensation of funds allotted to them by EPTA. It was only in the early 1960s that this situation was remedied by abolishing agency targets, introducing country targets, and thus giving the right to the recipient countries to express their needs based on their development objectives and priorities.

Lacking experience in managing development aid on such a large scale, EPTA underperformed in the early years and later overbudgeted thus leading to a financial crisis. As almost 40 per cent were in national currencies EPTA also encountered serious difficulties in the management of currencies. It was only later with comprehensive reform of its financial procedures that EPTA gained its momentum and by the end of the period covered here grew quite rapidly. However, EPTA's overhead costs remained rather high throughout the period. By the end of the period, agreement on the UN role in multilateral aid, its financing from voluntary contributions, indicative country targets and the right of recipient countries to determine their own needs were in place.

However, EPTA could not resolve problems in two areas. Firstly, it could not come up with a meaningful methodology for project evaluation. The TAC and ECOSOC were obsessed with the impact of an EPTA project on economic development of a country. This was difficult to assess because EPTA assistance usually formed a small part of not only of the overall national development effort in a country but in some cases EPTA input was not necessarily the most important input in a national project. Conceptually, there was also divergence between an 'EPTA project' and a 'national project'. The package of inputs provided by EPTA to a national project were considered as a project in EPTA's operations. The TAB emphasised evaluation at the EPTA project level but it did not offer a suitable methodology to do that. Another issue related to coordination at the country level. Despite prolonged debates and numerous resolutions coordination at the country level between EPTA, participating agencies and other international aid giving agencies was rather poor. The principal responsibility for coordination was placed on country resident representatives and several attempts were made to define the nature and scope of coordination, the role of resident representative and responsibilities of agencies but this problem could not be solved fully.

The creation of the Special Fund was largely a counteraction by donor countries to the demand for SUNFED by developing countries for financing of non-self-liquidating projects. The Special Fund had no country targets and operated on the basis of project budgeting. This was more like the initial UN Regular Programme of Technical Assistance. The Special Fund suffered from chronic problem of poor delivery and implementation. Later developing countries did manage to establish a Capital Development Fund but it had very scant resources as developed countries did not support it. At one point, the Secretary-General was asked by the developing countries to study the potentiality of transforming the Special Fund into Capital Development Fund. The Secretary-General's response was that the resources available to the Special Fund already fell short of demand for its assistance. The fact is that the Special Fund could not spend all the money it received during the seven years of its existence.

Towards the end of the period, there were now three programmes—UN Regular Programme, EPTA, and the Special Fund—running concurrently. There was undoubtedly considerable overlap and duplication of activities among them and, therefore, their merger into a single entity (UNDP) was a step in the right direction. The merger also held the promise of substantial economy in overhead costs. In the beginning the merger was not totally complete. In UNDP, the Special Fund and the technical assistance components continued to be administered separately until their merger in 1970 with the adoption of the Consensus.

Since the creation of UNDP there have been some major reforms in the conceptualisation and administration of technical assistance.

The resources of UNDP and consequently its Programme continued to increase and towards the end of 1960s the Administrator of UNDP foresaw the possibility of resources doubling over the next four years. He was concerned about the capacity of UNDP to provide timely and effective support to a rapidly expanding Programme. "The very dynamic growth of UNDP," observed the Deputy Administrator, "had inevitably strained the framework and functioning of a structure which had not originally been designed for an operational task of such magnitude."[1] He, therefore, submitted a report to the fifth session of the UNDP Governing Council on the assessment of needs for assistance and UNDP's capacity to carry it out. At the sixth session of the Governing Council, he suggested a capacity study and provided its terms of reference. Subsequently, Sir Robert Jackson was commissioned to prepare the report.

Sir Robert Jackson prepared a comprehensive report entitled: "A Study of the Capacity of the United Nations System."[2] "The essential purpose of this study," said the Administrator, "was to determine how the United Nations system could be strengthened so that within the next five years it could carry out a Programme twice the size of the present Programme. This was not an unattainable goal in view of the four-fold increase in the capacity of the United Nations system during the decade of the 1960s."[3]

Sir Jackson viewed the present machinery as too complex, impossible to control and coordinate, and thus inhibiting development cooperation provided by the United Nations system, especially UNDP. He did consider a complete integration of all parts of the UN system but concluded that "consolidation of all component parts (UNDP and agencies) into a single organisation—is not within the realm of possibility."[4] He, therefore, focused his report on restructuring of UNDP. In his report, Sir Jackson identified the constraints on the existing capacity of UNDP, worked out a comprehensive framework of a development cooperation cycle, explained its each phase in detail and provided elaborate analysis and recommendations for action. Following discussions of his report by all the parties, the UNDP Governing Council adopted a 'consensus' at its 9th and 10th sessions

---

1. DP/5. Volume I and II.
2. E/4782: Report of the ninth session of the Governing Council of UNDP, Ch.VI, paragraph109.
3. *ibid.*, paragraph 105.
4. DP/5. Volume I., Foreword.

which was based on Sir Jackson's report.[5] This was later endorsed by the ECOSOC and the General Assembly.[6]

This consensus marked a revolutionary step in the restructuring of UNDP. The consensus elaborated the entire process of development cooperation and provided detailed guidance on each phase of that process. It amplified and crystallised concepts of country programming and indicative planning figures. It made far reaching recommendations for the organisation of UNDP. The present organisational structure of UNDP owes its origin to the recommendations of the Consensus.

Later, the Governing Council, at its 24th session, took a decision on the role and activities of the Programme[7] based largely on a report[8] submitted by the Administrator of UNDP. The decision spelt out in a comprehensive manner goals and objectives of the Programme, new directions for the Programme, responsibilities of the Administrator, cooperation expected from the agencies and appealed to the governments to contribute towards increase in resources and "bear in mind the need for coherence in the United Nations development system".[9]

Since its creation, UNDP has expanded its Programme considerably and has opened several new dimensions of technical cooperation. It has sought and nurtured new partners in development cooperation. It continues to provide strong support to the least developed countries and invests in building capacity in recipient countries. It now shares large responsibility in the programme on Millennium Development Goals. It has set up Thematic Trust Funds contributions to which are earmarked by donor countries for particular projects or countries but they are claimed to supplement and not compete with core resources.

---

5. E/4782 and E/4884/Rev.1: Reports of the UNDP Governing Council at its 9th and 10th sessions. For a complete text of the Consensus, see Annex to the ECOSOC Resolution 1530 (XLIX) of 22 July 1970.
6. See ECOSOC Resolution 1530 (XLIX) of 22 July 1970 and GA Resolution 2688(XXV) of 11 December 1970.
7. E/6013/Rev.1, para 139. Also Annex to ECOSOC Res.2110(LXIII) of 3 August 1977.
8. DP/261.
9. Paragraph E(iii) of the decision.

While so much progress has been made, there are, I believe, several major issues on which further progress is desirable. First, there is the issue of the centrality of UNDP.

The UNDP was conceived as a central funding agency responsible for mobilising resources and for their programming and coordination in the UN system. This goal has not been achieved yet. The participating agencies have their own programmes of technical cooperation financed from their regular budgets. These programmes started long ago before the creation of UNDP. The question of merging all technical cooperation activities of the UN system into one single entity was discussed extensively in the ECOSOC and TAC in the early 1960s but the agencies had considerable support in these legislative bodies to prevent this from happening. Sir Robert Jackson, in his capacity study, had also considered the question of consolidation but concluded that it was beyond the realm of possibility. However, the UN legislative bodies keep repeating periodically[10] the *mantra* of UNDP universality and centrality without taking any concrete steps to attain that goal. The proliferation of technical assistance activities in the system has created problems in coordination and hindered a unified approach and response to emerging crisis or challenges. Consolidation of all technical cooperation activities in the system is, therefore, essential to promote coherence, consistency, harmony and effectiveness of the system's Programme. Such consolidation should include only the technical cooperation activities of the agencies that are financed from their regular budgets and not those that are financed from voluntary contributions made to them by their Member States for specific purposes. After all UNDP has Thematic Trust Funds and so there is no justification to deny it to the agencies which also receive voluntary contributions for specific projects or programmes in the area of their competence. In the UN, the question of such consolidation belongs to the realm of politics. But UN has rarely abandoned an issue for failure to reach agreement. With sustained efforts and patience some compromise has always been found. There is need for this effort now. UNDP is now managing several dimensions of technical cooperation,

10. See ECOSOC Resolution 1981/59 of 22 July 1981. Governing Council decision on the Role and Activities of UNDP, E/6013/Rev.1. and GA Resolution 32/114 of 15 December 1977.

has assumed responsibilities under the Millennium Development Goals and it needs to be poised to assist especially African countries as they receive larger volume of assistance as envisaged at the recent G-8 summit.

Secondly, the question of coordination at the country level between UNDP and agencies and between them and recipient countries has never been fully resolved. Almost each year it was on the agenda of the ECOSOC and the Governing Council of UNDP and continues to be on the agenda of the Executive Board of UNDP. There were several studies in the past by ACC and TAB which resulted in drafting and redrafting of the rules of the game and of the relationship between UN resident representatives and representatives of agencies. This problem becomes more complex with the expansion of the Programme accompanied by new dimensions of technical cooperation. As recently as 2004, at the annual session of the Executive Board the Administrator of UNDP identified five reform tracks; one of which was "strengthening the resident coordination system and increasing its accountability to drive strategic coherence and outcomes."[11] The success in this field will, of course, depend on the substantive and administrative capacity in the office of the resident coordinator to co-ordinate technical cooperation at the national level. But to a large extent coordination or lack of it is also a function of the continuing conflict of interest between UNDP and agency representation in the field. In this sense, the problem of coordination is related to the lack of centrality and universality of UNDP. In a co-ordinated framework, the question of coordination should become much easier to manage. There is value to the assistance agencies render to governments in the formulation of projects in their respective fields. What is important is to discourage 'salesmanship' by participating agencies at the national level.

Thirdly, like coordination, evaluation of programme implementation has also been an issue discussed by the legislative bodies year after year. There is need to recognise that except perhaps in the fields of agriculture, education and health, quantitative measures of results or impact of several types of projects financed by UNDP cannot be developed. For example, impact of assistance for

11. E/2004/35: Report of the Executive Board on work carried out during 2003, p.27.

policy and administrative reforms, for human resource development and for institution building and other such activities can be better considered in terms of detailed follow up. In the past, evaluation efforts centred largely on processes, procedures and counterpart support. In response to urgings of legislative bodies to strengthen result oriented evaluation and refinement of performance indicators the Evaluation Office of UNDP has made considerable progress. It continues to improve evaluation methodology, focuses on followup, provides support for building evaluation capacity within the UNDP and at the national level, and attempts to link evaluation to policy and implementation. It also publishes a Journal 'Essentials', which is devoted to lessons learned based on evaluation evidence.

While all this work in UNDP is good and must continue as a cornerstone of efficient and effective management of technical cooperation, there is need for an independent office of Evaluation. Such an office would be an arm of UNDP but independent of its management structure and oversight. This office would be akin to the office of an Auditor General at the national level. The Head of this office should be appointed by the Secretary-General in consultation with the Administrator of UNDP. He should report directly to the Executive Board of UNDP. A good model to follow is the Evaluation Department of the IMF. Such an office could undertake selective but comprehensive studies on a variety of subjects like country studies, coordination, cross-country analysis of common projects, delivery mechanisms, and, to wit, even internal evaluation in UNDP. It should not duplicate the work carried out by UNDP. Properly staffed and with a clear and coherent mandate, such an independent office can make very valuable contribution to an understanding of the working and evaluation of technical cooperation activities.

Fourth, there is the question of partners in implementation. In the past, specialised agencies were exclusively given the task of implementing projects in their respective areas of competence. Over time this has changed. Specialised agencies do not enjoy that privilege any more. UNDP believes in introducing competition in the execution of projects. UNDP does assign considerable work to the agencies but it also tries to reach parties in the private sector, other international agencies and executes some projects on its own. The execution by private parties has two-fold costs. Firstly, it is more expensive because most of such parties are found to be located in developed countries where costs are high. The extra costs involved cut into net programming resources available to developing countries. Secondly, it has opportunity cost to the extent that the experience of agencies is not utilised. Privatisation of project execution in UNDP with a view to bring in more competition is a misguided concept. Privatisation makes sense when there is already a competitive market in place. There is no such market where rights for the execution of UNDP projects are traded. In the execution of UNDP projects, private parties are usually chosen on the basis of past experience or familiarity. Sub-contracting can be done by the agencies also. It is highly desirable and beneficial to rely mainly on unrivalled cumulative empirical knowledge and experience of specialised agencies and to give them responsibility for oversight of projects and also continue to encourage government execution. It would be difficult for UNDP to affirm its centrality without having full confidence in the participating agencies which are integral parts of the system. The UNDP should also cease to implement projects on its own. It is not customary for a funding agency to implement its own projects. UNDP started doing this for multi-sectoral projects arguing that no single agency had all required skills to implement such projects. But then neither has UNDP which usually sub-contracts them out and performs essentially managerial functions which a lead agency can also do. But the main argument against this arrangement is that a funding agency will not be perceived to evaluate objectively implementation of its own projects. And this could affect the entire process of evaluation. It is better for UNDP to stay above board and demonstrate uniform application of evaluation standards to all projects. The World Bank does not implement its own projects which are mostly implemented by recipient governments. However, The World Bank does supervise and ensure that all procedures are followed and required standards are met. The Bank is then free to undertake evaluation of performance in projects.

Finally, something needs to be done about the decision making process and structures in the UN. There is no parallel elsewhere. Officials in the UN have to work with 191 countries. Although the General Assembly is the supreme decision making body, it delegates its work to several subordinate legislative bodies. For example, in the area of technical assistance, UNDP, in the first instance, reports to the Executive Board which then reports to the ECOSOC which reports to the Second Committee of the General Assembly which may either endorse the decision of the Second Committee or send it back for further reflection. The amazing part of this is that each body, as it gets larger than the original decision making body, discusses issues all over again and expresses its views in the form of resolutions until the process ends in the Second Committee of the General Assembly. The incremental value added at each stage is usually very small. It is therefore not easy for the UN officials either to persuade each body to accept the original decision or to make amends which they consider are essential. So the act of delegation by the General Assembly does not make much sense. It actually elongates the decision making process and becomes very time consuming. In operational activities like technical assistance, the General Assembly should vest complete responsibility for policy and oversight in the Executive Board of the UNDP and the Executive Board should submit its report directly to the General Assembly which will have an opportunity to make any comments or changes. This will simplify and expedite the decision making process and also facilitate speedier implementation of the Programme.

Index

A

F

G

H

I

J

K

L

Q

R

S

T

U

V

W

Y